BUSY CHILDHOOD

THE CENTURY CHILDHOOD LIBRARY
Edited by John E. Anderson, Ph.D.

BUSY CHILDHOOD, by Josephine C. Foster, Principal of the Kindergarten and Nursery School and Professor of Child Welfare, University of Minnesota

HAPPY CHILDHOOD, by John E. Anderson, Director, Institute of Child Welfare, University of Minnesota

HEALTHY CHILDHOOD, by Harold C. Stuart, M. D., Assistant Professor of Pediatrics and Child Hygiene, Medical School and School of Public Health, Harvard University; Visiting Physician, Infant's Hospital, and Associate Physician, Children's Hospital, Boston, Massachusetts

Off for a Good Time

The Century Childhood Library
JOHN E. ANDERSON, Editor

BUSY CHILDHOOD

Guidance Through Play and Activity

BY

JOSEPHINE C. FOSTER, Ph.D.

PRINCIPAL OF THE KINDERGARTEN AND NURSERY SCHOOL
AND PROFESSOR OF CHILD WELFARE
UNIVERSITY OF MINNESOTA

Student's Edition

D. APPLETON–CENTURY COMPANY
INCORPORATED
NEW YORK   LONDON

To my daughters,
MARIAN AND HARRIET,
AND ALL THE BUSY CHILDREN OF
THE NEIGHBORHOOD

"We approach all problems of childhood with affection. Theirs is the province of joy and good humor. They are the most wholesome part of the race, the sweetest, for they are fresher from the hands of God. Whimsical, ingenious, mischievous, we live a life of apprehension as to what their opinion may be of us; a life of defense against their terrifying energy; we put them to bed with a sense of relief and lingering of devotion. We envy them the freshness of adventure and discovery of life; we mourn over the disappointments they will meet.

"The fundamental purpose of this Conference is to set forth an understanding of those safeguards which will assure to them health in mind and body. They are safeguards and services to childhood which can be provided by the community, the State, or the Nation—all of which are beyond the reach of the individual parent. We approach these problems in no spirit of diminishing the responsibilities and values or invading the sanctities of those primary safeguards to child life—their homes and their mothers. After we have determined every scientific fact, after we have erected every public safeguard, after we have constructed every edifice for education or training or hospitalization or play, yet all these things are but a tithe of the physical, moral, and spiritual gifts which motherhood gives and home confers. None of these things carries that affection, that devotion of soul, which is the great endowment from mothers.

Our purpose here today is to consider and give our
mite of help to strengthen her hand that her boy and
girl may have a fair chance.''—Addresses and ab-
stracts of Committee Reports, entitled *White House
Conference, 1930* (The Century Co., New York,
1931), p. 6.

With these words, Herbert Hoover, President of the
United States, opened and defined the purpose of the White
House Conference on Child Health and Protection, held in
Washington at his invitation in November, 1930.

Attending the Conference were three thousand scientists
and practical workers interested in every phase of child well-
being. Prior to the meeting, committees worked for more than
a year collecting data and preparing reports. Out of the Conference there came the Children's Charter,[1] a bill of rights
for American children, and an imposing series of volumes
containing the detailed reports of the various committees.
Although these reports were not written from the viewpoint
of the parent, they contain a wealth of information of direct
concern and value to parents.

It is the purpose of the Century Childhood Library to make
much of this material available to parents in compact form.
In the preparation of the three volumes *Healthy Childhood,
Happy Childhood,* and *Busy Childhood* which constitute the
Library, the authors have drawn liberally upon the publications of the White House Conference both for quotations and
for material. The authors were all members of the Conference.
Dr. Stuart, author of *Healthy Childhood,* was Vice-Chairman
of the Committee on the Growth and Development of the
Child in the Medical Section of the Conference; Dr. Anderson, author of *Happy Childhood,* was Chairman of the Committee on the Infant and Preschool Child in the Section on

[1] The Children's Charter is reprinted on page 28, H. C. Stuart's
Healthy Childhood (D. Appleton-Century Company, Inc., New York,
1933).

Education and Training and was also a member of the Committee on Psychology and Pediatrics in the Medical Section; Dr. Foster, author of *Busy Childhood,* was a member of the Committee on the Infant and Preschool Child in the Section on Education and Training. The authors have not only had personal experience as parents but have also had a wide professional experience with children and are acquainted with the basic scientific literature. Dr. Stuart is a pediatrician with a background both in public health and in the medical care of children; Dr. Anderson, a psychologist whose work has lain mainly in the field of child development; and Dr. Foster, an educator who, though actively concerned with the education of the young child, is also interested in the activities of older children.

In *Healthy Childhood,* Dr. Stuart shows how parents may assist the child in acquiring a healthy body. The mother's preparation for parenthood, the principles of nutrition and of feeding, the provision of rest and activity, the control of infection and immunity, the care of the child in accidents are presented. Of especial note is the chapter on the care of children at various ages. In an appendix, the diseases of children are described in simple language. Dr. Stuart not only brings to the parent a clear view of the many practical problems arising in the physical care of the child; he also makes vivid the significant rôle played by medicine in reducing mortality and illness rates and gives an understanding of the human body upon which the child depends for his attack on life.

In *Happy Childhood,* Dr. Anderson, after a description of the equipment with which the child approaches living and the child's methods of learning and of meeting emergencies, shows how parents may assist the child in acquiring control over himself and his environment. The discussion of simple habits such as eating, sleeping, and elimination is followed by a treatment of fear and security, of love and affection, of self-

control and discipline, of language and reality, of intelligence
and knowledge, of social behavior and social esteem, and of
sex education and the quest for a mate. The quest for independence—emotional, intellectual, and vocational or economic
—is described. Practical methods of treating the child as an
individual and of training gifted and handicapped children
are next presented. A discussion of the influence of the home
and of parents is followed by a discussion of the child's quest
for happiness. Through the entire book one sees the child in
his dynamic quest for maturity as he moves in orderly
fashion from the dependence of infancy, through the experiences of childhood and adolescence, to the self-reliance of
adulthood.

In *Busy Childhood,* Dr. Foster, after pointing out the importance of occupation and play in the development of personality and character, moves on to the discussion of the play
of the infant and the vigorous play of the young child,
describing in some detail the games and activities so important for physical and mental development. Toys, play
equipment, social and dramatic play, intellectual play and
participation in family activities, play during vacations,
travel, and special days are presented in turn. A special
chapter is devoted to occupations and activities for the ill or
convalescent child. Practical illustrations and descriptions of
games and activities are given throughout, together with lists
of books, music, and play material for all ages. The volume closes with a section on home and school coöperation.
Dr. Foster has described the varied activities and interests of
the child and has given many concrete suggestions for enriching the life of the child.

Practical as these books are, they are more than books to be
read casually. Each will be found of use as a manual or
reference book to which the parent can turn again and again
for assistance. Each volume has its own separate index, followed by a brief combined index for all three. Although they

constitute a series, each volume is complete in itself and can be used independently of the others.

An expression of appreciation of the labors of the White House Conference on Child Health and Protection is unnecessary in a series of books in which each page gives evidence of indebtedness. It is the hope of the authors that not only much of immediate practical significance in the daily care of the child will emerge from the reading of the books, but that an underlying philosophy of child care and training, expressive of the point of view of the White House Conference on Child Health and Protection, will be made manifest. Authors and publisher alike express the wish that the volumes may contribute to the understanding of the child and so assist parents in rearing healthy, happy, and busy children.

PREFACE

The present volume attempts to bring to parents and teachers the most recent material which is available in the line of children's play activities, particularly that compiled in thirteen volumes published under the auspices of the White House Conference on Child Health and Protection.

The writer is indebted to Neith E. Headley and to Marion L. Mattson, the head teachers in the kindergarten and the nursery school in the Institute of Child Welfare of the University of Minnesota, for the many contributions which they made to the original outline of this book and for their criticisms of the manuscript at various stages in its development. Thanks are also due to the many friends who allowed the writer to search their snap-shot albums for pictures, to some who actually took pictures of their children to illustrate particular points, and particularly to George E. Luxton of the Minneapolis *Star* for the use of a number of his prints.

CONTENTS

CHAPTER I

The Parents' Responsibility. The Influence of Environment. The Home. Assuring Safety in the Environment. Securing the Best Physical Conditions for the Child. Providing a Desirable Mental Environment. Providing Desirable Activities. The Importance of Play. Teaching the Child to Play. Planning the Child's Play. The Possibility of Too Much Play. Advantages of Learning to Play Alone. Summary.

CHAPTER II

The Tiny Baby. Early Play. Toys Which Any House Affords. Exercises for the Baby. The Second Six Months. Keeping Toys Clean. Playing with Mother. Possible Dangers in Play for Babies. Summary.

CHAPTER III

A Place to Play. Play without Apparatus. Play with Simple Apparatus. Play with Outdoor Apparatus. The Value of Active Games in Improving Posture. Games and Sports. Summary.

CHAPTER IV

The Selection of Toys. The Commonness of Various Toys. The Child's Supply of Toys. Summary.

CONTENTS

CHAPTER V

CHAPTER VI

CHAPTER VII

CHAPTER VIII

CHAPTER IX

CHAPTER X

CONTENTS

CHAPTER XI

CHAPTER XII

CHAPTER XIII

LIST OF ILLUSTRATIONS

BUSY CHILDHOOD

Chapter I

THE WHOLE CHILD

As one year follows another, we find ourselves using familiar words in a sense in which we have not used them before. Only a few years ago, for example, the word *park* meant only a grassy place—with a few trees, shrubs, and flowers—open to all people; now we *park* automobiles; we *park* our books or umbrellas; and some of us go so far as to *park* our gum! In like manner, the word *child* for years conveyed to us the thought of any individual child as a unity, an individual; but now in order to express the same meaning we must needs say *the whole child*. The term has been devised to indicate that the child is not being considered from the somewhat biased, one-sided point of view of the specialist but from all angles and taking everything into consideration after the fashion of the old "general practitioner."

The Parents' Responsibility

In the other volumes of this series Dr. Stuart and Dr. Anderson stress the importance of two sides of the child which we ordinarily conceive of as chiefly the parents' responsibility.[1] After he has reached adult life, it is largely the individual's own concern whether he looks out for his health, whether he overeats or under-exercises, whether he lives under too great a strain, whether he becomes sluggish and a burden to himself and society, or whether he does the opposite of these

[1] Harold C. Stuart, *Healthy Childhood* (D. Appleton-Century Company, Inc., New York, 1933). John E. Anderson, *Happy Childhood* (D. Appleton-Century Company, Inc., New York, 1933).

things. There can be no doubt, however, that in the early years, the physical condition of the child is the direct responsibility of the parents. Although frequently the social graces which make a person acceptable in certain groups are deliberately acquired through the conscious effort of the individual himself, many of the fundamental habits—the habits of eating, of sleeping, of elimination and the like—are more the business of the parent than they are of the child.

All too often parents assume that their task is done when they see to it that the child is in good physical condition and has acquired certain essential habits. In other words, the parents watch over the child's eating, over his sleeping, over his elimination, and to a lesser degree over his social relations, but for the rest of his existence they take no responsibility. As soon as the child goes to school, the hours of parental control or contact are greatly lessened. Indeed, the school child sometimes sees his parents only at meals or when they supervise his cleaning up and going to bed.

Parents are obviously responsible to some extent for choosing the environment in which the child lives; they are surely responsible to the limit of their ability for promoting the child's health. Other duties which are not so universally recognized are responsibility for providing desirable mental surroundings for the child, for providing him with opportunities for the best types of activity, and for teaching him to use those opportunities to the best of his ability. The present volume is an attempt to show in what ways the home may help the child in these sometimes untouched hours, as well as in the hours which are directly concerned with the child's physical care and habit-training.

The Influence of Environment

The environment in which the child grows up has a lasting influence on all his later life. Even the physical features of the landscape sometimes affect us to a considerable degree. A woman who had been brought up in a prairie State had great difficulty in getting used to a new home in Montana. Her comment was, "At first it seemed as if I couldn't stand that mountain in my backyard; I just ached to push it out of the way so I wouldn't feel so crowded; but now that I have lived there eight years, do you know, I'd feel lonesome if that mountain was taken away." So the child who grows up near the ocean, near a lake, or near a coal mine will have all his future experiences colored to some degree by his early memories.

The Home

Most of us have to live in places which are far from ideal, but the White House Conference suggests [2] some points which we can keep in mind if we are selecting a new home. The neighborhood should be one which is "primarily residential" and "should be protected by zoning laws." The best location for a home is on a minor street which does not invite through traffic and which is "within relatively easy access of churches and schools, and civic, cultural and shopping centers" and not "unduly near railroads, aviation landing fields, public garages, stables, dumps, marshes or obnoxious industries." There should be in the neighborhood some provision for play, "either in individual yards, or in yards thrown together, or in accessible and safely approached neighborhood playgrounds, adequately equipped and supervised." The house lot itself "should be wide enough so that each room will have sufficient light from open spaces on its own lot, . . . should be properly graded or drained so that there will be no standing water," should be planted with trees and shrubs to "provide an attractive setting and furnish shade and privacy." It goes, perhaps, without saying that the house should be well built in every respect. "The house should be so designed and

2 *The Home and the Child* (The Century Co., New York, 1931), p. 13 ff.

placed upon the lot as to provide for adequate sunning and
natural lighting of all rooms. . . . Houses to be safe should
be resistive to fire. There is a considerable loss of life annually
of children in America because of the prevailing practice of
building houses that are not fire-resistive. . . . The room arrangement in the house plan should be such as to make it
possible to avoid waste motion, to save unnecessary steps and
to facilitate housework. . . . Each room should have adequate
natural ventilation." Radiators "should be screened so as to
protect children." If a nursery is provided, "the floor area
should allow at least eighty-four square feet for each child.
Artificial lighting should be high and indirect. . . . Since
most of the child's play is on the floor, hardwood floors or
floors overlaid with battleship linoleum or cork are recommended. The bed space for the child should be away from the
area in which the toys are kept. . . . Steep stairs should be
avoided. Landings should be broad. Triangular turns on
stairs are unsafe and undesirable. Handrails or balustrades
within the reach of young children should be provided on all
stairs, including those leading to the cellar and attic. All
stairs should be adequately lighted and where there are young
children it is often advisable to place gates at the tops of
stairs. . . . Some place should be provided as a playroom for
children. In case the extra room cannot be afforded by the
family a corner of a bedroom, nursery, enclosed porch, or of
some other room, or in the case of older children a portion of
a well lighted and well ventilated shed or attic may be used
for this purpose. . . . Low drawers and cupboards or other
special provision should be made for children's playthings.
There should be adequate provision for privacy for each
member of the family. Each child should have a place where
he can be quiet and undisturbed and have an opportunity for
uninterrupted study of home lessons or for reading or playing. There should be a workshop in which the men and boys of
the house can putter. This usually can be located in a dry,

sunny, well ventilated basement, shed, garage, or attic."
The actual physical environment is, then, important but the way the environment is used is still more important. The perfect house which is kept by the "perfect housekeeper" is a thing of horror, of good intentions gone wrong; the perfect house which is used to the utmost is a thing of joy. The White House Conference [3] suggests: "The smooth-running, ordered household contributes to the development of children for two reasons: first, because it frees the time and the energy of the adult members of the family for the needs of the children, and prevents those situations, always detrimental to development, which arise out of haste and irritability; second, because it provides an environment in which both boys and girls may develop a wholesome attitude toward home life and prepare for their own future home-making."

Assuring Safety in the Environment

The child's physical environment must not only be healthful; it must also be safe. It is obvious that the streets of the present day are dangerous places and that every child should have some other play space provided. If this other space is a playground, it should be furnished with reasonably safe apparatus, strongly built and kept in good repair; if the play space is an indoor playroom or gymnasium, such hazards as "steel or concrete pillars, posts or other obstructions projecting over the playing floor may be dangerous. Padding such projections often removes the hazard." [4]

One hazard which has been reduced greatly in recent years is that of drowning accidents. The American Red Cross has taught first aid, and "each year more children are being taught to swim and better supervision is provided by trained life guards at swimming places. As a result, although the

[3] *The Home and the Child*, p. 5.
[4] *Safety Education in Schools* (The Century Co., New York, 1932), p. 19.

number of children who are using our swimming pools, beaches, and other bathing places has increased many fold during the last decade, there has been no appreciable change in the number of drowning fatalities.'' [5]

Some of the suggestions which the White House Conference makes for the teaching of safety at home are: [6]

"Straighten rugs so others will not trip.

"Pick up trash and place it in proper receptacle.

"Avoid standing in rockers, playing on stairways and high places.

"Avoid sitting on window sills or leaning against glass doors or screens.

"Go upstairs one step at a time.

"Learn dangers of sewing machines, wringers, washing machines, electric fans, lawn mowers, and other machines used in and about homes.

"Avoid tasting contents of bottles and eating unfamiliar berries."

Securing the Best Physical Conditions for the Child

The physical environment will often be selected before the child is born. Once that is chosen, the family can turn its attention to assuring the best physical conditions for the child himself. Health is of great importance to any individual. Under the discussion of the school health program the White House Conference says:

"Health is a condition that permits the individual to realize the fullest development and expression of his best self, to render his best service, and to achieve his greatest happiness. It is a condition of organic soundness and adequate physical, mental and emotional functioning. . . . It is true that some men of poor health have made great contributions to society. In some instances poor health may have been an incentive to greater effort for a time. Yet it is possible that such success has been in spite of the condition rather than a result of it, and that with good health the period of service would have been extended and the individual's contribution greater. Under normal conditions, society should condemn scientists, teachers,

[5] *Safety Education in Schools*, p. 4.
[6] *Ibid.*, p. 26 f.

preachers, business leaders, or any other public servants, who lose their health or their lives prematurely thru their own indolence or neglect. . . . On the other hand, devotion to health for its own sake, and a constant search to attain it for personal welfare, seldom leads to any lasting contribution to society."—*Administration of the School Health Program* (The Century Co., New York, 1932), p. 13.

Not only does good health make for a more efficient and happier individual, but it may also act as a preventive of bad behavior. A study of delinquents [7] reports that "there is ample proof . . . that the existence of certain physical defects, diseases and peculiarities has an important bearing upon the incidence of misconduct. . . . The peculiarity may act secondarily in the sense that it serves to set the child apart, to make him different from others, for example deformities which impel the child to abnormal conduct as a means of fulfilling those natural ambitions he feels are thwarted by his physical defect." Then, moreover, there are "such things as unusual stature, physical peculiarities that may seem trivial to everyone but the child himself, poor vision, and similar difficulties that make school and other success beyond easy attainment. Important as are these possible physical factors there is danger in overemphasis upon them. . . . Deeper, more ominous and more significant is the child's attitude about the physical disability. . . . Nowhere in the field of delinquency is a finer art required than in this matter of aiding the disabled child to meet his disability without bitterness, his handicaps without defeat."

The foregoing quotations stress the fact that important though physical surroundings and physical condition of the individual are, still more important are the mental environment and the individual's state of mind. All too often we toss the problem of the unhappy or the irritable child to one side with the thought that "she comes by it naturally," "he gets his terrible temper from his grandfather," or something of

[7] *The Delinquent Child* (The Century Co., New York, 1932), p. 28.

the kind, without ever asking what we, as parents, can do to help the child to a healthier and happier attitude toward life.

Providing a Desirable Mental Environment

Probably the mental environment provided by the family, intimate friends, and playfellows is the most important influence in the mental life of the child, and the influence of the family begins its work first and continues longest and most steadily. As one group phrases it:

"As a foundation for a satisfying life, every child needs to be wanted, loved and understood. He needs to feel that he is accepted and belongs because of his own individual place and values in relation to the rest of the group. As he grows and develops, he will have an ever widening sphere of affection which starts with the mother, the father, and other members of the family, and later extends to those outside the family group. To the individual child this is security. . . . If we think of security as a growing, developing state which is not limited to a static relationship in one's own family group, it is important to consider the child who finds himself caught in too close, too dependent a tie on those in whom he found his earliest needs satisfied, and from whom he has never been able to reach out to a wider security in his relations to other people. . . . Growing up to become a responsible adult involves not only the expression of one-self but that expression in relation to one's social environment. With all children the earliest social environment is the family and it is, therefore, the child's relation to the needs of that group that determines much of his later relationship to other social institutions, such as the school, industry, the state. . . . If a child's earlier and most intimate groups fail him, he will, while still very young, go forth into his community to satisfy his longing for affection, appreciation, companionship, and adventure, and will respond to what he finds there with an immature evaluation. That which attracts and satisfies him the most may be the very thing that will make him socially unadjusted, delinquent or criminal. . . . In his inner feelings or emotional life the delinquent very often is found to be unsatisfactorily adjusted to other personalities or conditions in his environment. It is frequently discovered that a delinquent is a creature of unsatisfied desires; he may be habitually unhappy, or only at periods;

he may have times of restlessness, known only to himself, or they may be exhibited openly. Feelings of frustration, of thwarting, are sometimes brought to light. The child may have a sense of not being wanted in some group or of not being trusted, or of not belonging. Perhaps he does not achieve success in his family group or in his school, or among his playmates."—*The Delinquent Child* (The Century Co., New York, 1932), pp. 25, 66, 82, 85, and 193.

Again:

"It is recognized that the more subtle influences of home life, such as the degree of intelligence and understanding on the part of the parents, the relationship of parents one to another and to the children, and of the children to each other, are the most important factors relating to the home to be considered in dealing with behavior problems."—*The Delinquent Child* (The Century Co., New York, 1932), p. 350.

We see, then, that a normal, happy home life is the most important factor in the mental health of the child. According to the White House Conference study of delinquency, there is some indication that the lack of such a home life is "a more significant factor in the delinquency of girls than of boys," but there can be little doubt that if we wish a child of either sex to develop into the highest type of individual, one of the first things to provide is a desirable mental environment. In this environment the affection of the family and the feeling that each individual fills an important place in the family group is of paramount importance.

Next in importance to the other members of the family come the playmates and friends.

"Whether a child lives in the city, the town or the country, whether he is privileged or under privileged, he seeks friends and chums of his own age and liking, and forms with them small spontaneous social groups. These may become clubs or gangs, or may exist without any name at all or the significance that names can imply. Even if altogether undirected and unknown to others, such groups have great value in the life of the child and seldom breed delinquency unless the community in which the members live offers opportunities and suggestions for it. . . . When the child can find near home, with companions

of his own choice, opportunity for all that his ever widening sphere
of craving and interests demands, when his community, including
all groups, private, municipal, commercial, holds as its greatest
asset the security and development of all of its children; when the
spirit of the neighborhood reflects our most ideal teaching, then will
the community help to minimize those behavior problems that handi-
cap the lives of so many children. . . . Many studies of delinquent
children have emphasized the importance of bad companions as a
factor in the problem [of delinquency]. Healy and Bronner believed
bad companionship to be a causative factor in delinquency in 62
per cent of 3,000 cases and stated that it varied little for the sexes."—
The Delinquent Child (The Century Co., New York, 1932), pp. 195,
224, 417.

We cannot so easily prove that good companionship is a
causative factor in desirable behavior, but few students of
children will deny that this is a fact.

Providing Desirable Activities

Now that, theoretically, we have placed our child in the
most desirable physical environment, with the best sort of
family life, and the most desirable of companions, shall we
leave him to his own devices? Some people would answer
"Yes," but most teachers and workers with children would
answer, "No. We must see that he has something to do." Our
grandmothers would have retorted, "Satan finds mischief for
idle hands to do" and would have launched a program in
which most of the day was filled with work of one sort or
another, often with little thought as to the value or the harm
which the work might bring to the child.

Even such work-enthusiasts as our early forebears would
hardly have countenanced exhausting work in factories for
any except children who were considered inferior and un-
worthy of an education or the finer things of life, but it was
not uncommon to find boys of twelve or even ten doing what
was almost a man's work on the farm. Now we find that the
"growing conviction that too early employment, except for

motivation and appreciation of the work done by others, shortens productive life by limiting the individual's chances for an education, and interferes with personal development and occupational outlook, has reversed the attitude toward the child as a potential worker." [8] Such statements sound perfectly sensible to most of us, and yet if some one asks us if the case of the boy working on the farm is not different, we are apt to reply enthusiastically, "Oh, farm work is quite a different story. There the child is working in the fresh air and sunshine and is merely getting healthful exercise from his work." Persons who are working on the question of child labor, however, often give a quite different point of view. The committee of the White House Conference which was concerned with the problems of child labor reports:

"Whether or not any particular type of work is harmful for children depends on many things: whether, for instance, the work is too heavy for their years and physical development, or too long continued; whether it is hurried and therefore conducive to overstrain and excessive fatigue; whether it is of a kind that requires unnatural postures for long periods, or causes overdevelopment of one set of muscles at the expense of others; whether it exposes the child to damp and cold, or necessitates continued work under a hot sun; whether it involves accident hazards; whether the children away from home are housed in healthful and sanitary accommodations.

"There is little definite information about the physical effects of work in agriculture. Undoubtedly many of the tasks done by children are quite harmless, provided that they are not carried on by too young children, or for too continuous a period. . . . Farm boys and girls do not develop symmetrically. . . . Farm boys in the Army camps were slower to respond to play stimuli and reached the point of fatigue more quickly than city boys in activities that required the use of the whole body."—*Child Labor* (The Century Co., New York, 1932), p. 253 f.

Henry S. Curtis, who has written extensively on play is quoted in the White House Conference report on child labor as saying, "Country boys and girls are apt to be round-

[8] *Vocational Guidance* (The Century Co., New York, 1932), p. 169.

shouldered and flat-chested, with forward-slanting heads. Boys who have done much hard work are usually awkward and clumsy, almost without that grace and suppleness that are characteristic of a child who has been trained through play. Country children generally have more stable nerves than city children. Their digestion is commonly good. But they are apt to be deficient in lung capacity and heart development.''

Too much work, then, or too hard work is likely to have a deleterious effect on the child's physical condition; no work at all may have a deleterious effect on the child's mental outlook. The question of what work the child can do in the household will be discussed in a later chapter.

It is perhaps obvious to the present generation of parents that no child should be expected to work for long continued hours. In fact, the so-called ''modern parent'' is often all too ready to concede that this is indeed the ''children's century'' and that children should be allowed to do as they like, which in the opinion of the unthinking parent is the same thing as ''playing'' all day at anything they choose. That the parent has any responsibility for this play is beyond their conception for they fail to realize the real significance of the child's play. The more we study the occupations of the child the more we see that many things which the child greatly enjoys, he could not easily learn by himself.

''Young people need not only to learn that which will enable them to earn a living but they need also to be taught resources and skills that will enable them to make a happy use of leisure and that will satisfy persons whose working life, because of its often monotonous and repetitive character, offers little that is satisfying.''—*Child Labor* (The Century Co., New York, 1932), p. 25.

''The developmental needs of the state and municipality arise from the responsibility of each generation to equip the coming generation for more effective living. This is the main purpose of education, of recreational opportunity, and of the protection of children and young people from conditions that may hamper their development."—*The Delinquent Child* (The Century Co., New York, 1932), p. 227 f.

The Importance of Play

The question then arises: Why is play so important? The answer may be given that play occupies the largest part of the child's life and is the great preparation for future living. One of the older theories of play stated that play was the "instinctive preparation for future serious occupation" and "an agency employed to develop crude powers and prepare them for life's uses." There is no doubt that play does to some extent prepare the child for his later life. Playing house is a sort of rehearsal of the things which the housekeeper does; playing ball may be the earliest training of the future baseball player; splashing in the bathtub is the simplest form of water-sport and may be the first enthusiasm of the life-saver. More than this, much that a child learns in play is of the greatest value to his later life. Through play he may develop self-direction, initiative, patience, persistence, courage, resourcefulness, concentration, ability to coöperate, power of inhibition, and many other qualities which are of inestimable import to his later relationships.

It is not wholly or even in great part because play may be excellent training for the future that the modern child psychologist is concerned with it. It is, rather, because play takes up almost all of the time of the pre-school child and a great part of the time of the school child that we should give it our serious attention. If an individual is to be an adequate or a superior adult, successful in his undertakings and well adjusted to the civilization in which he lives, then that person needs to have had a happy wholesome childhood filled with worth-while activities. And of all the activities of childhood, play is the most worth while. The successful adult is, nine times out of ten, the person who was a successful child, and

by successful child we mean not the child who works steadily
to prepare for his future maturity but the child who gets
most out of and puts most into the life of the present. Although it is a fine thing to prepare for the future, some people
never stop the preparation but spend their entire lives in the
preparing with no years left for fulfillment. So, with an eye
on the future as a matter of course, let us train the children
to live the present to the utmost of their ability and let us
remember that each day is important not only as the forerunner of the future but as the present day itself. As Lee puts
it, "Play is to the boy what work is to the man—the fullest
attainable expression of what he is and the effective means of
becoming more." [9]

Teaching the Child to Play

Odd as it may seem, most children have to be taught how
to play—taught not only how to play games but also how to
indulge in the formless, ruleless, merry frolics that remind us
of the play of kittens and puppies. Usually, of course, they receive their training at the hands of older playmates. Sometimes this is good training, sometimes it is bad; practically
never is it the most desirable training. The very young uncle
often brings a rattle to a new-born baby and seems surprised
and rather disgusted when the baby does not grasp it and crow
with joy. The same uncle may be disappointed when an older
child does not at once grasp all the possibilities of a new toy.
The fact is that most of us have to learn the possibilities of
any form of play sometimes through numberless repetitions.
What adult gets the utmost possible fun out of a deck of
cards the first time he sees one? They are nothing but a series
of rather stupid-looking designs bearing consecutive numbers
and varied somewhat by a few pictures. What boy or girl fully

[9] J. Lee, *Play in Education* (The Macmillan Company, New York,
1926), p. viii.

enjoys a tennis racket when it first arrives? The child who is given a tennis racket or a golf club will have some fun hitting balls, but he will at first miss the greater fun that will come when, after some instruction and practice, he can actually play tennis or golf.

We do not mean to imply that, with every new toy, the adult should supply a set of exact directions. Quite the contrary, for the child needs plenty of time to investigate a toy and to discover its possibilities. It may be that he will discover uses for the toy which do not occur to the adult with his cramped imagination, though it is equally possible that he will fail to work out the most satisfying forms of play which a given toy may provide. If, for example, a child is given one of the wooden penguins now on sale at many of the five-and-ten-cent stores, he may be months in discovering that the penguin will walk if it is placed on a smooth slanting board and he may thus be missing a great deal of the fun that particular toy has to offer. But it may very well be that this individual child is not particularly pleased with that activity of the penguin and may be happier pretending that the penguin is an eagle who flies through the air, builds his nest high in the bookcase, and so on. If this is so, let the adult content himself with showing the child that one possibility, thereafter permitting him to follow his own interests.

It has been said many times that we Americans do not know how to play, that we take our play much too seriously, that we do not run for the fun of the running but for the sake of surpassing some one else or for the sake of surpassing our own previous record. The White House Conference suggests on this point:

"The competitive motive often approved by educators helps foster feelings of inadequacy and inferiority in the vanquished, and equally often, undeserved feelings of superiority and triumph in the winner. Nothing is worth doing merely in order to beat someone else. An activity first of all should be worth while in itself. The question is not how many pupils did you beat, but how well can you do it, are you improving, or can you do it as well as you need to."—*The School Health Program* (The Century Co., New York, 1932), p. 67.

Some children seem to have a natural liking for games and enter into any new play with zest. Other children hang back and spend their time watching from the side-lines. Frequently this reluctance to enter the game is the result of a child's fear that he will not do as well as the others, in other words it is due to a feeling of inferiority which is, in turn, due to lack of practice. If such a child can be given practice, he too will enter wholeheartedly into the game. Just as many people learn to like olives only after eating them repeatedly, so many people do not like games until they have played them many times. As in all other learning, the pleasant outcome has the greatest influence on the individual's desire to repeat the experience. So, if you are teaching children a new game, try to make sure that their first attempts at it are interesting and that they bring satisfaction. Exorbitant praise at the first attempts of the baby to pronounce a word or at the first attempts of the older child to toss a basketball into the basket may be the inspiration for long-continued attempts to perform the act again and more satisfactorily.

Another kind of training which it is sometimes necessary to give a child is in learning to be a good loser and a good winner. There is probably no one attribute more important to the member of a social group than the ability to accept defeat pleasantly, as all in the day's work, and to accept victory modestly, as something that one is happy to have but which does not, as the children say, "turn one's head."

Another rule which is of paramount importance in any sort of play or game is to "play fair." Children often give each other the strictest training in this regard; they simply will not tolerate any one who cheats. Adults, in too great affection for a child, often openly cheat themselves to help the child win unfairly. This is poor training. We all smile in-

It's Fun to Watch Other People Do Things Too

dulgently at the little old lady cheating herself at solitaire. At her age and in that game it really makes very little differ- ence how she plays or what rules she makes for herself, but the person who is playing with other people must learn to stick to the rules, play fair, and accept the outcome as of no im- portance save as it shows how hard he has tried and how far he has succeeded.

Planning the Child's Play

Not only do we need to encourage children in the kind of play which seems best for them, physically and mentally, but we also need to plan their free hours so that they get a varied experience. The girl who spends all her spare time with dolls and the boy who spends all his play time with a bat and ball are not attaining the all-round experience which they need. Although deep-rooted and lasting play interests are highly desirable, we must make sure that the children are not missing opportunities for experiences which might actually prove to be more interesting than the dolls or the bat. When a child's play loses its spontaneity or when long periods of inactivity and apparent lack of interest appear, the wise parent will ar- range for him to enter into some new activity. Often, of course, this must be done tactfully. Interest in stamps will often arise from hearing some adult tell how he has found certain very interesting stamps for his own collection; in- terest in football may start from seeing older boys play; interest in cooking from being asked to help mother on some special job, and so on. The greater the range of the child's play interests, the better rounded is his development, and the less likely he is to be bored with himself or the world.

In the succeeding chapters of this book, we have tried to suggest a few of the innumerable forms of happy and de- velopmental occupations which are available for the child, and we have tried to remind the parent and teacher that play is often more interesting when an adult enters in too. Perhaps the best rule for teaching a child a new way to play is: Play with the child yourself. After children are familiar with a game, particularly if there are several who know it, they will carry it on by themselves, but the learning period often passes more quickly and more happily if the adult helps out.

The Possibility of Too Much Play

There is a word of warning which perhaps should be sounded at this point. Although we believe that all the games and plays and activities which have been suggested here are desirable for the child, we offer them as suggestions and hope that parents will select the ones which seem to fit their particular situation rather than attempt to try them all. It is just as serious to overplay as it is to overwork. It is just as serious for the child to have too much supervision as it is to have too little, so may we plead at this point for some time each day and some days each year for which there is absolutely nothing planned. In this modern age we often tend, in our anxiety to give the child all the available opportunities, to crowd him so with appointments that he is hurried from one thing to another without a moment to get his breath or to relax and think over the things he has seen. A few weeks ago a friend reported that her child was becoming more and more irritable and had completely lost her former sunny disposition. The family physician, when consulted, inquired into her out-of-school activities and found that for weeks every afternoon after school had been taken up with some special appointment or, if not that, with going to the home of some friend for play and for dinner. The physician prescribed an entire week of coming home directly from school and playing there all alone. After three days of this régime, the child's former disposition returned and she was once more enjoying life. When this incident was being discussed among some friends, a father spoke up and said his child of ten was also doing too much. The mother retorted that she wasn't doing too much at all, that she was merely having three swimming lessons a week; attending one girl-scout meeting, one girl-reserve meeting; joining one Sunday school group one week-day evening every other week, and taking a trip to the dentist every other week to get her teeth straightened. Until the previous week, she had had a music lesson each week and a half hour's practice on the piano each day. What a schedule for a child who was spending supposedly "full" days in school already! The child does not separate work and play as definitely in his mind as does the adult. School, dancing lessons, tennis, and trips to the dentist are simply "things to do," so that, while we may feel that some of these are definitely forms of recreation and thus in a different category from the others, we cannot count on any one seeming like true "play" to the child.

Advantages of Learning to Play Alone

One form of play which should be provided for every child is "playing alone." (See Anderson's *Happy Childood*, Chapter X. Also Stuart's *Healthy Childhood*, Chapters X and XIII.) The well-adjusted individual must be contented without companions just as he must be contented with them. This is partly because there will be periods in the life of every person when he will be alone and there is no need for him to be unhappy merely on that account. It is also partly because the peace and quiet of playing alone is a great restorative of poise and of serenity. There is no one other treatment for temper tantrums, for scrapping, for irritability, for any sort of social difficulty which can compare with a short period of isolation. When a group of children (or adults) are having difficulty in getting along together, there are two very simple methods of restoring peace and good will: one is to provide food, the other is to provide a short period of separation. An orange or a glass of milk, two or three minutes in a room alone, or the same length of time in absolute relaxation in a room where there may be others but where there is quiet, will calm almost any storm arising in the play of young children. The child who learns to play happily by himself without losing the joy of sometimes playing with other children, has an accomplishment which will stand him in good stead all his days.

Summary

In summary, we may say that the home-education of the "whole child" is concerned not only with the planning of the physical environment in which he lives and the attainment of the best physical condition possible for him, but also with his mental or social environment and with his occupations. The child's home activities are of the greatest importance to his development and well-being and should be planned by the parents with such care that he will have enough interesting things to do but not too many.

Chapter II

THE PLAY OF THE INFANT

THINKING adults now realize that the period of infancy (see Stuart's *Healthy Childhood,* Chapters V and XV) is one of great importance for the ultimate development of the child. For some time parents have been reading uncounted pages of good advice on the care of the baby's health and consulting the pediatrician regularly with reference to food, clothing, and prevention of disease. More recently parents have become concerned over the formation of habits, mental attitudes, and emotional "sets" in the baby. No longer do we say with the immigrant mother, "All the baby, they cry for one year." We feel, on the contrary, that when the baby cries something must be wrong and we check up on his health, his physical comfort, and finally on his activities. Occasionally we find a baby who is obviously bored with his existence, restless for the want of something to do, without the ability to correct the difficulty, and without a parent observant enough to recognize his need. Although no one can say at just what hour a baby begins to play, all mothers would agree that, by the time the baby is a year old, he is playing a good deal.

The Tiny Baby

The day-old baby is apparently a rather insensitive creature. He does not hear; he sees only vaguely; he probably does not smell or taste; and he is not disturbed by pin pricks or small cuts. It is no wonder, then, that he shows no activity which we can call play. It is possible for an adult to play without movement, as by day-dreaming whether in fanciful imagining or in reminiscence of past pleasures. The tiny baby, however, has had so little experience that we cannot believe he can amuse himself by thinking, even when he seems to be pondering on the sorrows of the world or the enigma of life. The only way, then, that a baby can play is through activity, through using his muscles. This means that he cannot play until he gains some control over the muscles of his body.

Shirley has shown, in her interesting study of twenty-five young babies [1] from their birth to their third year, that the first muscles over which a baby gains any control are those of the eyes. Most babies make fleeting attempts to follow a light by the time they are four days old. At the age of four weeks these same babies look at a stationary light, and in another week they look at persons, or at least at the face and hands of persons who come near them. Before twelve weeks are past they have noticed their own hands. During these same weeks the babies are kicking and squirming, working their arms and moving their heads. They are also making quite a bit of noise: at first a thin piping and squeaking, later a lusty cry, and frequently a screaming when handled by strangers. With such a limited range of vision and of movement, the only reactions which could be classified as play are the watching of moving objects or persons, the waving of arms and legs, the exercising of the voice, and the investigation of his own fingers.

During the first quarter year of life, the baby may well be let alone for the greatest part of the day. He is gradually getting control over his various muscles and growing accustomed to the "blooming, buzzing confusion" about him. No attempt should be made to hasten his development. In the first place, such attempts are usually met with failure; in the

[1] Mary M. Shirley, *The First Two Years* (The University of Minnesota Press, Minneapolis, 1931).

second place, actual harm may be done to the child by putting stress on bones, ligaments, and muscles which are not yet sufficiently developed to stand the strain. If he is the first child in a family, he will probably suffer from one of two extremes. The parents may fail to realize his weakness and his disabilities and so may provide too much stimulation, too much excitement, too much handling. In this case, he may develop into a fussy, crying child who expects attention at every moment of the day. On the other hand, the parents may have been so impressed with the necessity for "scientific" upbringing that, while they attend meticulously to his physical wants, they fail to give him any companionship or to give him the foundation for future play. The White House Conference has shown that the oldest child is given toys earlier than the younger ones.

A five- or ten-minute period every day in which the mother or father encourages the baby to play will not only be a happy time for both of them but will actually help the child in the months to come. Just before the bath is probably the best time for this "play." Strip the baby's clothes off and let him lie naked on a bed in a warm room. He will kick and squirm and wave his arms and legs with much more freedom than is possible with even the loosest and most comfortably arranged garments. Then talk to him in a pleasant low voice, avoiding very loud or sudden noises. The baby will become accustomed to your voice, will learn to listen to the modulations of tone, and will really be taking the first steps toward understanding spoken language. Hold your hand gently against the soles of his feet and feel him kick and push. You are encouraging him to exercise his leg muscles. Try every once in a while the old familiar, "This little pig went to market, this little pig stayed home, etc." Often a baby of four or five months will be entertained by this play. While he is still spending his days lying on his back it may be possible to provide something for him to look at, such as stationary pictures on the ceiling.

The White House Conference found [2] that the percentage of infants who are allowed to play on the bed unclothed varies with the occupational class to which the father belongs. In the following table, Occupational Group I includes the various professions, Group II the big business men and managers, Group III the small independent business men, Group IV the farmers, Group V skilled laborers, Group VI semi-skilled laborers, Group VII unskilled laborers.

PERCENTAGE OF CHILDREN WHO PLAY ON BED UNCLOTHED

Occupational Group	Age, 1 day–5 mos.	Age, 6–11 mos.
I	81	58
II	68	46
III	49	54
IV	30	38
V	46	49
VI	46	30
VII	40	70

Early Play

Such activities as the tiny baby's free moving on the bed may seem little enough like recreation, but soon—between the ages of three and six months—we find a number of activities which more clearly display the element of play. The baby of this age discovers his own hands and fingers one hand with the other. His muscular coördination is so poor that he does not always succeed in clasping his hands at the first trial, but after repeated attempts he can wave his arms about in a clumsy fashion and bring his hands in contact with each other. Sometimes he slips and bats himself in the face with his fist. This blow may even have enough force to startle him into a cry. More frequently it happens that, during the waving of his arms, he brings his hand into contact with his

[2] *The Young Child in the Home: A Survey of Three Thousand American Families.* This report has not yet appeared in book form (1933).

mouth and starts sucking his thumb, as he will any object held to his mouth. The overanxious mother may throw up her hands in horror at this, but the experienced mother knows that, in the average child, "thumb-sucking" is merely a passing phase of his education which will disappear when he acquires the muscular control necessary to grasp a toy. Most children take much more delight in a rattle than in even a very superior thumb. A rattle, you see, makes a noise, and a rattle can be thumped against the side of the crib without unpleasant pain! A rattle which is merely a large celluloid ring can be held in both fists and affords great joy to many a baby. Rattles with small handles are not nearly so satisfactory because a baby can grasp objects only when he uses his whole hand, and he has great trouble with anything requiring fine coördination of finger muscles. The White House Conference shows that the rattle is the first toy of practically all babies. While no child uses it under one month of age, it is popular with 69 per cent of those between four and seven months.

Although the rattle is the typical toy for an infant, there are dozens of other things which he enjoys and which he should be given. He should be allowed to handle objects of many shapes and colors, objects that are fairly heavy and objects that are light, some that are rough and some that are smooth, and so on in great variety, omitting of course those that are sharp or in any other way dangerous. It is only by investigation, by feeling of, looking at, listening to, even by smelling and tasting of things, that he can learn about the world around him. Rubber animals meet many of the baby's requirements. They are easy to grasp, light enough to be lifted without strain, and they can be dropped on the face without harm; they are easily cleaned, they provide excellent chewing, and many of them can be made to squeak. Care must be taken about the whistle in these animals, however. If it is at all loose, it must be removed so that there is no chance for the baby to get it into his mouth and throat.

Toys Which Any House Affords

Many objects which are of the greatest interest to a baby are found around any house. A clothes-pin is just about the right size to be grasped and shifted from one hand to the other. When the baby is a little older he will enjoy pushing the open ends of two clothes-pins together so that they will hold. Empty spools, strung on a string or tape, make one of the oldest of baby toys and one of the most satisfactory, for spools are a convenient size for him and they will slip back and forth along the string in an interesting manner. A bunch of keys affords almost endless amusement and considerable experience in variations of shape. Large wooden beads and other smooth objects, hung from the edge of the crib or from a ribbon stretched across the crib, provide excellent opportunity for practice in reaching, grasping, or kicking. Before the child is six months old he has usually begun his long-to-be-continued interest in paper. As a baby, however, he is not interested in the possibilities of using paper for drawing, cutting, and folding, as he will be in the years to come. His first interest in paper is in tearing, crumpling, and rattling it. A stiff writing paper which will not tear is not nearly so satisfactory, from his point of view, as is a newspaper which can be shredded with ease; but whether it be brown paper, newspaper, or tissue paper, it will be enjoyed and destroyed with all the signs of great interest and entertainment. Another material which affords joy is cloth, usually the child's own clothing or bedding. Even though this cannot be torn up, it can be picked at and chewed in a most earnest fashion. Other materials, like the wood or metal of the crib, the tray to the high-chair, and the mother's hand, which cannot be torn or even chewed with any degree of success, can be clawed or scratched. And then there are the joys of the bath. To be sure the baby is probably still being supported on mother's arm, but he has discovered the fun of splashing, and he works his arms up and down against the water in a vigorous fashion that is usually most distracting to mother.

During the second quarter of the baby's first year, he is becoming increasingly interested in the people around him. More and more he enjoys having his mother talk to him, and he frequently gurgles, babbles, and laughs in response. He seems interested not only in the tones of her voice but in the expressions of her face as well. His gaze now wanders around the room and fastens on curtains swaying in the wind, on the canary hopping in his cage, and on the sunbeams lighting up various pictures or bits of furniture. He is attaining better control over his own body, especially his eyes, head, and arms, and consequently he is gaining some mastery over his immediate surroundings and is manipulating them, to some degree at least, to suit himself. In other words, he is playing.

Exercises for the Baby

Tisdall [3] has suggested some regular exercises for the baby which may well be considered as plays. Regular exercises are suggested for babies from five to twelve months of age, particularly for those troubled with constipation. Just before the baby's bath he should be laid naked on a firm table which has been covered with a blanket. The temperature of the room should be about 75°. Dr. Tisdall's four exercises are given below:

"Exercise 1. The baby is laid on his back with his feet toward the mother. The mother then grasps the baby's hands with her own and pulls the baby toward herself, thus helping him into a sitting position. The exercise should be repeated two or three times. The baby tries to help himself up, which strengthens the arm, shoulder, neck and abdominal muscles.

"Exercise 2. The baby is laid on his back with his feet toward the mother. The mother then simply grasps both feet with her hands and

[3] F. F. Tisdall, *The Home Care of the Infant and Child* (William Morrow & Co., New York, 1931).

gently resists any movements that the baby may make with his legs. This resistance usually stimulates the baby to kick all the more. The exercise should be continued one or two minutes. It serves to strengthen the leg muscles.

"*Exercise 3*. The baby is laid on his back with his feet toward the mother. The baby's legs are raised up and the calves grasped near the ankle with the mother's thumbs on the inner side and her closed fingers around the outer side of the baby's legs and toward the baby's face. The baby's feet are brought toward his nose with knees straight and the thighs in contact with the abdomen. This exercise should be repeated three or four times. It tends to strengthen not only the leg but also the abdominal muscles. It is of particular benefit to babies with constipation or distended abdomen.

"*Exercise 4*. The baby is laid on his back with his feet toward the mother. The legs are grasped by the mother midway between the knees and the ankles with the mother's thumbs at the front of the baby's legs and her fingers circling around the outer and back part of the calves. The legs are then lifted up until the lower part of the baby's back is not only off the table but the body and legs are almost in a vertical position with only the baby's head and upper part of the shoulders on the table. The baby is then allowed to return to its original position. The exercise should be repeated 2 or 3 times. It tends to strengthen the trunk and spinal muscles. There are many other useful exercises but the above four serve to strengthen the majority of the baby's muscles."

The Second Six Months

The baby stops being a "tiny baby," a completely helpless individual, by the time he is six or seven months old and is able to sit up alone. He now gets considerable amusement from watching people, dogs, and cars as they pass on the street. He is interested in watching the other people in the room with him; he throws his toys onto the floor and then peers over the edge of his high-chair at them; he makes responses to other people that are clearly social in nature.

One of the most satisfactory pieces of play material for a child of this age is an ordinary teaspoon, or a spoon of slightly larger size. It can be grasped firmly by a small fist,

Water Play in a City Yard

A Wagon Is Used by Children of All Ages

can be chewed, and can be used for pounding a pan, a table, or any other handy bit of furniture. If the spoon is highly polished, some children will be fascinated at the image of themselves which they find in the bowl. Almost everything in the baby's environment will inspire him with a desire to pull at it. If the result is amusing, as it is when he pulls mother's hair, or the window curtain, or the table-cloth, he will be apt to try pulling it again at some other time. Other objects furnish just as much pleasure when they are pushed. Many a parent carefully builds an elaborate block tower for the baby, only to see it knocked over at once. Mother and daddy often fail to realize that the baby has no fun in admiring the high tower; the only fun is in making it fall down. So, too, a rocking-chair will be pushed for the joy of watching it rock, or a swinging door will be pushed, sometimes with unfortunate results. Toys will be thrown to the floor for the fun of watching and hearing them fall. It is not nearly so amusing when mother ties the toys to the high-chair to save herself the trouble of picking them up off the floor, for part of the fun seems to be in watching some one do just that. During this second half of the first year the baby continues to enjoy tearing up paper or thin cardboard boxes. Anything in which he can dig his small fingers is interesting. Soap is perhaps the most satisfactory medium for this activity, but dough or bread or a cold boiled potato are just as amusing from the point of view of the baby. The thoughtful mother will find many materials about the house which provide the baby with ample opportunity for investigation.

By the time the baby is nine months old he has usually begun to exhibit some interest in pictures. He is also getting interested in fumbling over the pages of books or magazines, and he gradually becomes able to turn the pages of his picture books. Unfortunately his interest in tearing paper is not limited to loose sheets, and so it is disastrous to put an ordinary picture book in his hands. There are, however, a number of good picture books printed on linen or linenette which are sufficiently durable to last for several months. At first the baby is not concerned if his book is wrong side up. A horse with its feet in the air is recognized as readily as one standing on the ground. An apple or a ball, of course, may be seen any side up, and it is merely adult prejudice that makes us turn the picture book around for the baby.

Practically all babies over eight months of age play with something. The White House Conference found [4] that 75 per cent of children between the ages of eight and eleven months played with rattles; over half of them played with balls or household utensils; almost half played with dolls; and about a third of them played with paper. Children of this age are also more likely to show interest in the toys of older brothers and sisters than are younger babies. The conference data show very little difference between the play of boys and girls, though there is some slight indication that the girls begin to use toys a bit younger than do the boys and that they play with a somewhat larger variety of toys.

Keeping Toys Clean

Toys or playthings which are given to the baby should be clean. It is impossible to keep the baby's hands and toys out of his mouth, and it probably would be undesirable to do so even if we could. Since the infant's mouth is very sensitive to pressure, he undoubtedly learns more at this time through manipulation with his lips than through any other part of his body. In view of the fact that all things are going to be carried straight to the child's mouth and the fact that the mouth is a popular reception hall for germs, it is obvious that the toys should be reasonably clean. To be perfectly cleaned, they would have to be boiled for several minutes, but that

[4] *The Young Child in the Home: A Study of Three Thousand American Families.*

would be the end of many of them. Play materials can, however, be cleaned so as to be reasonably safe by washing them in soap and hot water once a day or whenever they fall on the floor. Materials, such as paper, which will not stand the hot water treatment, we can at least keep as free as possible from human contamination. A fresh newspaper is one of the cleanest articles which comes into the house, except for the outside sheet which should be removed before the other pages are given to the baby. Play materials which do not fall in the washable class can be kept off the floor and kept from contact with the hands of other people. When two babies are together, we frequently find the mothers exchanging their toys for the sake of variety and forgetting that, if one child has a slight cold, this exchanging will usually assure the development of a cold in the playmate.

Playing with Mother

Babies of eight months frequently show definite pleasure in frolics, enjoy plays that make noises, and pat or smile at their own image in a mirror. In another month or so these babies will be ready to coöperate in simple plays with the mother, the type of thing which Froebel years ago called "mother plays." Now the baby is ready to be taught the tricks so dear to the mother's heart. He will wave bye-bye and clap his hands. He will respond to the question, "How big is the baby?" by thrusting his arms high in the air, if he has been taught to do so. For these games the baby responds to the tone of the voice and the intonation, not to the actual words of the parent. One mother, who had taught her baby to respond to "How big is the baby?" was amazed to find that he reacted just as readily to the Swedish cook's "Hur stor är babyn?" and to the German neighbor's "Wie gross is das Kind?" In each case the question was put by a smiling adult and the baby responded promptly. Without doubt, he would have stretched his arms up just as energetically if the mother had asked, "How old is the dog?" with the same voice and facial expression.

The finger plays which the young baby most enjoys are those involving rather large movements. "Pat-a-cake" is great fun when the mother takes the baby's hands and puts them through the proper motions for rolling and patting and "marking with B" and so on. "Wash the lady's dishes," if played with gently swinging arms, is also satisfying. The plays where the mother touches the different parts of the baby's face, as in "Here sits the Lord Mayor," [5] are amusing, but they may tempt the child to try to focus his eyes on an object which is too close to his face and may sometimes mean that a careless adult finger carries infection into the baby's mouth. "Creepie mouse," with the tickling fingers traveling up the baby's body, is often too exciting unless it is played very gently with the suspense not too long drawn out. If the adult is too slow in getting the fingers up to the baby's neck, the child may get a bit hysterical in anticipation of the tickling. Perhaps the most popular game of this age is "Peek-a-Boo," or "Where is baby (or mother) gone?" In this game the baby knows perfectly well what he will see when the hands are removed. Perhaps the point of interest is in this feature, for I doubt whether the game would amuse the baby at all if, when the hands were removed, he should see something entirely strange. To be amusing, the elements of the joke must be familiar to us. Perhaps "Peek-a-Boo" is the

[5] The verse for this old game is:

"Here sits the Lord Mayor;	(forehead)
Here sit his two men;	(eyes)
Here sits the cock;	(right cheek)
Here sits the hen;	(left cheek)
Here sit the little chickens;	(tip of nose)
Here they run in,	(mouth)
Chinchopper, chinchopper,	
Chinchopper, chin!"	(chuck the chin)

simplest form of joke. At least it is the joke which is understood at the earliest age.

We see that a baby plays first with his eyes, watching at the start things in his immediate vicinity, then objects and persons farther off in the same room, and after a while following the movements of people, animals, and vehicles on the street. Before such visual play is at all perfected, the baby has begun to indulge in motor play, moving the parts of his body, grasping and moving objects, and the like. There is still a third way in which the baby plays, and that is with his voice. The first cries of a baby are instinctive and undifferentiated. Later they begin to express hunger, anger, pleasure, and other emotions. Still later the baby uses his voice as a plaything. He gurgles and babbles to himself while lying on his back all alone in the room. These noises are the foundation of his future language and the mother can help his vocal development as well as please him by talking to him and encouraging him to repeat the noises he has made and to imitate others which she makes. If the baby says "gug" and mother says "gug" back to him, he will often echo "gug" again. This, the simplest of conversations, is highly enjoyed by the child. Later on he will try to imitate some sound which the mother makes and so will start learning words. Some day he happens to say "Dada," which mother promptly interprets as "Daddy." Then she praises the baby and makes a great to-do over him. When he learns that whenever he says "Dada" he gets much attention, he has learned the word whether he has applied it to the right object or not. There seems to be no doubt that this early play with sounds can be definitely encouraged by the mother who is sufficiently interested to spend a moment or two during the day talking to the baby. The first truly social play appears either as smiling at mother or nurse when they come near or smile at the baby, or in babbling when some one talks to him. Most babies will babble when they are talked to at two and a half months, will babble when alone at three months, will laugh aloud by three and a half months, and will jabber enthusiastically by ten months either to persons or to their toys.

Possible Dangers in Play for Babies

Important as early play is, there are certain dangers in giving the child too much opportunity for play. A warning which all mothers might do well to heed is: Don't tire, over-stimulate, or excite any infant. The child who has a great many different toys or experiences thrust upon him may become a fussy child who cannot be satisfied with a little. The baby who is taken out every day in a baby buggy soon counts so on that ride that he frets and keeps every one upset, if a rainstorm or a visitor keeps him at home. From the point of view of the baby, it is probably much better for him to get his airing sitting quietly on his own porch or in his own yard than by being bounced over the sidewalks and streets. When, however, taking the baby out for a ride is the only way in which the mother can get an airing or a friendly chat, then the whole matter is on a different basis. The writer knew one baby (a first baby) whose mother started taking her out for a ride each day when she woke from her nap. In the course of these rides the buggy passed over various sorts of surfaces, and it did not take the baby many weeks before she was fussing as long as she traveled over smooth cement sidewalks, was more content when the paving was of bricks, and was perfectly satisfied only when the buggy was pushed over a rough cinder path. As the baby grew older she bounced the buggy herself whenever the traveling was too smooth to suit her. So in the case of playthings, the more a child is given the more he demands and the less joy he gets from what he has. There is no doubt that by the time the baby is three or four months old he should be played with, cuddled, and talked to for an occasional period, but there is also no doubt that it is better to keep these periods fairly short.

Another warning is: Do not keep all of the baby's toys around him. He will tire of them, if he sees them every day. Whenever you notice that he is ignoring some toy, try putting it away for a week or two. The probability is that he will greet it with enthusiasm when it reappears. If there are too many things around, the baby will shift from one to another, dropping each in turn and looking for something else. One mother watched her son of a year and a half at his first Christmas tree. When he was given the first present he was delighted and started in to play with it at once. He was even somewhat annoyed to be given another present. This, however, was also interesting, but just as he started to play with that, another was thrust upon him. At that point he gave up trying to play with anything, merely taking one present after another as they were offered and storing them to one side. When the presents had all been given to him, he was annoyed at the stopping of the flood and proceeded to cry because he was given no more. The same type of response may be observed in the smaller child. Too many toys mean that no one is really enjoyed.

Summary

During the first few months of a baby's life, the only play he needs is an opportunity to kick and move without the hindrance of clothes. Gradually, however, he becomes interested in simple toys, and by the age of eight or nine months he is usually happy to manipulate many sorts of materials. Before the close of the first year, the child will be ready for simple plays with his parents and will respond to remarks which they make to him. Throughout the entire period of infancy, the baby should be given opportunities for physical and mental development, but he must be protected from over-stimulation.

Chapter III

VIGOROUS PLAY

JUST as the radio-day starts with the toothbrush drill and the "daily dozen" so, perhaps, should any discussion of the play of young children start with what we ordinarily call physical exercise. Vigorous play which involves the use of the whole body is now taken so much as a matter of course in the training of any young child that few people need to be convinced of its value. It is worth while, however, to recall the benefits which the child derives from physical activity. The committee of the White House Conference which made a study of the health of the school child lists the objectives of physical education as follows:

"To contribute continuously to the development of nerve and organic power, as shown in muscular development, neuro-muscular control, normal increase in growth, increased endurance and rapid recovery from fatigue; to contribute to the development of good posture through suitable environment, equipment, and activities and by wholesome attitudes; to develop continuously the fundamental physical skills used in daily life and in recreational activities, such as running, jumping, climbing, striking, throwing, and dodging; to have, thru physical activity, increasing opportunity for experience in creative expression, as in developing games, revising rules for games and developing rhythmic plays; to develop continuously skill in, and a wholesome attitude toward, many natural activities in order to insure participation in physical activity during leisure time; to develop increasingly, leadership, followership, and cooperation,— qualities which encourage good citizenship."—*The School Health Program* (The Century Co., New York, 1932), pp. 210 f.

As the child develops, he gains control over the large muscles (see Anderson's *Happy Childhood*, Chapter IX) of the body before the coördination of his smaller muscles is at all satisfactory; that is, he can handle his entire arm, leg, or hand fairly well before he can use his fingers accurately. His play follows along with his development, of course, and so his early play is concerned largely with the use of his large muscles.

A Place to Play

For the average home, large muscle play is practically always synonymous with outdoor play. Except for the rare house which is equipped with a playroom large enough to allow for considerable free movement, indoor play must be chiefly of a type which involves only a comparatively small amount of gross movement. The home which provides space for swinging, for performing on a bar, for somersaulting, even for fighting, is an unusual place in these days of crowded living. All strenuous forms of play are better if indulged in out-of-doors in the fresh air and sunshine, but if they cannot take place there, then better have them indoors with fresh air, at least, than not at all. For many of our northern cities, outdoor play in the winter for very young children is largely impossible.

Every child should be provided with adequate outdoor play space where he is free from the hazards of the street. From the point of view of the welfare of the children in a family, a yard which is supplied with good play apparatus and which offers space for running games and ball play is far more desirable than any amount of carefully groomed lawns and attractive flower-beds. If both can be provided, so much the better, but if there is room for only one, let it be the playground. Frequently the city child must rely on public parks and playgrounds. More and more in city planning we are coming to feel that a city with small parks, dotted here and there throughout the community, is better for adults and children alike than the city where all the park area is concentrated in one big, beautiful stretch which gives a great deal of pleasure to those living near it but is completely inaccessible to hundreds, living beyond walking distance and without money for the necessary car-fare.

The White House Conference suggests that "there should be a playground within a quarter of a mile of every home, with a hundred square feet per child, and athletic fields which serve the older people within a mile radius. There should be recreation parks and museums and libraries. These opportunities should be under the guidance of a park and recreation department, within the city government, composed of men and women of vision. . . . Young and old should be served by playgrounds and recreation centers on an all-year basis. . . . Every activity that has value, that ingenuity can devise, should be offered the citizens." [1]

Figures on the places in which children play show, as we might expect, that younger children are more apt to be restricted to the home yard than are older children. There seems to be no difference in the size of radius within which boys and girls are allowed to play without supervision. When the different socio-economic groups are compared, we find that, with the exception of the farming group, "the tendency is somewhat greater for children in the lower occupational classes to be restricted to the home or home yard, and for children in the upper classes to be restricted to the home yard or the block. There is also a slightly greater tendency for children in the lower socio-economic groups not to be restricted at all in their place of play." [2] We read further that, as places to play for children from the age of two on, "playgrounds and the street increase in relative importance. During the school years more boys than girls play in the street and vacant lots, while equal proportions of both sexes play in parks or

[1] *The Delinquent Child* (The Century Co., New York, 1932), p. 213.
[2] *The Young Child in the Home: A Study of Three Thousand American Families.*

playgrounds," and "children in the lower classes are more likely to play in the street or vacant lots while those in the higher classes are more likely to play in parks." [3]

One committee of the White House Conference, in questioning parents on the subject of outdoor play, found that over 90 per cent of children play outdoors at least every other day.[4] If all the records were taken in summer, there is no doubt that the percentage would climb to one hundred for all who are not sick, while for the winter months in the northern States the percentage would undoubtedly be considerably lower, especially for the younger ages. Their figures give the median numbers of hours of play spent out-of-doors in the spring (taking all the figures for the week and including data for Saturday and Sunday as well as school days) as follows:

HOURS SPENT OUT-OF-DOORS

Age	Boys	Girls
1 to 2 years	5¼ hours	5¼ hours
2 to 3 "	6½ "	6½ "
3 to 4 "	6½ "	6½ "
4 to 5 "	7¼ "	7 "
5 to 6 "	7¼ "	7 "
6 to 8 "	8½ "	8 "
8 to 10 "	8¼ "	7½ "
10 to 13 "	8 "	7 "

From this we see that for young children the greatest amount of outdoor play comes at ages six and seven. Up to that age both sexes gradually increase their outdoor play time, and after that age they gradually decrease it. It also appears that until the age of four there is no sex difference in the amount of time spent out-of-doors, but from that age on the sex differences become gradually greater from a play time for boys which is a quarter of an hour longer than that for the girls at the age of four to one which is a whole hour longer

[3] *Ibid.*
[4] *Ibid.*

for the boys at the age of ten. "There is no difference between the economic classes in the number of hours children spend in outdoor play, except that the children of the farming class spend about one-half hour longer than the others do." [5]

Play Without Apparatus

Walking.

When most adults think of large muscle play, they think of the big organized games like basket-ball or football, but as a matter of fact much of our large muscle play is carried on without either rules or apparatus. There is, for example, all the play connected with walking. While walking to an adult may be merely a means of moving from one place to another; and while to the person accustomed to an automobile, it may seem to be a task or even a punishment; to the young child walking is a fascinating occupation, an art to the mastery of which he aspires. The elements of walking appear very early in the alternate kicking of the baby's two feet. Usually the infant creeps before the end of his first year, struggles up to his feet a few months later, and not long afterwards is moving about the room in an uncertain stagger. By the age of two, the child has gained a pretty fair mastery over his legs, and although he is easily toppled over, he is walking well enough to do it most of the time automatically. He trots around with apparent joy and seemingly for no other reason than for the pleasure the movement gives him, for he will make trip after trip around a room, or preferably through a series of rooms, without ever stopping to play with anything or to give interesting objects more than a casual glance. He stands on tiptoe for fun, and climbs over or around any bit of furniture that may be handy.

Older children do not usually go for a walk alone for the pleasure of the walk as some adults do; but at almost any age,

[5] *The Young Child in the Home: A Study of Three Thousand American Families.*

a group of vigorous people can be collected for the fun of a "hike." Such walking is more interesting if there is a particular goal, perhaps a meal at some inn, a football game to watch, or some special person to visit; the walk is also more pleasant if the scenery is unusual or of interest for some reason. Walking by itself may become too monotonous. Two men, who had never seen the wheat fields of the Northwest, once started out for a week's tramp through the prairies of North Dakota. They walked three days west and then turned back and, at the end of the week, announced that they never wanted to see another wheat field. The country was so flat that they saw nothing but wheat; the only routes were a level road between wheat fields and a railroad track between wheat fields. The railroad track proved to be somewhat the more interesting of the two for it required a little attention if they were not to trip occasionally over a tie. At the conclusion of the tramp the two veteran hikers agreed that walking alone did not provide sufficient pleasure and that the walk must include some variation in points of interest.

As he develops the child indulges not only in walking and trotting for pleasure; he also takes up all sorts of more complex types of advancing in space. He loves to march with a simple rhythmic accompaniment of singing or piano, especially if he can carry a flag or wear a paper hat. He pretends to dance when music is offered. At first he has difficulty in keeping his balance when he lifts a foot off the floor, but it is not long before he can caper away in fine style. Usually by the time he is in kindergarten, he has learned to skip and the joy in skipping lasts for many years. Often, at first, he skips on one foot only and learns the rhythm of skipping with both feet only after many trials, but once he does learn it, it remains his favorite form of locomotion for a year or two. Watch a group of children coming out of a grade school. Perhaps they will come in groups, walking very slowly and conversing with each other in great seriousness, but if there is a picnic on foot or a special treat waiting at home, they will skip, hop, or leap. Two or three children together will amuse themselves for hours working out complicated rhythms of skipping, three skips with the right foot to one with the left, two skips and a jump, or alternate hopping and jumping, until we feel that Milne had had considerable experience with children when he wrote of Christopher Robin's hopping, "whenever I tell him politely to stop it, he says he can't possibly stop."

Jumping.

The jumping of the small child usually consists in just jumping off the lowest step or jumping over a box or a line. Some children love to jump so much that any step or platform is an incentive too strong to be resisted. Not long ago a church congregation of fond parents was listening with alternate pride and anxiety to a group of children reciting verses on Children's Sunday. Their attention was caught by a small three-year-old girl who had held her place in the group on the pulpit platform just as long as she could withstand the temptation of the floor below her. The child, solemnly and with utter disregard of the audience, stooped and jumped off on to the floor, then trotted around to the side and up the steps to repeat the performance, after which she returned to her place in the singing group apparently perfectly satisfied.

Since the child may get a hard bump at the end of a jump, until he learns to land on his feet with a spring, some schools provide a "jumping pit" or a "jumping hole" for children of three or four years of age. To make such a pit, simply dig a bowl-shaped hole in the ground, some three feet deep and four feet across, and fill it about half full of sawdust or sand, or (in summer) completely full of hay. The sawdust, sand, or hay is soft enough to break the child's fall, but it provides all the thrills of a jump. The sawdust and sand must, of course, be kept light and soft; if they are trodden down, frozen, or matted with dampness, their usefulness is gone. Another form of jumping which breaks out every spring is jumping rope. Although girls seem definitely more interested in this form of play than do boys, both sexes enjoy it. The play may be made more complicated by having the ends of the rope swung by two children, while a third does the jumping. Such play requires good timing and rhythm from all three children and is good practice in coöperation. But the jumping does not stop there. The older brothers and sisters jump to see who can jump the farthest or the highest, and this competitive jumping develops into the high school and college contests in the broad jump and high jump.

Swimming.

Another play of movement and equilibrium is found in swimming. Here we have the added interest of water and the competition with a different element, but a great part of the joy comes from the movement of the body and the control of sets of muscles. The baby loves his bath and takes delight in splashing the water all around. The small child prefers to wade in the lake or the ocean. If the shore has a gentle slope, so that the water deepens gradually, and if there is no strong undertow, there is little chance that the young child will go out beyond his depth. Even children who are able to swim a little, will spend many hours in the water without getting wet above the waist. Children who ordinarily demand set games and considerable play material are perfectly content to be turned loose on a sandy beach in bathing suits. Sometimes the play develops into some sort of simple dramatic play, like building sand houses and playing house, or into a very simple play in which the water provides a surprise. A play of the latter type was devised by two small girls who hit upon the notion of pretending they didn't know there was any water there. Hand in hand they walked down the beach, talking busily about what a lovely walk they were having and how they were dressed in their best clothes and so on until they were well into the water. Then they would exclaim, "Mercy! We are walking in water!" and scamper out. When the child really learns to swim, a whole new field of activity is open to him, and he has the thrill of moving about in water which is over his head, the satisfaction of floating, the excitement of diving or of swimming under water, and so on.

Rolling.

A form of locomotion which is seldom used but which sometimes provides much fun is rolling. The baby learns to roll before he learns to sit up, and he shows considerable interest in rolling back and forth across the bed, provided he does not roll off. The older child often rolls aimlessly around on the floor, while he is waiting for something to turn up or deciding what he wants to do, but about the only real exercise in rolling comes for children—usually of kindergarten or early grade years—who cannot resist any grassy slope, down which they come with speed and squeals of joy increasing as they near the end of the incline.

Locomotion with Variations.

Variation in plays of locomotion comes with the introduction of various complications. There is, for one thing, locomotion in difficult places. Walking on a flat surface like a sidewalk becomes a matter of course after a time, while walking on the top rail of a fence or on its substitute, the walking board, may be a source of thrills. One of the simplest of walking boards may be made from a six- or eight-foot piece of lumber, four inches wide by two inches thick (the common "two-by-four"), used just as it comes from the lumber yard. When it is laid flat on the ground, this board is as wide as the foot of the two-year-old child. A plank narrower than the sole of the shoe of a very young child makes balancing too difficult a feat. When the child is a little older, the performance may be made considerably more difficult by turning the timber on its edge, thus giving a walking surface only two inches in width. The performance may be made still more difficult by raising the ends of the walking board off the surface of the ground, nailing cleats under the ends, or placing the ends of the board on boxes.

Walking becomes a game for the older child, also, when he pretends that, if he steps on a crack, he will be poisoned or will "break his mother's back" or will suffer some other dire calamity. City children often play that they must not step on any cement block in the paving which either has the maker's stamp on it or is in a row with one bearing the maker's stamp. The game has the possible added problem of coming across two "poison rows" together, in which case a very wide jump is required. This type of game, in which the places stepped on are strictly limited, may be adapted to indoor use by making the rule that one must not step on a rug or on the bare floor (the particular rule will have to depend on the amount of rug space and bare floor in the given house), or in the requirement that, although the child may step anywhere, one hand must always be touching wood, and so on.

Maintaining Equilibrium.

Besides the play of walking, there are the other games involving equilibrium. What child does not long to stand on his head and to walk on his hands? The effort to turn somersaults appears when the child is quite young. He usually rolls to one side at first, but after a while he turns straight over and finally somersaults both forwards and backwards. Attempts at walking on the hands meet with success only in the later years, if at all, but still there is the fun of trying. The fascination of standing on one's head seems to lie partly in the joy of attaining the difficult balancing and partly in the amusement of seeing common objects upside down. The feat is probably most easily learned by starting in a heavy arm-chair, warranted not to tip over. With the arms of the chair to help steady the body a bit, and a cushion for the head, this stunt can be accomplished by the average child of five or six. Perhaps the child's next step is to stand on his head in a corner of the room with the walls to help steady him, and then to learn to stand on his head against a single wall. Beyond this point, many never progress, and the child who learns to stand on his head in the middle of the playground is bound to be the object of many admiring and envious glances.

Play with Simple Apparatus

Variations of Walking.

There are variations of walking achieved by the introduction of apparatus. One of the oldest of such play materials is a pair of stilts, in the use of which the child must keep his balance high in the air. The smallest children may have very low stilts, while the older children will demand higher and higher ones. A contrivance called "Spring Shues" was recently put on the market and seems to be very popular with children of the jumping age. This device helps them to jump higher and farther than they are naturally able to do. Other appliances which vary locomotion and make it more interesting are skiis, snow-shoes, and skates. Roller-skates should not be omitted from the list. Probably some children are given roller-skates before their ankles are strong enough to bear the pull of them. One pediatrician has said that by the time the child is seven, he should be in condition to use roller-skates, if he does not wear them too long at a time. The smaller roller-skates, designed for younger children, are so light in weight that the children easily lose their balance on them.

Vehicles.

Although they would not be classified strictly under the term *walking,* there are many other plays which involve types

Skating Is Great Fun

of locomotion. There is, for example, the "scooter." This machine may be bought ready-made, or it may be manufactured by any child who is at all handy with simple tools. It is made simply by attaching the wheels of one roller-skate to the ends of a wooden platform some four inches wide and from eight to fifteen inches long and nailing a wooden upright to the front end of it. A simple handle may be added to the top of the upright, and the child can then sail blithely down the hill. Some little skill in maintaining equilibrium is necessary for progress on this vehicle, but there is little or no danger of falling for the platform is close to the ground and the child can stop at any moment simply by putting one foot down on the ground. Then there is the popular velocipede or tricycle. This machine is steady on its three wheels, but the child has to learn to work the pedals and to steer. More difficult to manage is the two-wheeled bicycle which requires considerable agility in maintaining proper balance. Although in some cities there may be the further difficulty of requiring children to ride in the street amid all the dangers of traffic, nevertheless, under the right conditions, a bicycle can provide great pleasure and much healthful exercise for the child of nine or ten or older.

Other forms of locomotion are found in boats. Rowing a rowboat and paddling a canoe are exceptionally good outdoor occupations for the older child who can swim and for the younger child who is accompanied by a capable adult. The joys of sailing and of running a motor-boat belong properly to the adolescent and, although the younger child may heartily enjoy trips in either kind of boat, his activity is limited rather than increased by their use.

Play with Outdoor Apparatus

Plays of locomotion may be further complicated and made of greater interest by the introduction of apparatus. The

White House Conference found [6] that the most common piece of outdoor equipment for a private family was a sand-box. About half of the families in the higher socio-economic classes provide a sand-box for small children. About half of the children on farms have a swing out-of-doors. Swings are not uncommon in the city; teeter-totters are less common; and slides are rather rare. Other pieces of outdoor equipment which were found by that study were tents, playhouses, rings, trapezes, and hammocks. A type of equipment for outdoor play which almost any home can furnish, but which very few do, is found in ordinary packing boxes. Nails should be removed from the edges or pounded in so that they cannot scratch or tear, and splinters should be removed as far as possible. A most interesting accessory to play with packing boxes is a ladder, five or six feet long, which may be stretched across two boxes to make parallel bars, or which may be used in the usual way for climbing high up. Even without the boxes a ladder furnishes many opportunities for play. It may make an excellent frame for several horses in tandem arrangement; it may serve as a teeter, and, of course, it may be used against a tree or building as a climbing device.

Climbing.

Of the sorts of play which use apparatus out-of-doors, perhaps climbing is the most popular. Whether or not we subscribe to the theory that a monkey ancestry accounts for the child's predilection for high and relatively inaccessible places, we must all admit that climbing is a fascinating pursuit for most children. The baby begins to climb before he can stand alone. Dr. Shirley found babies climbing on to chairs and stools and, with a little assistance, climbing up adults as they would up a telegraph pole. Climbing up steps is a common diversion, and climbing on to chairs and tables is in high

[6] *The Young Child in the Home: A Survey of Three Thousand American Families.*

favor. The low, spreading apple tree offers untold opportunities to the country child for the joy of climbing and for the mastery over gravity. It may also serve as a background for all varieties of playing house or playing school, or as a delightful isolation in which to enjoy a well-loved book. The "Jungle Gym" and its simplified brothers, designed for the use of younger children, offer the city child excellent chances to climb. We find also, various combinations of upright and horizontal ladders; bars of various sorts; ropes for climbing, with or without knots to help the ascent; and, for smaller children, steps leading up to the slides.

Shacks.

Some urban children have access to a tree in which a tree-house can be built. If the parents make sure that the structure is strong enough to support the weight of the children likely to use it, a tree-house will provide days upon days of happy occupation and useful work. Sometimes a tree-house is reached by home-made stairs; sometimes by a ladder of wood or rope; sometimes the occupants merely climb up the tree to it. The most fun is a tree-house whose means of access, usually a ladder, can be drawn up after the occupants are in their home, so that other visitors can enter only when and if the owners are willing to lower the ladder to them.

If children cannot have a tree-house, perhaps they can have a "shack." This sort of playhouse, when planned for younger children, is easily provided in an old piano box with one side or a part of a side left open for an entrance, but when the children get to be eight or nine or ten years old, they will enjoy much more a playhouse of their own making. Sometimes a very large packing box can be found for the foundation; sometimes nearby trees may be used as the uprights of the building; and sometimes the whole shack has to be built up piece by piece. There can be little doubt that the more work the children do on the structure themselves, the greater is their interest, enjoyment, and profit. Although the shack may be planned as a club-house, a meeting place for the gang, or a doll-house, the greatest fun is after all the work on the house itself. When the house becomes so nearly perfect that there are no improvements left to be made, the play with it gradually subsides into occasional visits. One group of ten-year-old boys, who made themselves a shack in a grove near their homes, became so interested in the subject of house-building (they were apparently inspired by two new homes being erected in the neighborhood) that they investigated the literature given out by heating companies and devised a make-believe heating system and then a ventilating system to go with it. By this time, the two ''systems'' took up so much space in the shack that it became necessary to build an addition to the shack itself to accommodate the four owners.

Swinging.

One of the most common forms of outdoor play apparatus is the swing. Statistics have shown that more accidents result from swings than from any one other common form of gymnasium apparatus. Usually the grief comes not to the child in the swing but to one who runs in the way and gets hit by the descending swing, which, of course, has acquired considerable momentum. The blow is a hard one, all too often followed by a second blow when the stricken child raises his head to see what hit him. If the swing is used, however, in a group which knows how to be careful of it, it will provide much fun and good exercise. The simplest form of swing is that which is illustrated in Harriet M. Johnson's *Nursery School Experiment*. All four corners of its board seat are supported by ropes and the seat itself is very close to the ground. The swing may be made still safer for the little tot if the supporting ropes are left long enough to drag beneath the seat like a brake on the ground or floor. Swings for all young children should be fastened permanently to the ropes, as in the cases where the

Even the Big Brothers Enjoy Shacks and Tree-Houses

rope passes through a hole in each side of the seat. Removable seats are dangerous for young children because they may get disarranged while the child is high in the air and cause him to fall. The two-year-old child is contented to sit in the swing, grasp the ropes firmly, and rock gently back and forth or at most be pushed by an adult. The older child learns to "pump" himself and to swing when standing up in the seat. Such complications add interest, as does the use of the same swing by two children, one standing and one seated. A variation of the common swing is seen in the single-rope swings. A single rope may sometimes be hung from a tree which offers no branch level enough to support a two-rope swing. A large knot at the lower end of the rope permits the child to sit or stand on it and swing. A single strand of the common "Giant Stride" provides a chance for climbing and swinging at the same time and also a chance for two children to use a single-rope swing at the same time.

Rocking.

Closely related to swinging is the activity of rocking. Tiny babies learn to love the rocking motion, if they are accustomed to sleeping in a cradle or to being rocked in their mother's arms. Adults frequently enjoy the rocking motion of a boat as it sails up and down the huge swells at sea. Children rejoice in the rocking motion under many conditions. Perhaps the simplest form of it is rocking back and forth, from toes to heels to toes, as we see many children and some adults do when they stand thinking for a moment. Our grandmothers and grandfathers in their youth had rocking-horses, those for the smallest children having a seat between two horses and those for the older child a seat on the back of a single horse on rockers. The modern editions of this play apparatus frequently give the rocking motion without the actual use of rockers. That the rocking-horse is not as popular as it used to be is shown by the experience of a school which provided both small rocking-horses and "Kiddy-Kars" and found that the latter were much more in demand. This is probably because the "Kiddy-Kars" allowed the children to move about the room, while the rocking-horses kept them in approximately the same place all the time. But for a child alone, a rocking-horse, not in competition with a "Kiddy-Kar," may supply much entertainment and be a great help in imaginative play.

Teeter-totters and see-saws provide many with the agreeable rocking motion. A teeter-totter to be used by young children should be so constructed that it is practically impossible to pinch small fingers between the board and the pivot. A very satisfactory small teeter may be made by nailing a smooth plank to a nail keg, so that as the keg rolls the board tips up and down. Other small teeters may be obtained with the rockers attached to the board. Variations of the teeter-totter and rocking-horse are found in the "rocking boat" which provides for two children at each end. There is little chance for accident in this contrivance, for the children have handles to steady themselves by, and there are no moving parts near their fingers. Another arrangement which allows a group of children to move backward and forward is the "rocking board." This is a long board, supported by a set of rockers at each end, and it moves backward and forward rather than up and down. Ten or eleven children can play on this at one time with little probability of pinched fingers.

Throwing and Catching.

Still another form of play which involves much use of the large muscles of the body is found in throwing, tossing, and catching. Although these activities are commonly thought of as part of the organized ball games, still there is much throwing and tossing and catching in the ball plays of the child alone. Most children of three or four enjoy a simple play with balls. Older children often pass through a stage of playing "bounce a ball" in which the most important element is catching the ball

Tricycles and Slides Can Be Purchased

Swings and Teeter-Totters Can Be Made at Home

as it bounces back from the sidewalk. Still older children enjoy throwing a ball against the wall of a house or garage and catching it as it returns. These older children also enjoy trying to hit some object with a ball or with a stone. Perhaps it is the same interest which causes them to try to hit a target and which develops later into interest in shooting with a toy gun, with a bow and arrow, and finally with a real shot gun or rifle.

Pushing.

By the time a baby is a year old, he has usually discovered that he can push certain small things around. This small degree of control over the physical universe seems to afford great delight and we find the toddler pushing chairs and stools, pushing doors shut, and pushing drawers in, sometimes with unfortunate results to baby fingers held over the edge. Even before he can stand up without help, the child enjoys pushing his own baby carriage or pushing a cart. The carriage and the cart help to steady him and serve as an aid to walking. When he has become independent in his walking, he will enjoy pushing doll-buggies, carts, and wheelbarrows. Probably the ideal instrument for this sort of pushing is the doll-buggy, for the handle comes in a convenient place and the buggy does not have to be lifted at all as a wheelbarrow does. Some parents, however, cannot overcome the feeling that a two- or three-year-old boy is a "sissy," if he has a doll-buggy. That point of view is unfortunate, of course, but these families can at least provide some sort of a thing on wheels which can be pushed with satisfaction. An English firm has recently put on the market a toy horse with wheels and an upright piece at the back which serves either as a back-rest for the rider or as a handle to push the pony by when the child is not riding it. Small carts are sometimes and large wagons are frequently pushed by children of eight or nine, kneeling with one knee in the wagon and pushing with the other foot. Whether or not the tendency to push other children is due to the desire to assert mastery over the environment, it is, of course, not a type of pushing to be encouraged, though it is one which is frequently met.

Pulling.

Closely related to pushing are pulling and dragging, and in using these types of activity we encounter all the common wheeled toys. Toy trains are perhaps the best example of this kind of toy and one which all children enjoy. For the littlest children, there are wooden and aluminum trains without wheels. The cars of these trains lock together simply and do not tip over under any ordinary conditions. They are thus well suited to the child of two or three. For the older child, the trains with wheels are more lifelike. They are, however, usually run by a spring or by electricity and so really lose their character as a toy to be pushed or pulled. Then there are carts, wagons, and wheelbarrows of all sorts. The best toys of this kind are the ones large enough to carry loads of blocks, sand, or whatever the child may want to move about. The small trucks and cars are a great help for many kinds of imaginative play, but it is only the big ones that involve the use of the large muscles of the body.

Digging.

Many a child at some time owns a small set of garden tools. Of these the shovel is the most popular. Shovels, whether for dirt or for snow, should be made of strong material, for a shovel that bends easily is no good at all. If the child is to do his digging in sand, he does not need quite so sturdy a shovel, and he may accomplish wonders with an ordinary garden trowel. If he is to dig in the earth itself, he will get more use and pleasure from a shovel strong enough to bear the weight of his foot, so that he may use it as he sees the gardener use his. And such fun as he may have in digging into the ground!

It is, to be sure, a little hard on a lawn, but most houses could set aside a corner of the back yard or a bit of the garden in which to let the child dig as he likes. When there is a fair amount of snow on the ground, there are, of course, untold possibilities for digging. In a very cold northern city, which ordinarily has many inches of snowfall during the winter, one mother devised a scheme for keeping her young children out-of-doors on days when they were not in school. She encouraged them to build trenches in the snow in the back yard. These trenches were deep enough to keep the bitter wind off the children and yet were interesting enough to keep them in constant motion and so sufficiently warm. The trenches had various branches and sometimes opened out into "rooms" where several children could stand together. The almost daily snow storms kept the children busy clearing out their trenches and adding new branches, and this group of children got much more of the fresh air and sunshine than most of the other children of that city.

The Value of Active Games in Improving Posture

All of the types of activity which we have been discussing —walking, jumping, swimming, rolling, balancing, swinging, climbing, rocking, pushing, pulling, and digging—are exercises which help to give the child greater control over his own body, while they are at the same time most entrancing occupations. The White House Conference Committee on Body Mechanics define their subject as: "the mechanical correlation of the various systems of the body with special reference to the skeletal, muscular and visceral systems and their neurological associations. . . . In recent literature the term *posture* is commonly employed synonymously with body mechanics, but . . . it is less descriptive and less inclusive." [7] The

[7] *Body Mechanics: Education and Practice* (The Century Co., New York, 1932), p. 5.

committee then go on to comment on the posture (see Stuart's *Healthy Childhood*, Chapter VI) of the children whom they studied. They report that the "body mechanics of the children studied showed a definite though slight relationship to age. . . . The youngest children (those under seven years of age) had better posture than those in the immediately succeeding ages. But at the age of seven and less than nine years, the percentage who had good posture . . . dropped from 5 to less than 1. In other words, the child when he enters school has a better posture apparently than he has after he has been in school for a while. In his so-called pre-school age, he is as a rule out of doors for a large part of the day and leads an active life. He then abruptly changes from a method of living conducive to robust, vigorous health, with presumably good muscle control to a less active, more sedentary occupation—going to school. This with the unaccustomed confinement, especially in seats and at desks (rarely properly adjusted) together with the strain of the usually sudden transition from play to work, undoubtedly contributes to weakened muscular control and therefore to poor posture." [8]

The moral of this finding surely is that the school child should be given just as much happy, vigorous, outdoor play as is possible at recess time, after school in the afternoon, and on Saturdays and Sundays. It is possible also to give children definite training in posture. The White House Conference writes:

"The experience of the children for whom two-year records are available suggests that the proportion of children free from structural defects whose posture can not be improved is less than 5 per cent and that some children require longer training than others. About nine times as many children improved in posture with training as improved without training. Since good posture once acquired (vacation periods excepted) was maintained, on the whole, over the two-year period of observation it seems reasonable to expect that with posture instruction continuous thruout grade school, the habits of

[8] *Body Mechanics*, p. 84.

good body mechanics will become fixed and lasting."—*Body Mechanics: Education and Practice* (The Century Co., New York, 1932), p. 96.

The same committee gives direction for the proper standing position: feet parallel, weight forward, waist flat, chest up and forward, chin in and head high,[9] and they suggest that such activities as throwing, tossing, rolling a ball, rowing, folk dances, and games will all improve the child's posture. Another committee of the White House Conference suggest that good posture may be encouraged by means of "suitable environment, equipment and activities and by wholesome attitudes."

Games and Sports

Many of the forms of physical exercise can be carried on by the person alone, but there are many other types of play which require the coöperation of at least one other person. Although in general children are not unhappy without companions before the age of two and a half or three, nevertheless, much younger children will often enjoy the occasional company of others. It has been found [10] that something like 82 per cent of children between the ages of one and two play fairly frequently with other children and that, as the children grow older, this percentage gradually increases until it reaches 98 per cent at the age of five. The youngest children usually choose playmates (or have playmates chosen for them) who are quite a little older than themselves, but as they grow older the ages of playmates come nearer and nearer together.

There are some plays in which the competition may be with the child's own previous record. One of the great advantages of golf for adults lies in the fact that, if no other player is at

[9] *Ibid.* (The Century Co., New York, 1932), p. 137.
[10] *The Young Child in the Home: A Survey of Three Thousand American Families.*

hand to furnish rivalry, the golfer can always and almost inevitably does compete against his own record. So in the case
of children we find boys spending hours trying to beat their
own records at the high jump, the broad jump, or the pole
vault. The younger children seldom show such an interest, but
as they grow older the interest becomes more keen.

Plays involving competition, but not necessarily team-work,
are found in all sorts of races and contests. The problem may
be simply to see who can run a given distance in the shortest
time, who can jump the greatest distance, or who can maintain some difficult bit of balancing longest. The question may
be: Who can carry most peanuts a given distance on a knife
in a given length of time? Or it may be: Who can carry most
potatoes on a teaspoon under similar circumstances? The players may group themselves in pairs for a wheelbarrow race in
which one player is the wheelbarrow, using his hands for the
wheel while his partner holds his feet off the ground and
they race with another pair; or again the players may form
pairs, with the left leg of one player fastened to the right leg
of his team-mate, while they run a "three-legged race" with
another pair similarly bound. Any slip in the rhythm of
either member of one of these pairs will usually result in an
upset. In the obstacle race, all sorts of obstacles may be introduced in the path of the racers. They may be obliged to
crawl through a barrel, to climb up a ladder, or to go around
a given tree a certain number of times, and so on.

Running Games.

The games which cannot succeed without the coöperation of
other children take many forms and appear in many degrees
of complexity and inflexibility of ruling. Perhaps the simplest
of these are the running games, in which there is no pleasure
unless the participant enjoys running. Tag is probably the
simplest of all. It can actually be played by two children with

only one rule—that the child who is *It* must touch the other child. As soon as the second child is touched, he becomes *It*, and the play reverses. The variations of tag are almost countless. Most of them involve some particular place or position of the body which renders a player immune from tagging. There may be, for example, one or a number of goals at which a player cannot be tagged, or he may be safe if he is touching wood, stone, or some other material; or when he is touching a tree; or when he is squatting down, or has his fingers crossed. These variations are usually named by their safety spots as "Goal Tag," "Tree Tag," "Stone Tag," "Squat Tag," and so on. One variation which older childen enjoy, but which needs to be played in an orchard or on a playground is "Hang Tag." In this game the player is safe if he is hanging by his arms with his feet clear of the ground. Only one player is allowed to hang in each place and if a second comes up to hang in that place, the first hanger must run on to some other place of safety. Then there are the skipping and running tags in which the *It* must skip or run.

A game which resembles tag to a considerable extent is the common "Puss in the Corner" or "Pussy Wants a Corner." In this game each child except *Pussy* chooses a corner or a goal in which he is safe. Then the players try to exchange corners without letting *Pussy* capture a corner. If *Pussy* succeeds in getting into any corner while player is out of it, that player becomes *Pussy*.

Some of the most popular games are those which require a great deal of running. The children of the kindergarten enjoy running for the fun of the movement with little thought of a race or of formal rules. Gradually they become interested in the "ring" or "circle" games in which the formation is always a ring of children, with one or two inside or outside that ring engaged in some particular activity. A typical game of this type is the old favorite, "Drop the Handkerchief."

The White House Conference suggests also [11] such games as "Brownies and Fairies," "Squirrel in the Hollow Tree," and "Run for Your Supper." For children in the third and fourth grades, the committee recommends games which involve running, jumping, dodging, catching, and throwing, games of the relay type such as "All Up Relay," "Shuttle Relay," and simple competitive games in which the competition is between two individuals or between an individual and a group, such as "Bull in the Ring," "Pom Pom Pullaway," "Bombardment," "Japanese Tag," "Three Deep," and "Duck on the Rock."

Directions for these games follow:

Drop the Handkerchief.

In this game one player is chosen to run around the outside of the circle formed by the others, with a handkerchief or a bean-bag which he drops behind one of the circle players. The object of the game is to drop the handkerchief in such a way that the circle players are unaware that it has been dropped. As soon as the circle player realizes that the handkerchief has been dropped behind him, he picks it up and tries to catch the one who dropped it while the dropper runs around the circle and tries to get to the place which has been left vacant by the child who is chasing him. If he succeeds in doing this, the circle player becomes *It* and the first *It* becomes a circle player; but if he gets caught, then he is exiled to the center of the ring until some one else is caught or until he can steal the handkerchief dropped to another player. Sometimes failure to reach the vacant place in the circle before being caught means merely that he must continue to be *It*.

Brownies and Fairies.

Divide the players into two teams, the brownies and the fairies, and have each team select one member as captain. Draw two goal lines on the ground some distance apart and have the teams take up their positions on these lines. The fairies should advance first to the center of the field of play and stand there in a line with their backs to the brownies. The brownies then creep very quietly up as near to the

[11] *The School Health Program* (The Century Co., New York, 1932), p. 211.

center as they dare. When they come very close, the captain of the fairies cries "Look out for the fairies," at which signal the brownies scamper for their own goal. All of the brownies who are tagged by the fairies then join the side of the fairies. The brownies then advance to the center of the field and try to tag the fairies. At the end of the game, the side with the largest number of players is called the winner.

Squirrel in the Hollow Tree.

In this game three fourths of the players stand in groups of three forming the "hollow trees." In the center of each tree is a player who is a squirrel and there is one other squirrel who has no tree. At a given signal, all the squirrels must leave their trees and try to find a home in another tree, while the odd squirrel tries to find a home too. The squirrel left without a tree is *It* for the next time. Sometimes the odd player, instead of being a homeless squirrel, is a dog who tries to catch the squirrels as they exchange homes.

Run For Your Supper.

All the players except one form a circle; that one, left in the center, is *It*. Walking around inside the circle, he stops and holds out his hand between two players crying, "Run for your supper." At this, the two run around the circle in opposite directions and the one who is the last to reach his place becomes the *It*.

All up Relay.

Divide the players into teams and line them up in single files with the leader of each team toeing the starting line. Some twenty-five or fifty feet in front of each starting line two circles are drawn three feet in diameter, with rims touching each other. In one of the circles, in front of each team three Indian clubs are stood. At a given signal, the first runner of each team runs to the circles, and moves the Indian clubs one by one into the other circle. He then runs back to his line and touches the next player. This player then runs up to the circles and moves the Indian clubs back into the other circle. In moving the clubs only one hand may be used; the other must be held behind the back. Any club which falls down must be stood upright again before the player continues. No player can cross the starting line until he is touched by the returning runner. The game continues until all of the players have run and the team whose players reach their original places first is, of course, the winner.

Shuttle Relay.

Divide the players into two or more even-numbered groups. Then divide each group into two divisions facing each other in single file at a distance of fifty feet or more. The leader of each file toes a starting line. At a given signal, the leaders on one side of the field run forward and touch the leaders of the files opposite them and then drop out of the play. The players who were touched then run forward, touch the head players in the file opposite and drop out of the game as the first runners did. The game continues until all the players have been touched and the last one has crossed the starting line across the field from him. The team whose last runner completes his run first wins the game.

Bull in the Ring.

One player is chosen as the bull, while the rest form a ring about him, holding each other's hands firmly. The bull tries to break through the ring, sometimes asking of each pair of hands, "What is this?" and being told "tempered steel," "hemp rope," "barbed wire," and so on. When the bull succeeds in breaking through some pair of hands, all give chase and the person who catches him becomes the next bull.

Pom Pom Pullaway or Hill Dill.

For this game considerable space and a fairly large number of players are desirable. The ground is marked off by two lines from one hundred to three hundred feet apart. The player who is *It* stands on one side of a line of the outer sections, and all the other players in beyond the other line. When all are ready *It* calls, "Hill Dill, come over the hill, or I'll come over after you." The players try to run across to the other line without getting tagged. The *It* tries to tag as many as he can before they get to safety beyond the line. Every one who is tagged then joins the side of *It*. *It* calls out as before and again everybody runs across the marked space, but this time, of course, there are a number of taggers. The calling and running go on until all are caught. Then the player who was the first one tagged by *It* becomes *It* for the next game.

Bombardment.

The players for this game are divided into two teams which stand on either side of a line drawn down the center of the field. Indian clubs, one for each player are stood in the field behind each defending team. Several balls are provided but not enough to have one for each player. Any sort of fairly soft ball may be used: basket-balls, volley balls, medicine balls, indoor baseballs, and the like. The object of the game is to throw the balls so as to knock down the Indian clubs of the other team, while that team, of course, attempt to catch the on-coming balls and protect their Indian clubs. Any Indian club which is knocked down by either friend or enemy scores one for the opposing team. There is no order in which the players throw the balls but any one who can catch a ball is free to throw it. No player, of course, is allowed to cross the center line. The game may be played within time limits and the team having most clubs still standing at the end of the time is then the winner; or it may be played with the rule that the team first losing all their Indian clubs is the loser.

Japanese Tag.

This game is different from ordinary "Tag" in that when any player is tagged, he is required to place his left hand on the spot where he was tagged, whether back, arm, knee, or foot, and hold his hand there until he succeeds in tagging some other player. The game is more exciting if there are two or three *Its* instead of the usual one, particularly if there are a large number of players.

Three Deep.

The players arrange themselves in pairs in a double circle, one behind the other, all facing the center. One player is left as *It*, and still another as the runner. The *It* tries to tag the runner. The runner may save himself by standing in front of any pair of players in the circle. This pair then is "three deep" and the back player of the three must leave the formation and be the runner who is trying to escape from *It*, the tagger. If any runner is caught, he then becomes *It* and tries to tag the other player.

Duck on the Rock.

This game involves accurate throwing, and running and dodging as well. One large stone is taken as the "rock" and each player is provided with a small stone for a "duck." The player who is selected as *It* places his duck on the rock. The other players stand at some distance behind a line and try to knock the *It's* duck off the rock. The throwers then try to recover their ducks and get back behind the line without getting caught by *It*. If *It's* duck is off the rock, he must replace it before he can catch any one. The first player who is caught becomes *It*.

For the older children, those in the fifth and sixth grades, the White House Conference recommends besides the group games and relays which the younger children play, also some games which involve simple team-work: games like "Corner Ball," "Newcomb," "Prisoner's Base," "Progressive Dodge Ball," besides such stunts as "Cockfight," "Knee Dip," "Single Squat," and others of the kind.

Corner Ball.

For this game, a space about thirty feet long and twenty feet wide is needed. A line divides this space down the middle and all the players, except two from each team, station themselves in a rough line some eight feet behind their side of the line. The other two players occupy the farther corners of the enemy's field which are called bases. One of the first team takes the basket-ball and tries to throw it over the heads of the other team to the player in one of the bases. If the man in the base succeeds in catching the ball, he throws it back to his own team. If the opposing team is able to intercept the ball, they score one point. Whether the ball is intercepted or not, the other team tries throwing the ball to one of their men on the bases. No player is allowed to cross the line dividing the field, but there are no other restrictions upon their movements.

Newcomb.

For this game, the field is divided in the center by a line and at a distance of about seven feet from this line, one on each side, other lines are drawn. The space between these lines is neutral ground, and the opposing teams are stationed on either side behind the second lines. The object of the game is to throw a volley ball back and forth across the neutral space without letting it touch the ground. A referee puts the ball in play from the neutral ground. He stands between two players, one from each team, who are allowed for this one time on the neutral ground. The referee tosses the ball up in the air and the two players try to gain possession of it. If the ball falls on the neutral space, it must again be put in play by the same method. Whenever the ball is allowed to touch the ground, the side which let it fall receives one score against it.

Prisoner's Base.

The players are divided into two teams, and each team is given a goal which is large enough to accommodate all the players on that side and a space for a prison in the corner of the playground diagonally opposite the goal. The object of the game is to tag members of the other team and place them in the prison. The game is begun by having some specified number of players from each side start running. Any player who is not on his goal may be tagged by a member of the other team who left goal later than he. When a player is tagged he is taken to the prison and the tagger is allowed to return to his own goal free. A prisoner may be released from the prison if a member of his own team manages to get to him without being tagged and then both are allowed to return free to their own goal. But if a runner is tagged while he is attempting to rescue a prisoner, then he too must enter the prison. The team which succeeds in placing all the players on the other side in prison wins the game.

Progressive Dodge Ball.

Three equal-sized courts are marked off in a rectangular field and an equal number of players is assigned to each court. The teams in the two end courts are the opponents of the team in the middle court. They do not oppose each other. The object of the game is to hit the opposing player with a flying (not a bouncing) basket-ball. Any player who is hit, must drop out of the game and leave the field. The ball is put in play by some member of the center team who throws it at some player in one of the end courts. After the ball has hit the ground or gone out of bounds, it may be recovered by any player and the play resumed, but no player may cross the boundary between the courts. He may take the ball only when it bounds or rolls into his own court. Whenever a player is hit with the ball, the referee blows his whistle and the game stops while that player leaves the field. The game then starts as at the beginning. A player is not out if the ball has previously hit another player, the ground, a wall, or any other object, or if the player who threw the ball stepped over his boundary line. This game is usually played in innings of five or ten minutes. At the end of each inning, the players change courts from right to left so that a different team occupies the center court each time. All players who have been hit, return to the game at the beginning of the new inning. The team which has had the fewest number of players hit at the end of three innings is the winner.

Cockfight

A circle some two or three feet in diameter is drawn on the floor or ground. The two contestants squat inside the circle with the hands clasped around their knees and a stick or broom handle held under their knees and above their arms. At a given signal each tries to tip the other over without, of course, leaving the circle.

Knee Dip.

Stand on the right foot, reach behind and grasp the left foot with the right hand. Dip and touch the left knee to the floor. Rise again. Stand on the left foot and repeat.

Single Squat.

Stand on either foot with the other stretched out in front. Sit on heel without touching the ground with hand or other foot. Use arms to keep balance and return to standing position, still on one foot. Repeat, standing on the other foot.

Hiding Games.

There are many games which combine running and hiding. The simplest of the hiding games have no running. Very small children of two will enjoy "Hide and Whoop" or "Hide and Coop." In this game one person blinds his eyes while he counts to a certain number (often to 100 by fives). Then he is ready to hunt for the others and they help him by calling out softly "Whoop" or "Coop." There is little competition and the joy of the game lies in the surprise when the hunter finds the hidden child. Often two children play this happily together, simply taking turns at being *It*. The game is most often played within doors. Other indoor hiding games are found in the ordinary "Hide and Seek" where several children hide, and the first one found is *It* for the next game. There is a variation which older children enjoy called "Sardine." In this game, only one player hides and the others all hunt for him. The first one to find the hidden player joins him in his hiding place without letting the others know what

has happened. Then when some one else finds the pair of players, he squeezes into the place, too, becoming thereby another "sardine." The play continues until there is only one player left who is not a sardine. This player then takes his turn at being the first one to hide.

Outdoor games of "Hide and Seek" usually involve running to goal. The *It* blinds his eyes at the goal and at the end of the required counting, starts out to hunt for the hidden players. If he finds one, he must run back to goal and call out, "One, two, three on Mary" or some such formula. If the caught player succeeds in getting to goal before *It,* he calls out "Free." The first player to be caught becomes *It* for the next game. The game may be hurried up after one or two players have been caught by calling, "All that are out, in free." This call has degenerated in some parts of the country into, "All's out's in free," and in at least one Scandinavian community into, "Ole, Ole, Oleson free!" Variations of the game are found in the method for timing the length of time the *It* must remain blinded. Sometimes it is by counting, sometimes by repeating some formula, sometimes by requiring the *It* to run and get a stick which has been thrown some distance and to bring it back to the goal before he can start hunting and chasing.

Other games which involve much chasing and hunting are common in all parts of the country, although different sections have their own variations. There are the games of the ring type in which the chasing is done in a limited area. "Drop the Handkerchief," and "Cat and Mouse," require most of the children to stand in a ring, while one child chases another. Then there are the games in which some one section of the ground is marked off to be defended by *It,* who may be Tommy Tiddler, or "The King," or the owner of "Dixie Land" in which case the other children encroach on his land and try to run on and off it without getting caught. If any one is caught, he, of course, becomes *It.* More complicated are the chasing

games, like "Run Sheep Run" and "Prisoner's Base," in which the group is divided into sides and in which the competition is of teams, rather than of individuals. "Blind Man's Buff" is a variation of the hunting game in which *It* is blindfolded and has first to catch another player and then to name him before he is counted as really caught. This game may, of course, be dangerous when played out of doors, and so is to be recommended only for indoor play.

Jumping Games.

Of games in which the main activity is jumping, there are not many. "Leap Frog" is probably the best known. In its simplest form it consists merely in having one player bend over, hands braced on knees and head down, while another player jumps over him by placing his hands on the first player's shoulders and jumping over with legs spread so as not to hit the stooping player. Complications are introduced by having a larger number of players, so that the leaping frog has several to leap over and then stoops himself in front of the last one. The player at the rear of the line then becomes the frog and leaps over all in front of him, and so on until the players weary of the game. "Leap Frog" may be turned into a race by dividing the players into two groups and seeing which group can vault over their entire row first.

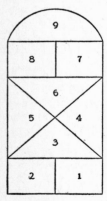

FIGURE I.

Another well-known jumping game is "Hop Scotch." This game is played with a diagram marked out on the ground or pavement. The diagrams vary a great deal and the rules for hopping, stepping, and picking up the stone vary also. One of the most common diagrams is shown in Figure 1. The directions are usually: The player takes a stone and tosses it into the space marked 1. He then hops into this space

on his right foot, picks up the stone without touching his left foot or either hand to the ground and hops out again. If he is successful in this, he then tosses the stone into space 2, hops on his right foot into space 1, then into space 2, picks up the stone as before, hops back into space 1 and out. During all this trip, he must not drop the stone or touch the ground with his left foot. Then he tosses the stone into space 3. He is now allowed to rest in 1 and 2 with one foot in each space. In the same way, after he reaches space 6, he is allowed to use both feet in spaces 4 and 5. As soon as he fails to toss his stone into the proper space, or as soon as he steps on a line or touches his left foot to the ground, he loses his turn. When he gets his next turn, he starts with tossing the stone into the space on which he failed before. The player who first gets to space 9 and back safely wins the game.

Another form of "Hop Scotch" requires much accurate hopping but no stone. Here the form is marked out in the shape of a snail. It is called "Ferris Wheel," and the coil is divided into squares which are large enough to give a child plenty of room for standing. The first player tries to hop in each square on one foot until he reaches the space in the middle, where he may rest on two feet. When he has rested a moment or two he hops back out of the spiral in the same way. If at any time he hops on a line or twice in the same square, he loses his turn; but if he is successful in completing the inward and outward trip without a mishap, he is allowed to select any one of the squares as his particular property. He marks the square with some special symbol, a cross or a circle for example, and ever after he is allowed to rest on both feet in that square while all other players are required to hop completely over it. The player who has most squares marked with his sign when all the squares have been taken, has won the game.

Games Which Involve Throwing.

Then there are the throwing and tossing games. These games often combine some other activity with the throwing, although the simpler forms such as ring toss, horse shoe, and bean bags do not. In bean-bag games the bags are sometimes tossed into a series of concentric rings marked on the floor, pavement, or ground and a score is attached to each particular ring. Sometimes the bags are tossed through different-sized holes in a board set up at an angle, with a score attached to each particular hole in the board.

A game that depends almost entirely on skill in tossing and catching is "Jackstones," in which certain numbers of the stones have to be picked up between bounces of a ball, or while one stone is being tossed in the air. This play has numberless variations, but will be found in some form in almost any place where there are girls of ten or eleven years of age.

The White House Conference has suggested [12] that many games may be used to improve the posture of children. Frequently games may be altered so as to require the players to carry bean bags on their heads. Such balancing demands excellent posture and control of body muscles. Thomas [13] says, "The balancing of something on the head tends to secure good posture, but is not sure to do so. A child may be able to carry his bag and still have a flat chest, and a protruding abdomen." Other games may be altered by adding the requirement that the children maintain a correct posture. Thus "Statues" and "Ten Steps" may be adapted to the use of body mechanics:

Statues.

In this game there may be one "statue maker" or the group may be divided so that half may be statue makers. The statue maker twirls the

12 *Body Mechanics: Education and Practice* (The Century Co., New York, 1932), pp. 137 ff.
13 Leah C. Thomas, *Body Mechanics and Health* (Houghton Mifflin Company, Boston, 1929).

others and then suddenly lets go. The person who is twirled then poses as a statue in the position in which he has been left by the twirling. The statue maker then decides which of the statues is the most beautiful. If under the definition of "most beautiful" the statue maker includes good posture, then this game becomes good exercise in body mechanics.

Ten Steps.

One child stands back to and some twenty feet ahead of the other players and counts aloud to ten. The players try to advance as far as possible during the counting. When the leader says, "ten," he whirls around and looks to see if any player is moving at that moment. Any player who is caught in movement is sent back to the starting line. The play then continues, and the player who first catches up with the leader becomes the new leader. If the leader sends back not only those caught moving, but also those who are standing with any fault in their posture, then this game becomes an exercise in body mechanics.

Games which include running and jumping help to give the child excellent muscular control, besides affording a great deal of fun. Kindergarten children love the running and leaping met with in "Jack be Nimble" and "The Little White Ponies."

Jack be Nimble.

Some small object six or eight inches high is placed upright on the floor. The players run single file and jump with both feet at once over the "candle" while all of them say the rhyme.

The Little White Ponies.[14]

A stick or window pole is laid across two low chairs or held loosely by two children about one foot above the floor. The other children stand in line at a far corner of the room. One after another the children in line run across the floor and leap over the stick as the others sing

[14] This game is taken from the *Manual of Games*, grades one to six, for the Minneapolis Public Schools, 1925.

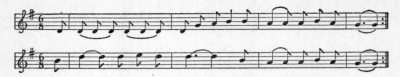

"The little white ponies are tired of their barn,
    And want to come out to play,
Now see them come out and jump over the pole,
    And gallop and gallop away,
    And gallop and gallop away,
    And gallop and gallop away."

Summary

Whatever active games are selected for the children or by them, let them be games which involve much movement of the whole body, what the physical educators call "big muscle" activity, and let them be played, whenever possible, out-of-doors in a playground which is big enough to allow much running without the necessity for dodging into the street and where the players are free to shout and yell to their heart's content. In other words, let the play be free and, so far as possible, unhampered by the restrictions of city life; let it be the real play of real children and not the formal movements of a group of puppets under close direction. There may be a general adult supervisor or playground director, but if the group of children is really enjoying their play, there will be little for the supervisor to do. He will not have to worry about encouraging active movement, for the average child left to his own devices is a strenuous young person; he will not have to worry about keeping up their interest, for the group will shift to a new game as soon as the edge of their enthusiasm for the old begins to wear off; he will not have to worry about making the children follow the rules and play fair, for there is no group in the world so quick to ostracize the player who cheats as a group of children engrossed in a game. The supervisor may, however, observe the games which the group likes best and be quick to teach them a new one or a variation on an old one when the need arises, and the supervisor will probably have to remind the children when it is time to go home, for time flies when an exciting game is on!

Chapter IV

TOYS

EVERY parent has at times answered the plaintive query, "What can I do now?" with a more or less patient, "Oh, go find something to play with." Whether or not this suggestion has the desired result depends in part upon the age of the child and in part upon the particular selection of toys which he has at his disposal. Interest in toys, starting as we have seen in the first year of life, continues to increase until it reaches its maximum by about six years and thereafter gradually subsides. In spite of the fact that toys are of great interest to the child for comparatively few years, during that time they are of paramount importance as sources of happiness and instruments for good physical, mental, and social development. The parent who expends considerable effort in the careful selection of desirable toys will be well repaid.

The Selection of Toys

For most people who are concerned with children, the mere fact that children like toys is sufficient warrant for providing them, whether or not any real benefit may be expected to result from their use. For persons who have made a study of children's development and behavior, however, the provision of toys is based on the recognition of the educational significance (see Anderson's *Happy Childhood,* Chapter IX) of such materials. The child's world may be roughly divided into people and things, and until he has learned how to get along with both of them, he is not an individual well equipped for life. Any sort of learning comes at first only through experience. In many ways it is simpler for the child to learn how to get along with things than it is for him to learn how to get along with people, for things are stable, constant, and inevitable, while people are constantly changing, uncertain, and moved by whims and feelings which are beyond the understanding of the child. A doll is the same yesterday, to-day and to-morrow; but mother may be the most indulgent of humans one day and a seeming tyrant on the next.

Although contact and experience with material objects is one method of getting acquainted with the world, the child's investigation of some of the objects about the ordinary house may result in the breaking of some valuable bit of china or in wrecking some mechanical device, even if it does not result in cuts and scratches on the inexperienced fingers of the investigator. If we limit the child to household articles which he cannot injure and which will not hurt him, his experience will be too limited and so we provide materials planned especially for him, that is, toys. Besides this learning of the physical properties of matter, toys may provide for learning of other sorts. From the use of toys which are miniatures of the equipment of the home—things like dolls, doll furniture, toy brooms, and the like—the child learns much about the actual use of such articles; from the use of other toys, such as balls, tools, and so on, he acquires muscular skill and dexterity; and from the use of such materials as paper, clay, and paint, he learns different forms of self-expression. From any play materials whatever, the child may learn how to share things with others and may acquire the general technique of social intercourse, or he may learn to appreciate beautiful things, or he may be inspired to exercise his imagination. The right toys, well used, provide the best possible material for the education of the pre-school child and one of the great sources of education for the child of any age.

In the selection of any toy or bit of play material, we should keep in mind such characteristics as attractiveness, safety, durability, and variety of use. Obviously, if the child does not like a toy, it is useless to expect that toy to furnish training or enjoyment. This fact is so self-evident that no one would think of selecting a toy which he thought a child would not like. All too often, however, the point of attractiveness to the child is the only quality which the adult demands. There are other qualities which should be considered in selecting toys. For example, no play material which is dangerous should be provided. Toys with sharp corners or edges of tin may cause painful scratches; blocks which splinter are undesirable; toys made of glass, although frequently most attractive in appearance, may result in more or less serious cuts. The fact that contagious diseases may be spread through woolly toys is of less importance to the home than to an institution caring for many children. It is better, nevertheless, even for the child who plays alone, to have toys which can be cleaned. We need not go to the extent of the young mother who boiled the baby's celluloid toys to kill the germs only to find that she had ruined the toys, but we can select, whenever possible, toys which can be cleaned with soap and water.

After we have chosen a toy that a child will like and one that will not injure him, there are still other questions to be asked. Will the toy last for any length of time? A great many of the cheap toys which are on the market break after a few days even when handled by the most careful of children; and when they have broken, there is nothing to do but to throw them away, for it costs more to have them repaired than it does to buy new ones. Moreover, if the child gets into the habit of having his toys break constantly and learns that each time they will be replaced by new ones, it is small wonder that he gets less and less careful about their use and thinks that it does not matter if he does step on the doll, for "Mother will get me a new one."

Another characteristic which increases the value of the toy

as play material is its adaptability to different sorts of play. A toy which can be used in just one way and no other is much less valuable than a toy which can be used in many ways. A good set of blocks will be used in hundreds of ways, at first just for piling up and knocking down, but later as accessories to all sorts of advanced play. Some writers believe that toys should be simple in design, so that they may serve as models if the child wants to make more like them. The toys should, of course, be selected with the particular child in mind. A toy which fits in with what the child already has or one which is appropriate to his interests is more valuable than one which is unrelated to either the child or his interests. A toy station and electric signal-lights will be great fun for the child who already has an electric train, but they will be utterly without value for the child who has no train. Materials for sewing will furnish hours of amusement for the older child who is interested in dolls, but they will mean nothing to the two-year-old.

The Commonness of Various Toys

The White House Conference [1] has listed the play materials which are found in over 75 per cent of the institutions for young children. This list contains materials which we have considered under other headings as well as under the present topic of toys, but it seems worth while here to quote their findings verbatim:

"*Day Nurseries.* Sandboxes, blackboards, balls, blocks, dolls, crayons, scissors, paper books, paper, pictures, doll furniture, paste, cloth books, doll dishes, toy animals, beads, brooms, picture puzzles, doll buggies, kiddie kars, sewing materials. *Nursery Schools.* Sandboxes, blackboards, slides, swings, tool benches, packing boxes, walking boards, balls, blocks, dolls, crayons, scissors, paper books, paper, pictures, doll furniture, paste, cloth books, doll dishes, toy animals, beads, brooms, clay, sand, doll buggies, wagons, kiddie kars, peg

[1] *Nursery Education* (The Century Co., New York, 1932), pp. 117 f.

boards, boards, hammers, goldfish, trucks, garden tools, nails, lumber. *Kindergartens*. Sandboxes, blackboards, balls, blocks, dolls, crayons, scissors, paper books, paper, pictures, doll furniture, paste, cloth books, doll dishes, toy animals, beads, brooms, picture puzzles, clay, sand, peg boards, sewing materials, paints, bean bags, hammers, plasticene."

If from this list of materials we discard those which obviously belong under our chapters on "Vigorous Play," on "Making Things," on "Play of the Intellectual Type," and on "Participation in the Activities of the Family," we find that the most common types of toys to be found in institutions for young children are: (in the order listed) balls, blocks, dolls and doll accessories, toy animals, beads, and peg boards. The same committee reported [2] that the most popular toys in the home were (in the order listed): balls, dolls, transportation toys, blocks, animals, and lastly mechanical toys. In this study it became evident that all sorts of toys are found more frequently in the homes classified as upper social groups. This difference is greatest in the case of toy animals and least for balls and dolls.

Balls.

One of the oldest and most universally loved of toys is the ball. We may not believe with Froebel that its greatest value lies in its symbolism for unity, but we shall have to concede that for the great majority of children balls of various sorts provide much good play and recreation. The White House Conference [3] has shown that the family's list of toys is more apt to include balls than any other type of play material about which inquiry was made. We find more than three quarters of the families, even those of day-laborers (the lowest socio-economic group), providing balls for their children. Although no child in the first three months of age

[2] *The Young Child in the Home: A Survey of Three Thousand American Families.*
[3] *Ibid.*

was reported as playing with a ball, a few children of four and five months and more than half of the babies over eight months of age had balls.

The baby likes a soft ball to roll and to crawl after. When he is a little older he enjoys rolling it back and forth to another person, preferably to an adult who can aim it and catch it when the baby pushes it wildly. Balls for the young child should, of course, be rather soft and should be large enough to be held easily in both hands. The old kindergarten balls were covered with colored worsted. This made them attractive and easy for the child to hold, but it meant that the balls became soiled in a very short time. Most people nowadays prefer a soft rubber ball which can be chewed and which can be washed as often as is desirable. As the child grows older, he learns to bounce the ball and often for a year or two girls, especially, pass through a fever of bouncing balls to the accompaniment of all sorts of verses and gestures. Some of these are merely devices to make counting the number of times the ball is bounced more interesting, such as "Charlie Chaplin stepped on a pin. How many inches did it go in? One, two, three, etc.," counting on up until the child misses. Others give different names to different complications, such as hitting the ball through a loop made by holding the skirt or bottom of the coat with the left hand, to the rhythm of "One, two, three, a basket, four, five, six, a basket, seven, eight, nine, a basket, ten a basket, postman!" The ball is struck through the loop of the arm whenever *basket* is mentioned.

After the years of bouncing balls, come the years of tossing and catching balls, and here we find the boys' interest much greater than that of the girls. In all the lists of children's games and children's activities we find ball-play of some sort holding the leading place for boys from the age of eight or nine on up. The tossing and catching games are sometimes played according to regular rules of the type used in kindergarten games, but when played by boys not under supervision, they are more apt to be mere practice in pitching and catching, leading to "one old cat," and finally to baseball itself. Baseball and its first cousin football take up practically all the play time of many boys. Basket-ball is popular with both boys and girls. The interest in play with balls does not stop with childhood or even with adolescence. In some more difficult games a ball is hit or struck in a particular way, and we find many adults playing hockey, tennis, ping-pong, and golf to say nothing of the thousands who get relaxation from watching others play baseball and football. In all of these games, the main point of the play is control over some sort of a ball.

Marbles.

The smallest ball used for play is found in the marble. The theoretical questions of whether children think of this toy as a form of ball, or whether they enjoy collecting a variety of marbles, or whether they are interested merely in the fun of controlling a moving object, is not as important as the fact that enjoyment of marbles is almost universal among children. The yearly appearance of these toys as soon as the snow melts from the ground is almost as definite a mark of the season as Washington's Birthday or Easter. The joy they bring and the training they afford in muscular coördination are obvious to any one.

Dolls.

Another toy which had its origin hundreds of years ago is the doll. According to the findings of the White House Conference,[4] after balls, dolls are next most likely to be found in the play equipment of the child. As in the case of balls, families of the higher economic groups more frequently provide these toys for their children than do those of the lower

[4] *The Young Child in the Home: A Survey of Three Thousand American Families.*

Spring Is Here

Football Is Fun for Girls Too

groups, but the difference is not great, running only from some 68 per cent of the day-laborer group up to 80 per cent of the professional group. Since even before the age of one year we find more girls than boys playing with dolls, we may assume that the lesser frequency of appearance of dolls compared with balls is due in part to sex differences, either real or superimposed by the parents. Dolls appear infrequently as the toys of babies less than four months old, but their use gradually increases with age until about half of the children one year old are supplied with dolls.

The baby's first doll is smaller, simpler in detail, and softer than the doll of the older child, but it is still a doll. For the child who is three years old or less, rag or cloth dolls are best. The fact that these dolls need not be elaborate in any way is evidenced by the love frequently bestowed upon a towel, knotted so as to suggest a head and long skirt. Any mother with a little ingenuity can fashion a very satisfactory doll out of an old stocking. Anything which has the general shape of a body and which has some suggestion of a face will do, provided it can be cuddled. Boys as well as girls enjoy dolls during the early years, and they would probably enjoy them longer, if it were not for the unfortunate teasing of older children. Although certain boys are not at all interested in dolls, there is no reason why the few who do enjoy this play material should be persecuted by teasing.

As the child gets older, the doll may well be more perfect in detail. Baby dolls are most popular, and if not a baby doll, then a little girl doll. Adult dolls are liked least of all, probably because the child knows too little of adult thought and interests to reproduce them in her play. It is possible to obtain some most attractive felt and cloth dolls which have good faces and in which the proportions of the body are true to life. Unfortunately, some of the best do not have the noise-making apparatus that gives the cry so greatly enjoyed by the children. Another detail which gives the older child con-

siderable satisfaction is the eyes that open and close. Real
hair that may be brushed and curled adds to the doll play,
and clothes that can be put on and taken off are the greatest
of joys. For many four-year-olds, the main pleasure in doll
play lies in the dressing and undressing. Composition heads
are more practical than china heads for although they are
not unbreakable, at least they do not smash as promptly as
the china ones. There are various good wooden dolls on the
market, large ones with steel joints that will survive harsh
treatment and small ones which stand stiffly on little pedestals
and which make a great addition to many kinds of block and
train play. Although such dolls are excellent for certain purposes, the fact that they are not soft and cuddly makes them
less satisfactory for playing house.

While the doll by itself is a joy to the small child, the
greatest pleasure soon comes to be in the make-believe plays
in which the doll takes a major part. For such plays the child
needs a few accessories in the line of doll furnishings of
which the most important is the almost indispensable doll-
buggy. If a mother has only a few dollars to spend on toys
for a small girl, she may well consider putting most of them
into a sturdy doll-carriage and then buying a very simple
doll to ride in it. The doll-carriage will provide all sorts of
play. It will offer an incentive to play with dolls out-of-doors
in good weather; it will provide for all sorts of travel and
transportation play; and it will probably help to bring
brother into the play, if only as a mechanic who must adjust
the wheels or repair the body of the coach. Next in importance
to the doll-buggy comes the doll-bed or cradle. Putting the
doll to bed is one of the great joys of doll play, and any household can produce remnants for doll sheets, blankets, spreads,
pillows, and pillow-cases. Through making the doll-bed, the
child may learn to make real beds. Then there are a whole
host of doll furnishings which will add to the pleasure of the
child. There should be, if possible, a toy dresser or bureau,

where the doll's clothes may be folded neatly away. There should be also some provision for tea-parties: a doll-table, a few chairs and, of course, dishes, aluminum for the younger, china for the older. Trunks and suitcases will suggest playing that the dolls are on a journey. The provision of a toy stove and kitchen utensils will encourage the children to pretend they are getting dolly's meals. Then there are hundreds of possibilities in a wash-tub, clothes-line and clothes-pins. In summer, dolly's clothes can actually be washed and hung out-of-doors; in winter, they can at least be washed in imagination (with perhaps just as satisfactory results).

Toy Trains.

Probably the favorite of the toys of locomotion is the train. Starting with the simplest wheel-less trains for the two-year-old, on up through the ordinary iron train which winds up and travels on a circular track, to the countless elaborations of the electric train, we have a toy which every boy and almost every girl enjoys. In collecting their data, the White House Conference grouped together all toys of transportation, but there can be little doubt that of this group toy trains make up the greatest number. In the possession of these toys we find a decided difference between the upper and lower socio-economic groups. It may be that, since trains are more expensive than balls and dolls, the poorer families cannot afford to buy them. The committee reports [5] that only 47 per cent of the lowest economic group provide its children with toys of transportation, while 85 per cent of the two highest groups are supplied with them.

Toy Animals.

More or less like dolls in their usage are toy animals of all sorts. As in the case of transportation toys, children from the

[5] *The Young Child in the Home: A Survey of Three Thousand American Families.*

upper economic groups are more apt to have toy animals than are the children from the less favored classes. The percentage of families in which children have toy animals ranges [6] from 35 per cent for the day-laborer group to about 80 per cent for the two highest groups.

The tiny baby enjoys a woolly cat or rabbit just as much as he does a rag-doll; and in many homes, a Teddy-bear holds the place of greatest affection. The Teddy-bear is apparently just as human as a baby doll and is soft and cuddly. Rubber animals we have already suggested as furnishing pleasure for the infant. At first the child is not at all concerned with the variety of animal. A toy elephant is just as satisfying as a stuffed dog. Later he may demand number and variety in his animals. One of the most popular sets of animals comes, of course, in the Noah's Ark. Here the interest seems to lie in two factors: first, in the animals themselves and second, in the fact that there is a receptacle, the Ark, in which the animals may be placed. All small children enjoy taking objects from one place and putting them into another, and a Noah's Ark provides an almost ideal set-up for this activity, for the animals may be marched in two by two, be put in singly, or in some other special manner. Then there are the various sets of wild and domestic animals, which may be obtained in wood or in composition. There are the wooden animals with movable legs like those of the Schoenhut circus, and there are wooden animals cut out of one flat piece of wood and perhaps mounted on a base. The better sets are those painted in the natural colors though these seem very drab when compared with the rainbow hues of some of the other sets. Animals may also be obtained in celluloid, china, rubber, and brass, but only a few animals are made in any one material, and they are not in correct proportion when compared with each other. The play with animals may be almost as varied as the play with dolls

[6] *The Young Child in the Home: A Survey of Three Thousand American Families.*

and will change from group to group, according to the familiarity of the children with farm life or with tales of wild animals and according to the interests of the particular individuals. Sometimes toy animals are of greatest interest when they are used in connection with toy dolls and villages.

Paper-Dolls.

The fascination of paper-dolls lies partly in the ease with which they may be acquired, simply by cutting figures from any fashion magazine, and partly in the possibility of making clothes for them without using anything more than paper, crayons, and scissors. The five-and-ten-cent stores offer a number of books of paper-dolls of various styles and sizes, some of which are accompanied by cut-out furniture for a paper-doll house.

Blocks.

A play material which is used in some form or other by all children is found in blocks. The frequency with which blocks appear in the homes of the different classes varies like that of other toys from least often in the lowest socio-economic group to most often in the highest group, the percentages being in this case 42 for the day-laborer group and 88 for the professional group.[7] It seems fairly evident here that the figures for the lowest group are too small. Many families are doubtless reporting only the manufactured articles and are not counting as "blocks" the empty boxes, pieces of wood, and the like which any child left to his own devices will collect and use. What is an empty packing box but a hollow block? It may of course sometimes be used as a box, but it is often used as something to pile up or to climb upon, in other words as a block. If this type of "block" were counted in, there is no doubt but that the percentage of families reported as offering blocks for toys would be greatly increased.

[7] *Ibid.*

The interest shown in blocks by the very young child and by the child who is considerably older develops into quite different forms of play. As they are used by older children, blocks supply material for constructive play to be discussed in the next chapter, but since they are also used as toys by younger children, we shall consider them here. The first blocks given to the child may be of any shape or material, provided they are free from splinters and sharp points. The most common form is probably the wooden cube, printed with letters or simple pictures in red or blue. As long as the child is interested merely in manipulation or in building up a pile of blocks to be knocked down at once, this sort of block meets his requirements. When he is old enough to want to build a wall of a building, the sets of cubes are no longer satisfactory. For this sort of building, the child needs brick-shaped blocks and a few boards, longer than the blocks and thin enough to serve as roofs and partitions. When the child is still older, he will enjoy odd-shaped blocks, triangles, curved blocks, and so on. The best sets of blocks are planned so that by putting two smaller blocks together, the child will have a piece that is the same shape and size as a larger block. Blocks thus selected offer much greater possibilities for planning and accurate building. One set of blocks which can be cut from the ordinary 2 x 4 timber and which has proved popular is made up of the following items:

> 12 blocks $3\frac{3}{4}$ in. by $3\frac{3}{4}$ in. by $3\frac{3}{4}$ in.
> 24 blocks $3\frac{3}{4}$ in. by $3\frac{3}{4}$ in. by $1\frac{7}{8}$ in.
> 12 blocks $7\frac{1}{2}$ in. by $1\frac{7}{8}$ in. by $1\frac{7}{8}$ in.
> 24 blocks $7\frac{1}{2}$ in. by $3\frac{3}{4}$ in. by $3\frac{3}{4}$ in.
> 12 boards 15 in. by $\frac{3}{4}$ in. by $3\frac{3}{4}$ in.

Children of six and seven are greatly interested in sets of blocks which can be fastened together by some simple means so that the resulting structure is sturdy enough to be moved around without falling to pieces. There are various sets of such blocks on the market, such as the "Hill Floor Blocks," the "Builder-Boards" and so on, but unfortunately they are rather expensive for the average family.

Every household, however, can afford a few blocks. When a load of kindling is delivered, hunt it over for bits of wood which will interest the child and plane off the splinters if necessary. Sometimes it is possible to get a small supply of odds and ends of wood from a firm which makes wagons or sashes and doors. The wood from these concerns usually comes already finished and is good hard wood in interesting shapes. One man ordered a load of odds and ends of wood from a wagon company, expecting to use it for kindling. The wood was dumped in the yard and when the man came home at night, he found that his boys and all their neighborhood friends had had so much fun with the pile already, that he finally abandoned about half of the load to the boys. He said afterward that he had never bought any play material for the children which gave as much pleasure and provided the same amount of occupation.

Most schools for young children provide some sort of large block, about 6 x 12 x 24 inches, for outdoor play. Such blocks may be made into a playhouse very easily and will not get knocked over or be as bothersome to pick up as are smaller blocks used out-of-doors. Packing boxes may well take the place of these large blocks for the private home, and will probably be of wider use if they are left, as they usually come, with one side open.

Nests of boxes.

Closely related to blocks are the nests of boxes which small children love. We said, in speaking of the Noah's Ark, that children like to put one thing inside another, and with the nests of boxes they have an excellent opportunity to do so. Such nests should be made of wood and not of pasteboard, for the latter is inclined to warp and, if a box will no longer slide into the one next larger, it is useless. The stronger the set is, the better, because the boxes will be piled up into towers, knocked down, sat upon, and, of course, fallen over. For outdoor play, some schools have had nests of large wooden boxes made. Although these are fairly heavy, they have good strong handles and may be lifted by one child, using both hands, or sometimes by two children working together.

Toys for Table-Play.

The toys which we have discussed so far have been those which require considerable movement on the part of the child. There are, however, a great many toys for young children which require little movement except of the small muscles, and these are often referred to as materials for table-play, meaning that they are usually used at a table. Small children are often given beads to string, and there is nothing which they enjoy more. They love to thread the cord through the beads and to wear the necklace after it is made. Children of two will be satisfied after stringing a few beads, but a year later they will string all the beads and may attempt a simple pattern. Usually the pattern is made by first using all the beads of one color, then all those of another color, and so on. Perhaps shape also will be considered, but only secondarily. If there is a sufficiently great variety in color and shape among the beads provided, the four- or five-year-old may work out a complex design, perhaps taking only one color and carrying the pattern through the arrangement of the different shapes of beads. Girls probably take more pleasure in beads than boys do, though when it is suggested that strings of beads may be used for necklaces and "sold" in a "jewelry store," the boys will be just as much interested in the development of an attractive design as are the girls.

A child's desire to stick things in and take them out is met very simply by the peg board. The old-style peg board is simply a board about 6 inches square with small holes at regular intervals and a large number of small pegs of various colors. This toy has always been popular with children and recently a number of interesting variations of the peg board have appeared. There is the "Peg Village," in which the pegs are topped with bits of wood roughly shaped as houses, trees, and flowers. There is the "Porcupine Toy," in which the pegs are stuck into a log-shaped stick, the "Peggy Pull" and "Cart-block Peggy," in which the toy can be pulled about after the pegs are inserted, the "Hoop Peg" in which the pegs are to be inserted in concentric rings, and so on and so on. Any one of these toys will fill a want in the life of a child of two or three or even four years old.

Certain toys are planned for their constructive features. The very small child is interested in the "Tinker Toy" and the opportunities it offers for thrusting sticks into holes, while the child a few years older may enjoy constructing some of the elaborate patterns which are supplied with the set or devising constructions of his own. A child who is much interested in the problems of making things, however, will probably not be satisfied with anything less complex than a "Meccano" or an "Erector" set.

A table-toy which delights many children is a rubber stamp. For the younger children, these stamps are usually outlines of animals. The small child greatly enjoys stamping them all over blank paper, sometimes making them into a procession, sometimes filling one sheet completely with prints of a particular animal. Older children will get more pleasure and considerable practice from the use of a set of stamping letters, with which all sorts of printing may be done. By the time a child is nine, he will be much interested in a typewriter and, if the family owns an old one or can afford to purchase a small one for the child, he can learn and enjoy a great deal.

Water-Toys.

Still another form of toy which, in general, requires little use of the large muscles are the toys for water play. Of course, the child sailing his boat in a lake or pond may be engaging in very vigorous exercise, but the child whose sailing is confined to the bathtub is not particularly active. The simplest form of water-toy is the celluloid fish or duck which entertains the baby in his bath. Then come the simple wooden boats, without mast or center-board. Then we have the boats which are not meant to be pulled but which are to sail by wind or some mechanical contrivance. The tiny celluloid boats which are moved by the action of camphor in lowering the surface tension of the water behind the boat are not really valuable as a toy, but the sail-boat which will move in the wind or when an electric fan is blowing on it, the boat whose propeller moves when the spring is wound up, and so on, offer the possibilities of races and of much coöperative play. Best of all boats are the ones which the child makes himself, at first merely shaping a flat bit of wood, later adding a mast and working out some method of keeping the boat upright, for a mast, of course, raises the center of gravity and tends to tip the boat over. Then there are the boats made of walnut shells or of pea pods which require careful manipulation and accurate placing of parts. Another play which involves the use of water is blowing soap bubbles, which teaches the child to control the rate of blowing to say nothing of teaching him not to soak the space about his bowl of suds. There is also the possibility of caring for or raising water-animals: frogs, turtles, snails, goldfish, and guppies. Many water-plays can be carried on reasonably well in the house. If, however, a real pond or a real brook is available, there is chance for all sorts of experimentation with dams and water-wheels.

The Child's Supply of Toys

After we have some idea of what kind of toys are most interesting to the child and most desirable from the point of view of his development, the question arises: How many toys should a child be given? No definite answer can be made, of course, but a general rule can be stated: The child should be provided with enough toys to keep him interested, but not so many that he is distracted by mere numbers. The presence of an enormous number of toys is bad from many points of view. The child who has a limitless supply of toys does not get the full enjoyment from them; he is careless of them, tosses them aside with little thought as to whether they will break or not, and he may thus learn to be careless of all his possessions. Then, too, if there is no limit to the supply, there is no necessity for the child to use any ingenuity or imagination. If he wants a boat, he thinks he must have a certain kind of a boat with all the proper paraphernalia. After he does get the exact boat he wanted, he may find that it isn't really such fun, and he may come to envy the ragged little urchin playing in the brook with a scrap of wood which is now a gunboat attacking an enemy fort and now the house-boat of a captured cricket. A further difficulty which arises when too many toys are provided is that the child is constantly distracted from his play by seeing other toys scattered about the room. If he is to get the full joy out of any toy, other toys should not be allowed to impede the play either by being actually in the way or by serving as a distraction.

Although we must be careful not to provide too many toys at a time for any child, we must also be careful to provide a sufficient variety. The White House Conference [8] showed that most children are given a fairly wide range of toys. The committee asked about the presence or absence of the follow-

[8] *The Young Child in the Home: A Survey of Three Thousand American Families.*

ing types of toys: balls, dolls, toy animals, blocks, tools, sand, mechanical toys, materials for hand work, and transportation toys. The median number of types of toys which were found in the homes visited varied from four types for the lowest socio-economic group up to seven types for the two highest classes. The three types of toy least apt to appear in a home are: tools, sand, and mechanical toys. Such a report is quite encouraging for, of all the nine types, mechanical toys are the least desirable as playthings, and sand is often impractical for indoor play. That tools have made their appeal to the families who are better educated and who have a larger budget is shown by the fact that they appear most often in the records for the two highest socio-economic groups.

Summary

In summary, we may say that for his best development the young child should be supplied with a reasonably large variety of toys, selected on the basis of interest to the child, safety, cleanliness, durability, and adaptability to various types of play. If such toys can be used in the fresh air and sunshine of out-of-doors, their value is thereby enhanced, but, even when used inside, they bring joy to the child and aid in enlarging his knowledge of the world about him, in developing his muscular control, and in giving play to his imagination.

Chapter V

MAKING THINGS

As they grow older, children gradually lose their interest in toys as such and require play materials which offer greater possibilities. When the older child does use dolls and blocks he uses them as accessories to some play of family life or of transportation and, although the toys add to the play, they are by no means essential. More and more the child wants to make things or to change the materials which he has. The materials which are best adapted for such usage we may call ''plastic'' materials or materials for construction.

The committee of the White House Conference which worked on the subject of the school health program writes:

"It is highly misleading to say that only the few can create. The ability to create is found in even the lowest and earliest instance of learning. It remains, in different degrees, a characteristic of all learning. . . . And creation enriches life. Nor is creation confined to art. All life demands it and illustrates it. To join things in a new way to meet adequately a sensed situation of any nature whatever is among the most enjoyable of experiences, and the more meaningful the surer the joy. Every person's life abounds in such opportunities. To help find the promising places for creation, to help build the wish to create, and to help find the means of better creation—than these the educator has no higher duty."—*The School Health Program* (The Century Co., New York, 1932), p. 17 f.

Play which involves making things is of value not only in offering great opportunity for enjoyment but in providing much instruction. As he gains control over the materials which he uses, the child is acquiring better control over the small muscles of hand and fingers. He becomes fairly adept at manipulating scissors, saws, hammers, needles, and crayons. He is learning much about the nature of clay or of wood or of whatever he is using, what it is best fitted for, what he can and what he cannot do with it. He is learning also to observe what he sees more carefully, for often it is not until he tries to reproduce a thing that he realizes how sketchy his knowledge of that thing has been. The mother, who tried to make a stuffed elephant for her baby and produced a thing which looked like a dog with a trunk attached to his nose, discovered before she finished that an elephant's front legs are longer than his hind legs, that his tail is very small, and that his ears do not droop over from the top. She had supposed she had seen elephants so many times that the construction of a toy one would not be difficult. And so the child who draws a house or makes a basket from paper learns a good deal about houses and about baskets. There is, moreover, always the possibility that some child may have unusual talent and that early familiarity with the implements and materials of some art will give him self-confidence and further his interest. While few of us can give much time to the search for the rare person of talent or genius, we should make a definite effort to give every child a chance to express his own feelings and his own experiences.

Self-Expression without Words

Children express themselves without self-consciousness and through many media. Most adults have gradually come to limit themselves to a vocal expression of their experiences. We tell some one else about what we have seen or done or read and stop at that. The child's vocabulary is so limited and his general command of language so poor that he often cannot describe his experiences in the way he might desire. Indeed, at times, words fail all of us, and we then fall back on gesture. Who can describe a spiral staircase or an accordion satis-

factorily in words without the use of his hands? The child
resorts even more readily to means other than language for
describing or reliving his experiences. A little girl of three
went to her older brother's school one day to hear a program
in which many of the children took part. On her return home,
she was unable or unwilling to tell her parents what she had
seen and heard at the school, but a little later she was found
dramatizing the experience in her playroom. There she had
constructed from blocks a stage with steps leading up to it,
and she was marching her tiny wooden dolls up the steps one
by one, making them bow to the imaginary audience, recite a
fragment of Mother Goose, bow again, and march down the
steps. The child then clapped heartily, bumped the next doll
up to the platform, and continued the program. She was
reliving her afternoon, and enjoying it all over again, although she did not have the language in which to give an
oral account of the proceedings. Another child, this time a
boy with considerable ability in using clay, came home from
a Christmas play and instead of discussing what had occurred,
modeled all the characters from clay and set up the first scene
as it looked when the curtain was raised. The mother realized
that her son had done an exceptionally good bit of work in
molding the figures, and a few days later she asked him to
let her save them only to find that they had already been re-
molded into a group of cowboys he had read about the evening before. Some children prefer one medium for self-
expression and some another; the opportunity is more
important than the particular material.

Sand.

The simplest of the plastic materials is sand, which is
frequently provided, at least for outdoor play. The White
House Conference found [1] that, while only 18 per cent of the

---

[1] *The Young Child in the Home: A Survey of Three Thousand American Families.*

families in the lowest economic groups had sand-boxes, some 60 per cent of the families in the highest group included them in their play equipment.

The two-year-old enjoys running his fingers through the sand and pouring it from one cup or pan into another. This interest in feeling of the sand lasts for many years. Hardly one of a group of adults sitting on a beach will refrain from fingering the sand and pouring it back and forth from one hand to the other. Sand which has been dampened has more possibilities than dry sand. It may be made into little hills or into sand cakes, the modern substitute for mud pies; it can be loaded into trucks, and so on. Any utensil put into a sand-box will be filled and dumped time after time. As the children get older, the sand play becomes more complex. The whole sand-box may be a series of roads over mountains, under bridges, and through tunnels; it may be a lake over which all sorts of craft sail; it may be a village with sand or wooden or cardboard houses, and so on. Sand is an ideal material for the base of such activities, and the public schools often use the sand-box for setting up an Indian encampment or a medieval castle.

All sorts of materials may be used to elaborate the sand play. For very small children, glass should be prohibited, but for older children, who can be careful, glass is an interesting material because it allows the grains of sand to be seen as they fall inside the bottle or jar. If the family uses a can-opener which leaves a smooth blunt edge on the cans, then any household can supply them in various sizes, either left as they come or painted. For small children, we may well provide individual aluminum pudding molds, colanders, spoons, trowels, funnels, small rolling pins, butter paddles, and small flat-bottomed wooden boats; for older children, measuring cups, small trucks and trains, toy houses, trees, bridges, animals, dolls, and the like. These accessories for the older children are more valuable if the child has manufactured them himself than if they are bought ready-made, and probably they are more valuable and more interesting, if they are acquired one by one and not in a set.

The most famous of sand-piles is the one described by G. Stanley Hall [2] years ago in which, for summer after summer, a group of boys elaborated their set-up and their dramatization of village events. The play started when two boys, aged five and three, found in a load of fine sand a "bright focus of attraction. . . . Wells and tunnels; hills and roads like those in town; islands and capes and bays with imagined water; rough pictures drawn with sticks; scenes half reproduced in the damp, plastic sand and completed in fancy; mines of ore and coal, and quarries of stone, buried to be rediscovered and carted to imaginary markets, and later a more elaborate half-dug and half-stoned species of cave dwelling or ice-house—beyond such constructions the boys probably did not go for the first summer or two."

This sand-pile attracted other boys and furnished the base of all their play for some nine years, gradually changing in form until it was entirely replaced by loam, and the play changed from simple digging and burrowing to the plotting of an entire village which was remade on the same plans year after year. With this village the congenial group played at reproducing the life of a real community. Each boy, representing one family and adopting the name and many of the characteristics of some man in the town, spent many hours whittling the members of his family out of wood, building barns, planting his fields of oats and wheat, and hanging elaborate gates at the entrances to his property. Town meetings were called whenever need arose; laws were passed when necessary; a supply of dollars and half-dollars was manufactured for the use of the inhabitants; and almost the entire life of a rural community was reproduced in the toy village.

[2] G. Stanley Hall, *Aspects of Child Life and Education* (Ginn and Co., Boston, 1907).

When the play was finally abandoned, after some nine years, the families felt that the boys had learned at least as much from their ''sand-pile'' as they had from their formal schools during the same period.

Hall summarizes the benefits which these boys derived from their play as follows: ''The spirit and habit of active and even prying observation has been greatly quickened. Industrial processes, institutions, and methods of administration and organization have been appropriated and put into practice. The boys have grown more companionable and rational, learned many a lesson of self-control, and developed a spirit of self-help. The habit of loafing, with its attending evils, has been avoided, a strong practical and even industrial bent has been given to their development and much social morality has been taught in the often complicated manner of living with others that has been evolved.''

Clay.

Clay and plasticene and modeling wax offer many opportunities for self-expression and creative activity. In most schools clay is selected because it can be more satisfactorily sterilized and because it will harden in a few days into permanent form. Clay, however, must be kept at the right degree of dampness, if the child is to produce work which satisfies him. Often this means that one jar is kept with very wet clay and a second jar with clay which has been drying for a day; it is easier to keep the general supply very wet and dry it a bit as is necessary than it is to try to soak up a large supply to just the right consistency at short notice. Clay, generally speaking, is not so satisfactory for home use. Many mothers object to the dust which powders off the dried clay and are unwilling to bother to keep it at the proper consistency. Plasticene is usually cleaner for home use. There is also modeling wax which may be softened in the hands, then molded and left to harden. It is clean to use but not as pliable as plasticene.

Nest, Snowball, Angle-Worm,
Cake. Age 4

Man Looking at His Garden.
Age 5

Dog. Age 7

Dish. Age 8

Candle. Age 10

Doll in Buggy. Age 10

Airplane. Age 11

Chessmen. Age 11

Clay Products at Various Ages

If clay or plasticene is used, the child's clothes and the furniture may be protected by providing an oilcloth apron and either an oilcloth covering for the table or a special board which is used for clay and nothing else.

Children of two and three enjoy manipulating clay, but they seldom show an end-product. They are happy to take a lump of clay and stick their fingers into it, or punch holes in it with a stick. Such activity is the forerunner of real modeling and should not be discouraged or hurried. The child of four and five will make simple objects. He will make "snakes" by rolling a bit of clay between the palms of his hands, bird's nests filled with tiny eggs, and "lollipops" or "suckers" with a roughly rounded lump of clay mounted on the end of a stick. Rolling-pins, doll knives, and modeling sticks help in the manufacture of these objects. Sometimes the child of this age will model recognizable animals, boats, or persons, and an occasional child will develop a group of related figures. As they grow older, children make such articles as candlesticks, small vases, strings of beads, and the like, which may be used and which are much more satisfactory if they are painted after they have been thoroughly dried.

Soap and some vegetables may be used by the youthful sculptor, though the fact that these substances necessitate the use of fairly sharp knives makes them less desirable media for the use of young children. Under proper instruction many children can learn, however, to use knives correctly and safely.

Wood.

Wood may be used in dozens of ways. Happy the child who has available a simple work-bench with real tools, at least a hammer and nails and a little later a saw. Odd bits of lumber are most interesting to the child of three or four. The older child is also interested in scraps of lumber, but he appreciates having some good wood, free from knots and in sizes which he can use without too much cutting. A few round wooden discs will suggest wheels and result in loved, though wobbly, wagons. Older children will be more elaborate in their carpentry and will make book-shelves and carts and doll-houses, while a group of kindergarten children, encouraged to work with wood, will produce chicken coops, suitcases, shacks, and even representations of animals and people.

The White House Conference shows [3] that many families do not provide tools for the use of their children. Since no record is made of the age of the children in the homes studied, we may assume that the lack of tools in some cases is due to the extreme youth of the children, but even allowing for this, there are many children of five and six and seven who lack opportunity for the pleasure and profit derived from the use of tools. About a quarter of the families of the lowest economic groups and slightly more than half of the families of the highest economic groups have tools for the children to use.

Paper for Drawing.

For fairly quiet constructive play there is no one kind of material which can be used in so many different ways as paper. It need not be expensive and should not be glossed. For drawing the regular manilla paper in a 12 x 16 in. size is most satisfactory. One of the ways in which a child most readily expresses himself is in pictures. Even the two-year-old glories in color and will entertain himself for some time with large crayons producing straggly lines and scribbles. Small hands cannot control fine materials well, so the ordinary crayon and pencil should be avoided, and the large crayons especially planned for young children and the large pencils with large soft leads should be used in their stead. Painting is more satisfactory, if the paper is fastened to an easel or pinned against the wall, with a newspaper beneath to catch the excess paint. Paints for the younger children should, of course, be water-

[3] *The Young Child in the Home: A Survey of Three Thousand American Families.*

colors,[4] which can do no permanent damage to clothing. Brushes for younger children should be large. A good cheap paper for children's painting is "unprinted news"; other cheap papers can be procured through the school supply houses.

Do not expect the child to paint a picture of an object which you present. Leave him alone at first merely to experiment with color. He will cover many sheets of paper with blobs and dashes of paint just for the joy of the color, but he will be learning some technique and may be forming his tastes for color combinations.

Study of the early drawings of children has shown a fairly regular sequence in their development, both in technique of handling the materials and in the representations produced. Scribbling appears as a preliminary stage, first formless wanderings over the paper and later zig-zags, spirals, and curlicues. These more advanced forms of scribbling are sometimes named and so form the link between the first aimless scratches and the later premeditated drawings.

Usually the child's earliest true drawing is a primitive representation of the human figure, at first appearing merely as a head and legs but gradually becoming more and more complete. Of the features, the eyes are most apt to appear, while the nose is frequently completely forgotten. Next in frequency come drawings of animals, particularly the four-legged domestic pets. Later on, birds and occasionally fish and butterflies are represented. Unlike the human being, which is always represented full-face at first, the earliest drawings of animals appear in profile. Such free drawing of children is almost wholly from memory. In fact, the presence of a model is often

---

[4] The bricks of paint in the boxes of paints commonly supplied by most toy departments are too small to be used satisfactorily with large brushes. A much smaller collection of "Show-card Colors" or of "Alabastine" will give better results. Alabastine gets dusty as it dries, but if the paintings are not to be preserved, it will please many mothers because it can be kept in its powdered form and a little mixed for use when desired.

entirely ignored, while the child reproduces the characteristics which stand out in his memory. Sometimes there will be introduced into the picture an astonishing amount of detail, some of which the child knows is there, though he cannot actually see it. His houses will be transparent; his chairs will show four lines of equal length for legs; and so on. One child covered a sheet of paper with blue paint and called it a picture of an airplane. When questioned as to just where the airplane was, he explained most seriously that it had "flown so far away you can't see it any more."

Not only are the early drawings of children incorrect in proportion and completely out of perspective, but they are without orientation, that is, some figures which are upside down or sidewise appear mixed with others which are correctly placed. Gradually such flaws disappear and they are never very important. The child tends to draw the things in which he is interested and, if other details are included, they are often small and inserted casually without concern as to their connection with the rest of the picture. The parent need not worry about the quality of the child's drawing, for the value of it lies not in its accuracy nor in its technique but in its function as a means for expression of the child's ideas and feelings.

Paper for Cutting.

Paper is useful not only as something to paint and draw upon, but also as something to tear and to cut. The infant enjoys tearing up newspapers. The older child may enjoy tearing paper, too, and will be amused at the odd shapes which result from irregular tears. He may become sufficiently adept at tearing paper to tear out any shape he wants—houses or animals or flowers. Most children find that tearing the paper accurately is much more difficult than cutting it where they will.

Unlike adults, children are just as ready to take a pair of

House, Fence, Stop-and-Go
Sign, Pants, Design, Un-
named, Tree. Age 3

House, Man. Age 4

Elephant, Squirrel, Cow.
Age 5

Girl and Ball. Age 8

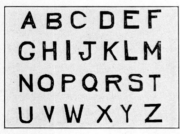

Alphabet. Age 11

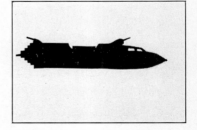

Rocket Ship. Age 11

Paper Cut-Outs at Various Ages

scissors and cut out a man from blank paper as they are to draw the man. In fact, such is the fascination of scissors, that many children prefer cutting to drawing. When the child is first allowed to use scissors, he wants merely to cut and he does not care where or what he cuts. If he has access to scissors but not to paper, he may destroy the sheets on his bed or may cut scallops in his clothing; if he is given blunt-pointed scissors and plenty of paper with the warning that only the paper is to be cut, there is usually no trouble. Remember that the unskilled fingers of the child have more trouble in manipulating a poor pair of scissors than do the more able fingers of the adult and so make sure that the scissors given to him are really good tools. The two- or three-year-old child is happy just to snip up a sheet of paper into small bits. He is interested in the process and not in the product. As he gains control over his hand and over the scissors he will begin to cut with an object in view. He will cut a house and delight in the door which may be swung open or shut, or he will cut a man and march him up and down the table. If he continues working with paper, he may gradually come to cut out things he has seen—a boat, a dog, a clothes-line with the clothes swinging in the wind. If paste is supplied as well as paper and scissors, the possibilities of picture-making are greatly increased, and with a plain sheet of paper as background, he may produce village scenes, historic events, and fanciful imaginings without the use of pencil or crayon or paint.

Paper for Folding.

Then there are hundreds of possibilities in folding paper. All paper-cutting and folding in the schools used to begin with the "sixteen-square" or "nine-square" fold. To get these effects, a square piece of paper is folded twice in each direction, creased down carefully, and then opened up to show that the creases have divided it into sixteen squares. For the nine-square fold, since most small children have trouble in folding the paper in thirds, the simplest procedure is to make a sixteen-square fold and then cut off one row of squares length-wise and one crosswise. A paper so folded may be made into a box simply by cutting down one side of each corner square and folding the side squares up at right angles to the middle one. It may be made into a square house by turning the box upside down, adding a chimney, and cutting doors and win-dows. It may be converted into a table by turning it up, as for a house, and then cutting away a bit from each side. Chairs may be made by using the nine-square paper, making a table, and then cutting an extra piece to be stuck on as back or back and arms. Such chairs will slide under the table if the chair legs are cut down a bit. The child who is limited in his paper construction work by having to fold his paper into a specific number of squares before he starts to cut, is not as free as he might be to use his ideas or to represent things not made in the shape of squares. The sixteen-square fold offers an easy way in which to start a child folding paper, but he should also be encouraged to do plenty of folding and cutting free-hand without the aid (or hindrance) of fixed creases.

There are many possibilities in curves too. A round saucer or a pan cover may be used as a pattern for a circle. Then if a line is cut on a radius of the circle in to the center, the cut sides may be lapped over to form a roof for a silo, an umbrella or, twisted a bit more tightly, an Indian wigwam. Trees may be made by winding fringed paper about a toothpick stuck in a cork, or by cutting out two flat outlines of trees and slitting one from the top downward, the other from the middle of the base upward, far enough so that they may be slipped to-gether to form a tree that will stand on its own base. The in-genious child of nine or ten needs only to be shown a very few types of paper construction to devise methods and arrange-ments of his own. If he is once shown some of the ways in which a standard may be put on to the back of a paper-doll or a calendar to make it stand upright, he will be at no loss to keep any of his structures erect.

The simplest kind of construction with paste is probably found in the strips of colored paper which come already gummed. All the child has to do is to moisten the end of a strip and press it against the other end of the same strip to make a ring or press it against another strip to make a longer strip. The inventive child will combine the strips to make all sorts of figures besides the obvious chain.

Pasteboard.

When paper construction work is not strong enough to satisfy the demands of the child, pasteboard may be substituted. Pasteboard boxes provide fascinating material. If mother is careful to save the boxes which come to the house, whether they are broken in places or are in perfect condition, she will find that most of them are used sooner or later. A sturdy box will make a delightful doll-house for small dolls or for paper-dolls. If it is turned with the open side toward the floor, it may be converted into a charming home by merely cutting doors and windows, pasting on shutters, adding a folded piece of heavy paper for the roof, and pasting a chimney on to the ridge-pole. Or it may be an adobe house for an Indian family, especially if a smaller box is added to the top of the larger one and a pasteboard ladder provided as means of access to the upper story. If the boxes are wanted for interiors, they may be turned with the open side toward the child, as if an outer wall had been removed, and then all sorts of furnishings may be made and arranged inside. A pasteboard box with a spool or button wheels will also make a satisfying wagon; or it can be turned into a delightful boat (for use on dry land only) by adding a mast, a sail, and perhaps a folded paper bow. A whole train of cars may be made from pasteboard boxes, using a round oatmeal box for the engine and square boxes for the cars.

Tissue Paper.

Tissue and crêpe paper are too limp to be used by themselves for construction, but, combined with other stiffer materials, these softer papers offer many possibilities. Dresses for paper-dolls, draperies for the cardboard house, trimming for May-baskets, and ever so many other things, may be devised in the variety of lovely colors available in tissue or crêpe paper.

Cloth.

Cloth is not as versatile in its uses as is paper, and yet, for many occasions, it is much more satisfactory. The most common use of cloth by children is, of course, for doll-clothes. These may be cut and sewed at the inclination of the child, but the older girl will find sewing much more satisfactory, if she is given a pattern for the dress she wants to make, is shown how to apply the pattern to the cloth, and is offered a little instruction in sewing. There are many kinds of sewing that are less difficult than making doll-clothes. The child may make a quilt for the doll's bed, either a patch-work quilt or merely a square of cloth with rough edges turned in and hemmed. Then there are bags to hold marbles, holders for grandmother for Christmas, and so on. As in the case of other materials, when a child first shows interest, he should be allowed a great deal of freedom in experimenting, in trying out the material, and discovering some of its possibilities and some of its shortcomings. Making costumes delights the heart of every child. Paper may be used for a costume to be worn only once, but, if it is to be used over and over, it should be made from cloth. There are various other kinds of work with cloth and yarn. Children will be interested in weaving rugs for the doll-house, perhaps in crocheting reins, and certainly in the kind of knitting in which the yarn is lifted over nails on a spool.

The needles and thread selected for the use of young chil-

dren should be sturdy. Children grasp the needle so tightly in
their attempts to control it, that any fine needle snaps into
bits, and they pull the thread so earnestly that it breaks in the
most inconvenient places. Kindergartens used to provide children with perforated cards for sewing. For occupation in an
idle hour, there can be no objection to these, but to consider
them as training in sewing or education in much else, is a different matter. The young seamstress will learn much more
from her early struggles with cloth and needle and thread
than from working with an outline of holes on a card.

Odds and Ends.

Every family throws away many things which have most
interesting possibilities to the child who is accustomed to using
a variety of materials. The average waste-basket is a place of
great promise to the child. Many charming advertisements are
thrown away every day because the mother does not see their
possibilities as furnishings for a doll-house or decoration for
a playroom. The gay linings of envelopes may be removed
with very little effort and tucked away for future use when
some bright bit of paper is needed. Large envelopes are in-
valuable as storage places for paper-dolls or sets of pictures.
Even the colored handbills which are left at the door make
good dresses for paper-dolls, gay sails for toy boats, and nu-
merous other things. The child can ignore the printing on these
bills with an ease which adults may well envy. Old magazines
may seem utterly valueless to a grown-up who has read them.
To the young child, the magazine with few or no illustrations
may become a fine scrap-book, for the even rows of printing
make an unobjectionable and even pleasing background. Sometimes it is fun to use different pages for different rooms of a
house, pasting all the things which would go in a kitchen on
one page, all those belonging to a bedroom on another, and
so on. For the pictures to paste into these scrap-books nothing
can be more satisfying than the gay advertisements of foods

and furniture and draperies that appear monthly in some of the better magazines relating to the home and housekeeping. Old newspapers are of use also. Children learn readily to spread them down when they are going to do anything messy that might injure mother's rug or table, or they can be used to make soldier caps, or paper chains, though in general they tear too easily to be as useful for these purposes as are the stronger papers planned especially for construction work. Brown wrapping paper has, of course, many uses: it makes a good background for pictures, and it may be used for folding or construction of various kinds. If wrapping paper is badly creased, a warm iron will usually smooth it satisfactorily.

Another source of material for paper construction is found in paper bags. The larger bags that come from the grocery store make most satisfactory masks when the features are cut out and the rest of the mask is painted or crayoned to make the face of a clown, an Indian, or a bear. A fascinating doll may be made by filling a paper bag partly full of crumpled paper and tying bits of string tightly about it to make the doll's neck and waist. The open end of the bag may be flared out to form a skirt, or split in two, twisted, and bound with string to make reasonably stiff legs. Extra pieces of paper may be added for arms and the whole doll painted appropriately and even dressed!

Old wall-paper may be used in many ways. If it is possible to get an old sample book of wall-papers, the children are assured a source of all sorts of patterns, designs, flowers, and so on, that may be used to decorate many a valentine, program, or place-card. Even if the sample book is not available, there will be paper left when the house is redecorated. Perhaps mother will want to keep large pieces to repair possible cracks and tears but surely the children may be given the bits of paper that cannot be used on the walls.

The waste-basket will provide many other things of use and of interest. Mailing tubes, elastic bands, and paper clips are often tossed aside carelessly, when they are sometimes the very thing the child needs for his work. A sturdy mailing tube has almost limitless possibilities. It may be a speaking tube, a megaphone, a telescope, or a tunnel, without any alteration at all. With slight changes it may be a smoke-stack or the body of a locomotive. The bolt upon which ribbon has been wound may become a wheel, or, with a pebble or two dropped inside, a rattle. The spool on which a typewriter ribbon has been wound is such a good wheel! The only trouble is that daddy is often too slow in providing three other wheels to go with it. The spools on which camera films come are good wheels too. The ordinary thread or silk spools are a little harder to work with as wheels, but they make excellent smoke-stacks, legs of chairs, parts of pulleys, or necklaces for the baby. Two of them nailed to the wall or to a board, at the proper distance apart, may form a broom-holder, or one of them the knob of a door.

Of wooden boxes, there are various kinds to be found in the scrap-basket of the ordinary house. Wooden cigar boxes are well made and may be used as blocks or may be decorated by the child and kept as a place of storage. Orange crates and apple boxes make excellent tables and chairs. An orange crate, stood on end, makes a fine base for a cupboard or a dressing-table. Laid on its side, it can be converted easily into a two-room doll-house. Peach baskets suggest fascinating cages for circus or zoo animals. Wooden butter and lard dishes may be developed into fine boats, a little clumsy as sailers, but attractive, nevertheless. Strawberry boxes may be used for many things, especially if they are first soaked in warm water for half an hour. The handles from discarded brooms and mops are a mine of wheels and axles. The tops of jars which have been broken need not be thrown away, for a good one will make a fine dish for paste or, if painted, perhaps an ash-tray for daddy for Christmas. A tin can without rough edges may be used in the sand-box, may hold paint, or may be converted into a flower

pot, while the cover will make a large wheel, if a big nail is
hammered through the center. Odd bottles, especially if accompanied by a cover or cork, are greatly prized. Corks may
be the making of a house-boat or of a duck with two tacks for
feet. Glass is fascinating because it is transparent, and the
child can look through it to see what is happening inside. A
wide-mouthed bottle, when partly filled with weeds and covered by a punctured paper, will make a fine temporary home
for a worm or a caterpillar. Other bottles will be filled with
gayly dyed sand or with the liquid mixtures of all varieties
with which all children love to mess around. Flour and salt
sacks carelessly tossed away, may be ripped up and washed to
furnish the material for all sorts of sewing, whether doll-
dresses, or costumes, or aprons, or covering for a wigwam, or
a top for a covered wagon. Old clothes-pins make delightful
dolls.

And so we could go on poring over the contents of the waste-
baskets in the ordinary home, finding thing after thing with
many, many possibilities for constructive work by the child.
We do not mean to suggest that every time a colored adver-
tisement comes to the house or every time a crate of oranges is
emptied, the child should be required or even expected at once
to make use of the waste material. But we do mean that there
are possibilities in all these things, and the child who has been
brought up to see them will be more happily and more use-
fully employed than the child who is told, ''Oh, that is no
good. You don't want that.'' Why cannot a special closet or a
special box be kept, into which the adults may drop things
which they no longer need or want, with the understanding
that the children are free to help themselves from that box
whenever they like? Margaret McMillan provides a special
heap of odds and ends in her nursery school in England. She
says: [5] ''Our green plots and ordered walks are good and

---

[5] *The Nursery School* (E. P. Dutton and Company, Inc., New York,
1921), pp. 47 and 106.

Many Discarded Bits of Household Equipment Are Greeted
with Joy

right, but who does not remember that he once liked to play in a big place, where there were no walks at all, and no rules? Therefore, a Nursery garden must have a free and rich place, a great rubbish heap, stones, flints, bits of can, and old iron and pots. Here every healthy child will want to go; taking out things of his own choosing to build with. . . . More than any other place our children love the great heap of stones and builders' rubbish that the masons have left behind them after building our extension.'' And if children of three and four can find material which they want in such a rubbish heap, certainly the boys and girls of nine and ten and eleven will find many more things suitable for their use.

Collections.

Most individuals at some time pass through a period of collecting. These collections range all the way from the ''sublime'' of the art collections of the great galleries to the ''ridiculous'' of the strings of paper-match covers displayed across the windshield of the automobile. Children's collections cannot, of course, reach the highest levels of excellence, but they may be decidedly worthy of consideration.

One of the most common and most educative collections is found in the stamp album. Interest in stamps leads directly to interest in the country from which the stamp came and is a great incentive to the study of geography. Collections of birds' eggs may lead to the study of the haunts and habits of birds, collections of shells to the study of shell-fish, collections of wild flowers to botany, collections of toy animals to greater knowledge of live animals, collections of autographs to clearer understanding of the contributions of the individual to society, and so on. Some children enjoy the opportunity for accuracy and completeness which certain types of collection offer. One boy, for example, who had a flair for statistics, one year collected all the possible kinds of milk-bottle caps. It happened that in his home city, each milk company used paper caps, stating the kind of produce (milk, cream, cottage cheese, etc.) which the particular container held and also the day of the week on which it was delivered to the house. The boy's mother filled many a request such as, "I need a whipping cream labelled Tuesday," or, "Saturday I wish you'd get cottage cheese." His original intention was to get an entire set of caps from each milk company in the city, but whether or not he achieved his desire I do not know. A few years later this same boy was keeping detailed lists, showing the prowess of each of the baseball players in the major leagues. Less profitable collections are those of pictures of movie actresses, often acquired by small girls who feel within themselves the possibilities of a similar career; those of playing card backs, cigar bands, cigarettes of various brands, odd bottles of various shapes, stubs from theater tickets; "guest" cakes of soap, stamped with the names of different hotels, and the like.

Summary

We find, then, that every child wants to express himself through making things. What he makes is of less importance than the opportunity to do some sort of creative work. Even "creation" which is mere collection of what others have done has value. Creation which is reproduction of what has gone before, creation which is a supposed improvement on present practice or a product of sheer imagination, is an experience which no child should be forced to miss.

Chapter VI

SOCIAL AND DRAMATIC PLAY

WE are apparently becoming more and more a social civilization; we know many more people and have to learn to adjust ourselves to many more than did our grandfathers and grandmothers. No longer are there thousands of farms and ranches almost completely out of touch with the rest of the world. The lone forest ranger, the lone trapper, and the lone prospector, who have contact with other human beings only at intervals of several months, are disappearing. In their place we find the forest ranger answering his telephone and exchanging bits of news with his chief or his friends, the trapper listening in on radio broadcasts of all sorts and perhaps sending out messages himself, the prospector using the services of a taxi-airplane. The automobile and the radio in particular have brought the inhabitants of the world closer together. To the rural people of Maine, for example, California and New Mexico are no longer vague localities at the other end of nowhere to which young pioneers trudge with little chance of returning; they are now places from which every year numbers of people tour in their cars and assist in the process of helping the whole country to get acquainted.

Not only are we becoming better acquainted with each other, but we are also probably becoming more like each other. It is certain that we are all eating foods which are more alike than ever before; we are using scouring powders and sitting in chairs which are the duplicates of those used at far distant places; and it is quite possible that the radio announcers may in time teach us all to talk with the same accent.

115

The Need for Social Training

It is, therefore, increasingly important for us to learn how to get along with other people. (See Anderson's *Happy Childhood*, Chapter XII.) The individual who has not learned the art of happy social intercourse is a misfit in the modern world. And it is, indeed, an art which has to be learned. The tiny baby is not at all a social being. Even the two-year-old has little social sense, though he prefers usually to be in the room with other people. The three-year-old, on the other hand, craves companionship and is at the beginning of his social education.

Most schools which are working with young children conceive of social training as covering a number of points. To be a socially well-adjusted individual, one must be to a certain degree self-reliant and independent, for the parasite and the clinging vine are no longer thought of as desirable types. The schools, therefore, stress self-help, the ability to do things for oneself. To be an acceptable member of the social group the individual must also be equipped for proper use of leisure time; he must have interests and hobbies which are worth while or which at least are not detrimental to himself or to others. Our ideal social being must, moreover, be satisfactorily adjusted to the group, must coöperate, take turns, obey rules, respect the rights of others, enter into the conversation of the group, and exhibit emotional control. In addition to the points already cited, the mature adult should have some intelligent understanding of the civilization of which he is a part. Much of the training for this desirable social behavior depends upon the instruction given by the adult and has been discussed in another volume of this series; but much of the training for the desirable use of leisure time comes through the simple trying out of many kinds of play activities and the gradual discovery of the keenest interests and pleasures of the individual. So, too, much of the training in social adjustment to the group develops simply and naturally as the result of playing day after day with other children.

For at least two reasons, then, it is important for the child of three or four or older to have playmates. In the first place, playmates are essential because only through playing and working with other children can a child learn to get along with other persons of his own age. Children want to play together and they are ready to sacrifice many things in order to be accepted into a group. They learn to give and take. They learn that one child cannot monopolize all the desirable characters or positions in a game without receiving that terrible punishment, ostracism from the group. Gradually after repeated trials of different sorts of behavior in the group, the child comes to learn what actions and attitudes will be tolerated and what will not. He comes to learn the difference between *my* possessions and *your* possessions, between *my* rights and *your* rights, and the more difficult distinction between *their* rights and *our* rights.

In the second place, there are many delightful plays which require the participation of a group of children, if the play is to progress at all. Sometimes, it is a play where there are several parts to be taken and where it would be awkward and confusing for one child alone to shift his character from one personage to another. Sometimes it is a game played with cards where each player should know only his own hand. If it is a game of chance, it may be possible for one person to play for each of several imaginary players without becoming confused, but in any game where ignorance of another player's holdings is necessary, it is, of course, impossible for one child to play it by himself.

The White House Conference [1] asked parents whether their children played with other children in their own home, whether they played with them somewhere else, or whether

---

[1] *The Young Child in the Home: A Survey of Three Thousand American Families.*

they did not play with them at all. Their data do not cover infants less than one year old, but show that some 18 per cent of children between one and two do not play with other children at all. This percentage drops rapidly. Of the two-year-olds only 6 per cent lack playmates and only 2 or 3 per cent of the three-, four- and five-year-olds are without playmates; from age six on the percentage is negligible. As we might expect, the younger the child, the more apt he is to play only at home whereas the older the child, the more apt he is to play with others both at home and elsewhere. Further data obtained by this same committee of the White House Conference [2] shows that only about 16 per cent of one-year-old children have a favorite playmate but that this number rises fairly rapidly until more than half of the four-year-olds are said to have a favorite playmate. There is some evidence that from the age of six on, girls are more apt to have a chum than are boys.

Imitation

Dramatic and imaginative play begins fairly early in the child's life. As a toddler he tries to bark like a dog or limp like a lame neighbor. Such play is at first, of course, very simple and consists merely in imitating some movement which he sees or which he has seen recently. As the child grows older, he reproduces in his play more and more complicated actions. Finally he comes to the point where he feels the need of other children to take the parts of various characters and the need of a few stage properties or the suggestion of a costume.

Dressing Up.

Dramatization of a simple form is found in the ever-recurring "dressing up." Girls are probably more interested in this process than are boys, though the latter are very ready

---

[2] *The Young Child in the Home: A Survey of Three Thousand American Families.*

to don an Indian suit or a fireman's helmet. The girls delight most in the cast-off clothes of members of the family. A discarded evening gown, an old pair of shoes, an out-moded hat, even a piece of the child's own clothing which is definitely outgrown, or the coat or hat of another child, will inspire hours of dramatic play. Costumes, whether originally planned for some other purpose or provided by a thoughtful mother, offer a great variety of play. Sometimes an old cape or a square of gayly colored cloth will furnish the entire play-wardrobe for several children and will be now silk now rags now furs to fit the shifting desires of the children. Dressing up is not an essential part of dramatic play, but it frequently adds greatly to the pleasure of the children and the costume itself may suggest all sorts of dramatizations which they might not have thought of by themselves.

Playing House.

Sooner or later children imitate nearly every occupation or activity which they see going on about them. Naturally enough, the activities of the household are the first to be dramatized and the ones that are most frequently seen in the play of children. "Playing house" is a play which persists in varying forms for years. In it, the children re-live their daily experiences. The play, which at first involves merely the pretense of sweeping or washing dishes, soon develops into a family play. There must always, apparently, be a mother and a baby. If more children are available, they may be given parts as other brothers and sisters, but more often they make up a second family and the two visit back and forth. Sometimes dolls take the place of the babies in the families and the children themselves all play the parts of adults. The play is usually more satisfactory if each "family" is allowed to "live" in a different room, so that they get the feeling of being somewhat off by themselves. The "house" which the "family" occupies may be merely a room in its ordinary state, but the play may seem more realistic to the child if his "house" is a real enclosure such as may be made from chairs and tables with a blanket or some other covering as a roof.

Some children get so much pleasure and satisfaction out of playing house, that they play it on all occasions. If they are out-of-doors, certain areas may be marked off as the houses of the different families with acorns or pebbles or twigs as children, if no dolls are available. Paper-dolls are, of course, used a great deal in house play, and they are particularly adapted for dressing and undressing activities, for any paper-doll may easily have a most elaborate wardrobe and may have her clothes changed in a second or two. An extreme example of children playing house upon all occasions was found in the case of two little girls who had been helping trim the Christmas tree. Among other ornaments for the tree were two German crêpe-paper dolls three or four inches in height. These had been hung on the tree with the other ornaments and when the decorating was complete, the children started at once to play that one doll lived in one "house" (really a branch of the Christmas tree) and the other in another house. For an hour or more the dolls visited back and forth, did their housework with imaginary utensils, telephoned for groceries, went shopping around the tree and admired the other ornaments, ate their meals, went to tea-parties, and so on, through the regular list of plays, all on the Christmas tree.

Playing Store.

Another sort of activity often represented in children's play is keeping a store and selling various articles to other children. If there is a long table, a table-leaf across two chairs, or an empty shelf of a bookcase which can be used as a counter on which the wares can be spread, so much the better; if there are paper and string for wrapping up purchases, the play is yet more interesting; and still further detail may be added by the use of "money." For the youngest children, pins or scraps of paper make perfectly satisfactory currency. Indeed sometimes the shopper merely pretends to drop something in the storekeeper's hand. But older children are interested in toy money of different denominations and in the process of making change. Grocery stores may be very well stocked, if mother will open her cereal boxes carefully so that they may be glued shut again after their contents are gone, if she will save empty spice cans, vanilla bottles, and the like.

Playing School.

The activities of the school-room, especially of the teacher, inspire considerable dramatic play. In such plays the favorite rôle is that of the teacher, the least popular that of a pupil. One group of small children organized a "school play" one afternoon and assigned the following parts—teacher, principal, janitor, nurse, dental nurse, and music teacher—only to find that there were no children left to be pupils, so they finally decided to dispense with the music teacher and have a pupil. Although the average age of this group was six or seven, they were not at all disturbed by the scarcity of pupils. An older group would doubtless have seen the incongruity and have tried to remedy it. The only equipment necessary for playing school is a row of chairs. If it is possible, however, to provide two chairs apiece to represent desk and seat, to provide a blackboard and enough paper and pencils to go around, the demands of the most exacting young "teacher" will be satisfactorily met.

Playing Indian.

Playing house and store and school are generally most popular with girls, but there are other dramatic plays which are of the greatest interest to boys. The most satisfying one is probably that of cowboy and Indians, with the stress laid on riding horseback and shooting. As a small boy, the child has probably played horse with a bit of rope for reins, but that is a very tame kind of "horse play" compared with the "horse play" of the cowboys. Often a stick will be taken as the horse and the boy will caper, prance, buck, and gallop to the accompaniment of the yells and whoops of the rider (the child's legs obviously taking the part of the bronco, his arms and voice that of the rider). The children taking the part of the Indians are provided actually or in imagination with bows and arrows and the cowboys with guns.[3] Sometimes the guns have been carefully fashioned from wood; sometimes they are rough sticks or twigs; sometimes they are there in imagination only. Some groups will organize warfare between the Indians and the cowboys and go through all the motions of hiding, hunting, slipping from tree to tree, shooting, and capturing members of the enemy. Boys who have read tales of Indian warfare may add such details as the council fire or the torturing of prisoners. The play will be furthered, if feathers can be found to stick in the caps or hair of the players or if Indian or cowboy suits are available.

[3] One of the toys most often found in the hands of boys of eight or ten is a toy gun or pistol. No toy has received more condemnation from pacifists, timid women, and from adults who are seriously concerned with the child's welfare. There can be no doubt that, in these days of lurid head-lines, there is a tendency for boys to play at "hold-ups" and at gang warfare. Any thinking adult will realize that familiarity with such plays for any length of time may so accustom the children to thoughts of murder that the actual crime will seem less horrible than it would normally. On the other hand, it is unfair to reject a toy completely because it can be put to undesirable uses. Many intelligent and really kind-hearted adults enjoy the fall hunting season. Here the use of guns constitutes a sport, a skill, in which the hunter is required to test his ability to predict the distance which, for example, a wild duck will travel while the shot from the hunter's gun is reaching the place toward which the bird is flying. A less trying test of ability is found in shooting at a target, a sport which almost any person will enjoy. If we can limit the "gun play" of children to pretending to kill dangerous wild animals or to shooting at a target, we are fostering a desirable skill; if the play persists in impersonating characters of the "under world" or exists merely for the sake of terrifying younger children, the use of toy guns should be prohibited.

Courtesy of the Minneapolis *Star* and George E. Luxton

Cowboy and Indian

Courtesy of the Minneapolis *Star* and George E. Luxton

Many Adult Activities Are Dramatized

Less Common Imitations

There are, of course, hundreds of other kinds of dramatization of activities which the child sees or of which he hears. A group which has just been on a trip will organize a detailed "travel play" and will take taxis, trains, steamboats, and ferries with the attending porters, captains, head waiters, engineers, conductors, whistles, baggage, and so on. Children who live in the neighborhood of a fire-house or who have watched a fire-engine go by will extinguish many an imaginary blaze with much clanging of bells and swishing of water. Children who have visited a zoo will turn into prowling leopards and growling bears. Whatever activity the child sees, whatever occupation he becomes acquainted with, will be reproduced in his play, provided only that that activity has much action involved in it. The bookkeeper, the minister (except for his activities in the pulpit), and the student do not appeal as do the farmer, the policeman, and the blacksmith.

Dramatizing Stories

Children like to dramatize not only their own past experiences but also certain stories which they have read or have been told. Even the three- and four-year-olds will play over and over the story of "Billy Goats Gruff." All they need is a plank or a box for the bridge and a child crouching beneath it. Kindergarten children enjoy playing "The Three Bears," building the necessary chairs and the beds out of blocks. Bits of Mother Goose are frequently dramatized by young children, for the action is quick and clear. On the other hand, books like those of A. A. Milne, where the interest lies in the conversations and in the exact wording, are acted out only infrequently, although some children will, of course, dramatize any story which catches their interest.

Children who have been to a theater will often reproduce bits of the play after they get home, or they may be moved to invent plays of their own. For children who read easily, simple plays especially written for children provide considerable entertainment and training. There are advantages in both the spontaneous, extemporaneous and in the memorized plays. The spontaneous plays may give an opportunity for the exercise of the imagination, and under a little wise direction they may teach the children some of the problems of the stage, but all too often they deteriorate into useless and pointless showing-off. If the children actually learn parts in a well-written play, they will learn something of good English and more of the plan of a plot than they possibly could through any unaided efforts of their own.

Whether the plays be spontaneous or learned, they have much more point if they are given before an audience. A real stage is, of course, an addition but by no means an essential one and all the thrills of a "first night performance" may be realized if only there is a curtain to be pulled or lifted aside.

Social Games

Before they reach the age of five or six, children seldom show much interest in real games—those in which it is necessary to follow set rules—but older children greatly enjoy games of this type and learn much from them. Each one learns, for example, to take his own turn and to wait while the other children have theirs; each learns to obey the rules and not to cheat; each learns to accept defeat pleasantly and to be magnanimous when he wins. While many of the best known and most popular games fall under the "Vigorous Plays" discussed in an earlier chapter, there are many social games which are best adapted for indoor use.

Dozens of them, such as the ones frequently played at children's parties, require no apparatus and yet provide much fun. We can do no more here than suggest some of the most common. Many are very simple, keep all the children busy, and are not ruined if some one child fails to follow the rules of the game. Such a one is the familiar "Queen Dido's Dead" in which the children sit in a ring and the action moves around the ring until all the players are in motion. The child who begins the play turns to his left-hand neighbor and says "Queen Dido's Dead." The neighbor replies, "Is she? And how did she die?" The first child answers, "Going this way," and shakes his right hand. The second child turns to his own left-hand neighbor, repeats the conversation, and imitates the action. All the time the child who started the play keeps his hand in motion too. At last all the children are shaking their hands. The original questioner starts again but this time his answer sets the left hand to shaking also. The play may be continued until both hands, both feet, and the head are in motion, or the starter may introduce such actions as winking, moaning, and the like. Children find it most amusing to watch every one in the ring going through the same sort of motions at the same time.

There are games in which most of the action, at least at any given time, falls to two or three children, although all of the group are somewhat active. In "London Bridge" two children form an arch with their hands, or stand upon two chairs and allow the others to march beneath their arms while they all sing the familiar "London Bridge is falling down." At the last words of the song they drop their arms and catch whoever is at that moment between them. That child is taken aside and required to choose between two articles named, each chosen privately by one of the members of the bridge. The caught child takes the place of the child whose article she has chosen. In a variation of this game the caught child stands behind the one whose article she chose, and the game continues until all the children are behind one or the other member of the bridge. Then the game ends in a tug of war.

For some games the entire group must be divided into two teams. In "Clap In, Clap Out," half of the players leave the room, while the other half stand behind empty chairs. After each of these players has chosen which one of the other group he wants to have sitting in his chair, the members of the outside group are allowed to enter one at a time. The first one to come in sits down in the chair which he guesses is reserved for him. If he guesses correctly, everybody claps and he is allowed to remain seated. If his guess is wrong, everybody hisses him out of the room. Another player is then invited to come in and the game goes on until all the chairs are filled.

Another humorous game is "Gossip." Here all the children sit in a ring. One, who is chosen as starter, whispers some remark very rapidly and very softly to his right-hand neighbor. No repetitions are allowed, and the neighbor must try to make sense out of what he heard and whisper it in the same manner to his right-hand neighbor. When the whispering has gone around the entire circle, the last person says aloud what he heard and the starter tells what he said in the first place. The difference between the two remarks is often striking and very amusing to the children.

A game in which all are in active competition is "Going to Jerusalem." In this game two rows of chairs are placed back to back down the middle of the room with one less chair than there are children playing. A march is then played on the piano or sung by the children. At a given signal—either the stopping of the piano or a bell rung by some person not in the game—all the marching children try to get seats. The child unable to secure a seat, drops out of the game. One of the chairs is removed from the row and the play continues until there are two children and one chair left. The one who secures that seat is the winner of the game.

Indoor Games of Skill

There are various tests of skill which are suitable for indoor use with a group of children. We have already said something of forms of "Hide and Seek." There are other hiding games in which the purpose is to find not an individual but some concealed object. "Hide the Thimble" is one of the oldest of these games and traditionally a thimble is the object hidden. The game may be made simple by placing the thimble where it can be seen without moving anything and by giving all hunters a notion as to how high above the floor the hiding place is. Another variation which makes the game easy is having the hider report whether the hunters are getting "warmer" or "colder," i. e., nearer to or farther away from the hiding place.

Many games have been devised which depend upon the accuracy with which the players can aim. One of the most common is "Ring Toss," which may be made easy or difficult by moving the post nearer to or farther from the players. There are other aiming and shooting games, such as "Indoor Golf" in which a golf ball is driven over and through various hazards. An aiming game, complicated by having the players blindfolded, is "Pinning the Tail on the Donkey."

Board Games.

The games which require special boards are interesting to many children. Any toy shop will offer many racing games, in which each player is represented by an airplane, or a yacht, or a train, and in which the progress of each piece is determined by shaking dice or spinning a pointer. Often the route of the racers is peppered with danger spots involving some penalty. The player may be told, "If you land at this point, your airplane has sunk, and you must return to the start and begin again." Or he may be told that stopping at certain points means making a detour or waiting there until the other players have had a certain number of turns. Thirty years ago there were many games of this type, in which the players all started at the "Little Red School House" or at "Home" and ended in the President's chair or on the gallows, according to the luck of the spinning. The more modern games provide less melodrama but not less fun.

One of the most popular and one of the oldest games to be played on a special board is "Parchesi." Although the rules for this game may be made simple or complex, according to the age and experience of the players, one rule which should be enforced on every player is that there are to be nothing but smiles when a piece is "sent home" to start again. Some children will be ready for checkers by the time they are ten or eleven years old; a smaller number will enjoy "Camelot." Chess is too difficult for most boys and girls of this age, though an occasional child may be ready to play the game with a player of ability equal to his own.

Card Games.

There are a number of good children's games which are played with cards. The most familiar is probably "Old Maid." Even the younger children enjoy this, though they are satisfied with drawing cards and matching them without the added interest of the old maid card. A four-year-old, playing a game of "Old Maid" with her mother and older brother, seemed surprised when the others objected that no "Old Maid" card was left at the end of the game. The Mother said, "I wonder if it is lost." Miss Four-year-old replied: "No. It's not lost. I left it in the closet on purpose so I'd be sure not to get it." Many children enjoy the game of "Snap" which requires quickness of speaking but which sometimes ends in an argument as to who spoke first; and many enjoy "Slap Jack" which requires quickness of movement and leaves no room for argument as to who slapped first because the hand of the other child comes down on that of the one who did.

Another card game which is less well known but which provides many hours of happy play is "Everlasting." For this, any and all of mother's old decks of cards may be used whether or not the decks are complete. The cards are dealt evenly among the players and one child begins the game by turning his topmost card face up on the table. Turns are taken in the ordinary clockwise direction used for most card games, with each child turning over his topmost card. The child who first turns up a card of the same suit as the first player's card but of a higher rank, is allowed to gather in all the cards which have been thus far placed on the table and to add them to the bottom of his pack for later use. Thus, if the first child turns up a ten of diamonds, the second a two of spades, the third a three of clubs and the fourth a queen of diamonds, the fourth player takes all four cards and then starts the play again by turning up another card. After the first round it sometimes happens that the child who turns up a card is also the one to capture it and the others. In this game the ace counts at either end of the scale. When it is the first to be turned, it may be taken by any other card in the suit; but when a king is the first card to be turned, the ace is the only card which will take it. The game is continued until one child has acquired all the cards that are being used.

The number of good card games is almost limitless. Simple forms of double solitaire or the old-fashioned straight whist may be greatly enjoyed by a group of children nine or ten years old. Usually the children who enjoy the more complex games are those who have had several years of experience with the simpler games.

Summary

The child's social development may be greatly facilitated by playing with other children. In such play he learns to be fair, to take his turn, to expect only his own share, to accept defeat pleasantly, and to win graciously. The child who has learned the joys of playing with others should be better able to make a game out of drudgery which he cannot escape, to throw his best efforts into his work, and to accept philosophically upsetting circumstances which he can neither foresee nor prevent.

Chapter VII

PLAY OF THE INTELLECTUAL TYPE

In most of the kinds of plays which we have discussed, the part which the parent plays is very small. If the mother provides opportunity, materials, and playfellows, her duties are largely over. Of course, she needs to be near at hand to prevent dangerous play, sometimes to answer questions and to settle difficulties; but the play itself will be of greater value to the child if it is not too evidently controlled by the mother or any other adult. Only by meeting his own difficulties, solving his own problems, and settling his own scraps can the child finally attain the goal of self-reliance and self-control. (See Anderson's *Happy Childhood,* Chapter IV.)

In the kind of play which we shall take up in the present chapter, however, the game is usually more successful if mother, father, and any other available adults join in it and do their best at it. The greatest joy and the greatest benefit from an intellectual game come from competing with others who are superior to yourself. The fact that there are great discrepancies between the various abilities of the group does not interfere with the pleasure which each player may get from the game, and there are few other ways in which the family as a whole may come together for a happy half hour as sociably as in some sort of guessing or memory game. These games have not been as fully covered in writings on play as have some of the more active games, and so we shall here suggest a good many with the rules for playing them.

Frequently discussions of the careers of great inventors or of great discoverers—whether of germs or of continents—may

131

be summarized in the statement that the great man had in-
tuition, made a lucky guess, or, in the slang of the day, "got
a hunch." The ignorant may assume that a correct guess
comes merely by chance, as in throwing dice, but those who
have followed the careers of the "good guessers" realize that
the probability that any guess will be correct depends partly
on the amount of information which the guesser already possesses and partly on his ability to "put two and two together."
The electric light was invented because Edison recognized the
fact that, if he could discover a filament which had certain
properties when under the influence of an electric current, he
would have a new source of light; certain of the outer planets
have been discovered because astronomers "guessed" that
some heavenly body must be in that position if the movements
of the other planets were to be explained; the part played by
the mosquito in the transmission of yellow fever was discovered because a doctor "guessed" that thus the transmission of the disease could be explained; the modern oil company drives a well wherever some geologist "guesses" that oil
will be struck. The common characteristic of all these successful guesses is that the individual is working not on pure
chance but on the basis of all his previous pertinent knowledge. This should mean that we can train children to be good
guessers, that is, train them to pick out the essential points in
any situation and base their predictions upon those, ignoring
more striking but irrelevent elements. Such training need not
be in any way formal. It will develop as the natural result of
many simple games which all children enjoy increasingly as
they grow older.

Guessing Games

A fairly young child is amused at trying to guess which of
the questioner's hands holds a coveted article. If, however, the
possibilities are practically limitless, as in the problem "Guess
what I am thinking about," then the chance for failure is so

much greater than the chance for success that, after a few attempts, almost any guesser would "give up." Even when the possibilities are limited, few persons over five or six years old enjoy making "a stab in the dark," a guess which is pure guess and whose probability of correctness cannot be heightened by thinking. There is some fun in guessing which hand is holding the tiny doll or the spool, if you have noticed that the questioner usually holds things in one particular hand or if you have discovered that he is apt to turn his eyes to the side holding the concealed object. As the children grow older, they become more and more interested in the games which involve more and more thinking; a guessing game which can be solved by thinking is really a puzzle and falls into the class with the cross-word puzzles over which people of all ages wrinkle their foreheads and with the detective stories which amuse some of the "highest of brows."

A number of years ago, the kindergarten began to teach the children to be more observing of what they saw and heard. For this purpose they devised a listening game in which the child is required to guess the name of a person from the sound of his voice. The person who is *It* is blindfolded and seated in the middle of the ring. One of the others comes up to him and says very softly, "Good Morning, Sarah (or John, or Peter)," and the blindfolded child answers, "Good morning, Henry," naming the child whom he thinks has spoken. As soon as the blindfolded child guesses correctly who has spoken to him, the person whose name has been guessed takes his place as *It*.

Variations of this game involve guessing by feeling instead of from sound as in the previous case. In this case the child who is blindfolded is required to name a person whom he cannot see, who does not speak, but of whom he may feel. This play may be varied by having him name an object from the feeling instead of a person. Children and older people as well may be amused by trying to recognize foods from their odor or taste only or to recognize songs from the rhythm, unaided by the pitch of the notes.

There are guessing games in which only a part of an object or person is seen. This game in its most common form may provide a great deal of fun. A sheet, with small openings cut in it at appropriate heights from the floor, is stretched across a doorway. After the players have been divided into two groups, one group is sent behind the sheet, and the lights are extinguished so that their shadows will not fall on the sheet. This group stand behind the holes in the sheet so that their eyes, noses, or mouths show through the holes, and members of the other group are required to state to whom the eyes, noses, or mouths belong. Usually the holes are numbered and each member of the guessing team records each of his guesses on a paper opposite the corresponding number. The person or the team making most correct guesses is the winner. In another stunt, the problem may be to guess who a person is from his shadow or from his profile (either thrown as a shadow on a sheet or from a picture previously taken against a bright background). Guessing individuals from their baby pictures, from a sample of their handwriting, from their gait, or from some other usually ignored trait, all may be productive of much fun.

Considerable thought may be required, if the problem is to guess what an object is from the description of it given by another player. This game is amusing to small children when only two persons play, each one in turn selecting an object and describing it in greater and greater detail until the other is able to name it. For older children, the game is much more fun, if there are several persons listening to the description and if there is competition to see who can guess it first.

"Twenty Questions" has been a favorite game for many years. Originally the person who was *It* was limited to just twenty questions and, when they were used up, he had lost the game if he had not guessed correctly, but most commonly the questioning is allowed to go on until the object is guessed. One player is sent from the room while the others agree on some object which he will be required to guess. The *It* then returns and questions all the other players in turn, asking only questions which can be answered by "Yes," "No," or "I don't know." Sometimes it is necessary also to allow, "I can't answer that." Suppose, for example, the object chosen is the heel on some one's shoe. Then if *It* asks, "Is it her shoe?" there is obviously no chance of saying "Yes," or "No," truthfully without unnecessarily misleading *It*. With older players, this exception need not be made. As soon as the object has been guessed, another player takes his turn at being *It*. The game is usually continued until all have had their turn at guessing. In playing with children of six or seven, it is well to select objects which will be within sight while the child is asking questions. With older children, objects which they have seen in some other place or at some other time may be used. With adults, objects which no longer exist, descriptions of historical characters, etc., will make the game a real contest of wits.

There are at least two similar games in which the guessing is not of an object but of a verb or adverb. The guessing of the verb is often called "Tea-kettle" or "Coffee-pot" because the verb is never mentioned but these words are substituted for it in the questions which are asked. One person chooses a verb, and the others take turns in asking him, "How do you like to Tea-kettle?" "Where are you usually when you Tea-kettle?" "Do you Tea-kettle alone or with other people?" and so on. Each of these questions must be answered truthfully by the *It*. When the verb is guessed, another player becomes *It*. In the game in which an adverb is to be guessed, one player selects an adverb (roughly, quickly, loudly, or something of the kind), and the others demand that he "Sing in the manner of the adverb,'' or ''Stand in the manner of the adverb,'' or ''Make a face in the manner of the adverb,'' and so on until the adverb is guessed.

All children like to rhyme and games in which the end-sound of the word is all-important are popular with young children. One player will say, ''I am thinking of a word which rhymes with *all*,'' and the others guess until the right word is found. A more elaborate play of this same type is called ''Crambo.'' In this, as in the simpler form, the play will start with, ''I am thinking of a word which rhymes with *all*.'' The answering player answers not with a simple guess but with another question, such as, ''Is it the part of a house that the front door opens into?'' The first player then answers, ''No, it is not a hall'' (or ''Yes, It is a hall,'' if that happens to be correct). The questioning continues, of course, until the right word is discovered.

Games of Observation

In our discussion of the value and interest in guessing we have said that a good guess depends partly on the person's ability to pick out the essential details in a situation. All too often we have to admit that, when faced with a given situation or event, we simply did not see or did not hear something which was vital to the comprehension of the whole. Just as failure to understand one particular word may mean failure to comprehend a joke, so failure to recognize some particular person or some particular object may mean misunderstanding a situation which is really important. It may be a sort of ''for the want of a nail a battle was lost.'' This ability to see everything which is to be seen may be of value not only to the individual, but it may also be the source of a great deal of pleasure for him. The person who knows what to look for and who is able to find it has a wealth of entertaining occupations at his command which the average ''mentally blind" person completely misses. Let us, then, encourage children to become good observers.

It is not uncommon to hear a mother remark of her child, "He notices everything; nothing gets by him." As a matter of fact, an enormous number of things "get by" all of us, as is shown every day by the testimony of reliable witnesses in court. To a certain extent individuals can be trained to observe and to report accurately. In the modern kindergarten, for example, we may find children playing a game of "Hide and Seek," in which the "hidden" object is in plain sight, and the question is merely who can see it first. At a later age, we find adults learning to read proof, that is learning to observe the errors in printing. In one game, which depends for its success upon accurate observation, a large number of objects is placed on a table and displayed for a very few minutes. The children are allowed to look at the objects as long as they are uncovered and then are asked to name or perhaps to write down all the things which they saw. A similar game, which involves accurate observation and the ignoring of irrelevant details as well, is the puzzle in which the problem is to find the "cat" or the "old witch" or whatever is hidden in a drawing. Children are, of course, unable to make these drawings for themselves, but the pictures can sometimes be obtained for them.

Games of Memory and Quick Recall

Our great discoverer not only picks out the essential points in the situation with which he is faced, but he compares them with those of more or less similar situations which he has met in the past. In order to do this, it is obviously necessary for him to remember past events accurately. There is probably little that we can do to "train" our memories, but we can learn the fun there is in testing ourselves, in seeing how quickly and accurately we can recall something. It is often fun to see how much we can remember, not just to indulge in reminiscence of happy or exciting or unpleasant experiences of past years, but to try deliberately to see how accurately we can remember new material which is presented to us. Older people may enjoy simply trying to see who can learn a given verse or bit of prose word for word in the shortest time, but children need to have more fun attached to the process of learning, if they are to enjoy such a contest.

Of the memory games popular with children, the most familiar is usually called "I Packed My Sister's Trunk." Here one player starts the game by saying, "I packed my sister's trunk and in it I put a pair of shoes." The second player takes up the game and says, "I packed my sister's trunk and in it I put a pair of shoes and a velvet dress." The third player adds an item of his own. The play goes round and round the circle with the list of trunk-contents getting longer and longer. If any player omits any item or names any in the wrong order, he is dropped from the game. The play continues until only one player is left. Other games very similar to this game are found in "A No-horned Lady," "Genteel Lady," "The Good Little Man," and so on.

The game "Beast, Bird, or Fish" (or "Fish, Flesh, or Fowl" or "Animal, Vegetable, or Mineral") requires the players to think quickly and accurately. This game may be played in either one of two ways. In the first way, one player points at another and says "Beast, bird, or fish?" and then names something, such as "partridge," and immediately counts aloud to ten as fast as he can. The player who has been designated by the pointing must classify the partridge by answering "bird" before the *It* has counted to ten. In the other form of the play, the *It* names not a particular animal but the class of animal and requires the other player to name a representative of that species which has not already been named by some other player. The question is, then,

"Beast, bird, or fish? Fish! One, two, three, four, five, six, seven, eight, nine, ten!" A more difficult form of the game allows the questions to be asked in either form, during the same play. The child who fails to respond before the questioner reaches ten becomes the next *It*.

Quick recall is also demanded by certain games played with anagram letters. The players divide the letters evenly, usually omitting *x* and *z*, and keep their pile face down in front of them. In its simplest form, the players may decide at the beginning that the question is to be of names of countries, or names of famous people, or characters in books, etc. Then one player turns up a letter so that the others can see it, and the one of them who first calls out the name of a country (or whatever has been chosen) beginning with that letter, is given the letter (or allowed to score one). The next player then turns up a letter from his pile. The player who turns the letter over is not allowed to guess, because he often happens to see the letter a moment ahead of the other players and so stands a better chance to guess first than do the others. In a more elaborated play, no general category is decided upon for the people or objects to be named, but each player selects his own. The first player may thus say, "This is to be the name of a president of the United States," and then turn his letter over. The second player may say, "This is to be the name of a kitchen utensil." The third may ask for a "vegetable" and so on, around and around till all the letters have been used up. The player with the highest score or the largest pile of letters wins.

For children who have mastered the technique of writing easily, still other memory games are available. In one of these, the letters of the alphabet are taken one by one and the letter *A* assigned first. Each player is required to write down all the animals (or all the rivers, or all the towns, or all the inventors) which he can remember beginning with *A*. When all have finished, or when some previously arranged time-limit has been reached, each player reads his list aloud and is given a score of "one" for each word on his list.

Games with Words

The person who is interested in language and in the vagaries of English words has at his command an almost limitless supply of entertainment. We may smile over the varieties of pronunciation met with in *cough, tough, plough, through, though,* etc., or we may try to list words of like sound but different spellings, such as *toe, bow, so, sew,* or we may chuckle over the unintended meaning given to a sentence by the introduction of a word of similar sound but different meaning, as when we hear the old lady say that her "Ford rode more comfortably since they got bloomer tires for it." Some families become interested in new words and make it a point at mealtime to ask each member for any unfamiliar words he has heard that day. The definitions of these words are then looked up in the dictionary, and the whole family take pleasure in pronouncing and in using the latest addition to their vocabulary. Such entertainment from words is, of course, usually incidental to reading, but we can play many actual games which hinge upon the use of words.

One of the old word games requires the recalling of adjectives beginning with each letter in the alphabet. The first player starts by saying, "I love my love with an *A,* because he is ———" and fills the sentence out with some adjective beginning with *A*. Each succeeding player repeats, using a different adjective. When no player can think of any more adjectives beginning with *A,* some one starts, "I love my love with a *B* because he is ———," supplying an adjective beginning with *B*. Hundreds of variations may be introduced by adding, "I met my love in *A*———" "I feed my love on *A*———" and so on. A variation which adds a personal touch and which is most amusing to children requires the first player to say "You have a face," the second player to ask "What kind of a face?" The first player replies, using an adjective beginning with *A* as in "an attractive face" or "an apelike face" or "an animal's face." The players may continue with *A* until all known words beginning with that letter have been used, or they may take successive letters, one using *A*, the next *B*, the next *C* on through the alphabet.

Anagrams is a very old word game. The common way of playing it is for one player to select the letters which spell some word without, of course, announcing what word he has chosen. He mixes the letters up and gives them to another player, who is expected to rearrange them to make the word. Another form is that in which the letters for a very long word are given out, and the player is required to rearrange them into several small words with no letters left over.

A game which requires rearrangement of letters to form words, but which does not require that all the letters be used, is "Making Little Words Out of Big Ones." This is usually played with paper and pencil, and all the players use the same big word. The goal may be simply the greatest number of words which can be formed, although the game is usually more interesting if the players take the different letters one at a time as initial letters. Thus, if the word chosen were *International*, the players would all work at first on words beginning with the letter *i*, and when each person had written down all the small words beginning with *i* which he could make from the big word, then they would compare their numbers of words. The score may be simply the number of words which each player has found, but the game is more interesting if the score for any word depends on the number of other players who found that word. Thus, if one player starts to read his list of words aloud and finds that there is one player who has failed to get his first word, he will receive a score of "one" on that word; if two players have failed to find that word, his score will be "two." Extra score is sometimes given for very long words; in this case, two-syllable words are ordinarily scored twice and three-syllable words three times what the score would have been for a one-syllable word.

A ride on any street-car will prove the popularity of one word game, the cross-word puzzle. It is possible to find some of these puzzles which have been designed especially for small children with the problem very simple and very few words crossing each other. From this simplicity on, there are all degrees of difficulty up to the type where the spaces are left unnumbered and where the definitions contain some sort of a joke or pun.

Another type of word game may be made up on the spur of the moment. The players may select two four-letter words, such as *coat* and *hash* and try to change one into the other by changing only one letter at a time and making an English word with each change. Thus *coat* may be changed to *cost* by substituting *s* for *a*, and later substitutions will give *cast*, *cash* and at last *hash*. Victory may be determined by the speed with which the words are transformed, or by calling the player who effects the change with the fewest steps the winner.

Still another form of word game is found in games of the type of "Peter Coddle's Trip to New York," [1] "Mrs. Casey Wants to Know," [2] and "The Old Maid's Birthday." [3] The game consists of a little booklet in which a story is told with a good many words omitted and blanks inserted to indicate the omissions. Then there are small cards with other words printed on them, one card for each omission in the text. One person is selected as "reader." The cards are shuffled and divided between the other players. Then the reader starts reading the story, stops at the first omission, and the player at his left reads

[1] Published by Milton Bradley Co., Springfield, Mass.
[2] Published by Parker Bros., Salem, Mass.
[3] See D. Canfield, *What Shall We Do Now?* (Frederick A. Stokes Company, New York, 1922), pp. 81 ff.

the top one of his cards to fill in the omission. The reading continues and the second player reads his topmost card to fill in the second blank, and so on to the end of the story. This game provides much amusement because, of course, the cards seldom fit appropriately into the blanks, and it is difficult to say whether the children are more amused at the incongruous situations which are described by this method or more pleased when a particular card happens to make sense at a particular point. The game is also a stimulus to reading and younger children will learn to read the cards quickly for the sake of being admitted to the game.

Another form of this same game is found in the game of "Funny Conversation Cards," [4] in which a set of cards carrying questions and a set carrying answers are provided. Both sets are shuffled and then are drawn off one at a time. First the top question is read and as a reply the top answer card. Thus we may find that the answer to "Do you consider yourself handsome?" is "You may as well guess at your answer. A fool must now and then be right by chance." From the child's point of view, the answers may fit too well and not be as funny as the utterly incongruous completions in the other games.

Number Games

It is the rare individual who finds numbers more intriguing than words, and yet almost any one can be entertained by some of the number games which, although less common than word games, are yet available. A wide-awake family can invent many more for themselves. In one of these games the person who has the first turn says, "I am thinking of two numbers which added together will make six" (or whatever number he chooses), and the others guess which numbers he has in mind. A variation is "I am thinking of two numbers which multiplied together will make twelve," and so on.

[4] Published by Milton Bradley Co., Springfield, Mass.

A simpler number game is called "Buzz." As commonly played, the players sit in a ring and start counting, the first saying "one," the second "two," and so on. Whenever a player should say a number which contains the figure "seven" or is a multiple of "seven," he must say "buzz" instead. Of course any number may be selected as the "buzz" number, but seven is suggested because it is one of the more difficult ones. The counting would then proceed "1, 2, 3, 4, 5, 6, buzz, 8, 9, 10, 11, 12, 13, buzz, 15, 16, buzz," and so on. The counting goes round and round the circle until some one slips, either by failing to say "buzz" when necessary or by saying it at the wrong time. This person is then dropped from the game which goes on, either starting again with "one," or going on from the point at which the error was made.

Puzzles

Puzzles of all sorts fascinate certain children. There is some evidence that ability to work them is to some degree a "special ability," just as musical ability is, but the interest in them is general enough to make it desirable to give every child, who is seven years old or more, a chance to work with puzzles. The simplest form of puzzles is found in the insets where there is just one place into which each piece will fit. Montessori's cylinders are a good example of the type of puzzle about which four- and five-year-old children are most enthusiastic. It is unfortunate that there are not more simple puzzles on the market. The nested boxes, nested Russian dolls, wooden eggs, and nested trays come close to being in this category.

Picture puzzles are made in all degrees of difficulty and, within the level of achievement, are interesting to most children. There are the common animal pictures, cut into rectangular strips; the somewhat more complicated pictures from

Mother Goose or illustrations from well-known stories, in which the pieces must be fitted for shape as well as for picture; and, of course, those cut into intricate designs and hundreds of small pieces. A still more difficult type is the pictureless stone puzzle in which the worker is required to arrange the pieces in the shape of a pattern which is provided. Since the patterns are smaller than the design made by the blocks themselves, and since they do not indicate the divisions between the blocks, some of them will test the most alert puzzler.

Various paper and pencil puzzles are available for young children. There are, for example, mazes of lines where the child is asked to trace with a pencil the shortest path from one point to another. There are also puzzles put out in which the page appears to be just a confusion of scattered numbers. The child is to take his pencil and draw a line from the number "1" to the number "2," then to the number "3," and so on to each number in succession. When all the numbers are connected, it is found that a picture has been outlined.

A fairly common pencil game which is more or less of a puzzle is "Tit-tat-to." For this a diagram is drawn on a paper in such a way that two parallel horizontal lines cross two equally spaced parallel vertical lines. From the squares so formed, the players take turns selecting first one, then another, for their own. They mark each choice with some special symbol which they have selected. The player who first succeeds in getting his symbol into three squares in a straight line, whether vertical, horizontal, or diagonal, cries, "Tit-tat-to, three men in a row," and wins.

Other plays of the puzzle-type are found in making patterns with parquetry blocks, beads, or sticks. This play, which usually starts merely with the copying of a pattern provided with the set of materials, may develop into invention and the making of new designs at the child's own fancy.

Riddles

Riddles fascinate the child of eight or nine. To be interesting to an adult, a riddle must be new, but children enjoy old riddles much more than new ones. They seem to take little pleasure in trying to work out an answer. Perhaps they would be unable to, but they can thoroughly appreciate the joke in the answer when they do hear it. Furthermore, the joy in riddles with which children are well acquainted does not depend upon being able to ask it of some one who has not heard it. On the contrary, a group of children can amuse themselves for some time by asking riddles which they all know and either seeing who can answer most quickly or even taking turns in answering.

A nine-year-old girl, who is highly entertained by riddles, was asked to select from each of her books of riddles the four which she considered funniest. From "Peter Puzzlemaker," [5] she chose:

Why are the tallest people laziest? *Ans.* Because they lie longest in bed.
When is a piece of wood like a queen? *Ans.* When it's made into a ruler.
Why is a little dog's tail like the heart of a tree? *Ans.* Because it's farthest from the bark.
Why does water get into a watermelon? *Ans.* Because it's planted in the spring.

From "The Big Trick and Puzzle Book" [6] she chose:

What is often returned but never borrowed? *Ans.* Thanks.
When is a black dog most likely to enter a bungalow? *Ans.* When the door is open.
Why is the letter *O* like a pain? *Ans.* Because it makes a man moan.
What is the difference between a wealthy man and a little dog's tail? *Ans.* One keeps a motor car and the other keeps a wagon.

[5] Plat and Munk Co., New York, 1929.
[6] Whitman Publishing Co., Racine, Wisc., 1929.

From the cards of a Knapp Electric Questioner [7] she chose:

What has four wheels and flies? *Ans.* A garbage wagon.
Why did the fly fly? *Ans.* The spider spider.
What is the difference between snow and Sunday? *Ans.* Sunday falls
  on the first day of the week and snow falls on any day.
What animal keeps the best time? *Ans.* A watch dog.

Charades

Another form of guessing game is found in "Charades."
Usually in this game the players are divided into two teams.
One team selects a word which can be divided into syllables
which are in themselves words: *polygon* into *polly* (to be represented by a parrot) and *gone; background* into *back* and
ground, and so on. The side which has chosen the word appears before the other side and acts out first one syllable, then
the other, and last of all the whole word.

A simpler form of this type of guessing may appear in a
game in which half of the players take turns in acting out
in pantomime some historical event, while the other children
try to guess what event is being reproduced. Extensive "properties" are not necessary for such dramatization, for rough
signs may inform the audience, "This is a mountain," or
"Here is a deep, very blue lake."

Summary

Games which involve competition in guessing, observation,
and memory; games concerned with words and numbers,
puzzles, riddles, and charades become more and more interesting to most children as they grow older. Younger children,
if the parents enter into such games with them, will acquire
a liking for this sort of mental amusement which may provide a great deal of pleasure for them in their later years. (For

[7] Knapp Electric Inc., Indianapolis.

a discussion of the importance of encouraging intellectual interests see Anderson's *Happy Childhood,* Chapters XI and XVII.) In addition to the games which have been suggested in this chapter there are, of course, many others, but usually a few suggestions are sufficient to help each family develop the games and the rules which will best fit their own situation. It makes little difference which particular games are selected, as long as they stimulate the child's thinking, observation, or recall. There are grown-ups who have reached the stage where thinking is an effort, but the normal child is an alert being, with his toes constantly set on the mark, ready to start any kind of a contest, and glorying in his own ability. Games of the intellectual type offer a most desirable and most satisfying kind of training in quick and accurate thinking, and it seems only fair to assume that occasional (not constant) indulgence in such plays may prepare the individual to think straight to the point and efficiently when he meets problems in his later life.

Chapter VIII

PARTICIPATION IN FAMILY ACTIVITIES

The Child's Place in the Family

THERE are many homes where the child is treated not as a
member of the family but as an outsider; homes where one
or two rooms are put aside as a nursery, and where, except
for passing down the stairs and out of the front door, the
child is never seen in the rooms in which the other members
of the family live. Often these are also homes into which children can never bring their playmates and friends. There are
others where the opposite situation exists; where the house,
instead of belonging entirely to the adults, belongs solely to
the children of the family. These are the houses where there
is never a pencil or a pin or a sheet of paper available because the children have appropriated them; where mother,
if she wants to hear anything, must postpone all telephone
calls until the children go to school or are asleep. Often these
are homes in which there is not even one comfortable chair
whose springs have not been broken through use as a piece
of gymnasium apparatus. In the first kind of home which we
have suggested, the child is not really taken into the family
as a member; in the second kind, he is made the sole end and
aim of all the family living and again is not a real member.
Only by sharing with the others can he attain the true status
of a member of the family. (See Anderson's *Happy Childhood*,
Chapter XIX.)

The homes in which each individual has his fair share of
the house itself, his share of the family pleasures, and his
share of the work and the responsibility of the family—those

are the happiest homes and the ones which best prepare the
child for taking his place in the world. This "fair share" for
the child will not mean an "equal share" necessarily. Certainly no one would want a small child to shoulder the same
amount of responsibility for the home that the parents assume,
but he can take some of it and be happier for it.

The committee of the White House Conference which
studied the delinquent child says:

"We ask you . . . to see that the individual is no mass of mere
bones, skin, viscera, surrounded by a group that looks in upon him,
his family, his church, his school and so forth, but rather that the
lives of these adults are so woven into his, are so intimate a part of
the life of the child that we can know the individual delinquent only
as we know his environment."—*The Delinquent Child* (The Century
Co., New York, 1932), p. 7 f.

We need not limit this remark to the "individual delinquent," for the influence of the family on the well-behaved
child is just as great as it is on the badly behaved one. Again,
in the same report we read:

"The guardians of the child have the duty to present in their own
lives such patterns of honesty, sincerity and courage as shall challenge
the child's emulation. In an age when mechanical devices bring distant wonders, and the spread of wealth provides ease and comfort
beyond our wildest dreams, it is of the greatest importance that all
adults realize that by no such trickery is the matter of wholesome life
produced. It is only in the example of sincere living that the child finds
the dynamic impulse for his own wholesome development."

In the family group it is expected "that the child shall
first learn to live with others, and have his early lessons in
the rights and power of the group." [1] To be a successful
group, the family needs "a sense of mutual belonging among
its members, and of an accepted place in the community; a
feeling of harmony among the individual members, a unity
or *esprit de corps,* due to the presence of common or mutual

[1] This quotation and the two following are from *The Delinquent
Child* (The Century Co., New York, 1931), p. 31 ff.

Fun for Grandpa and Bobby Alike

Many a Game Is More Fun When Grown-Ups Play Too

ties; economic stability, including enough of the essentials of food, shelter, clothing, and protection to allow the individual members of the family to feel that what they possess compares favorably with the possessions of other families in the social milieu which they consider their own. . . . In a family where the interplay of relationship is based on a healthy acceptance of one another and on an integrated, harmonious *esprit de corps,* any apparent conflict between the urges of the individual and the needs of the group may never become so crystallized that any individual feels that he is undergoing hardship." The schools are now said to realize that the child is "no isolated museum specimen but one clothed mentally and physically by his family; nicknamed mentally and physically by his neighborhood; bent mentally and physically by all those burdens involved in the earning life of himself and his family." Many other recent publications stress the point that the child can be thought of only as a member of his group, and for the young child this means only as a member of his family. It follows that the thoughtful parent will give the child the finest opportunity for learning from his family, which means giving him a real place in it while he is still young.

The Child's Share of the Home

Although the child's share in the house itself will vary with the size of the house and the size of the family, practically every child can have a bed of his own and a corner of his own where he can leave his toys and know that they will not be molested. Sometimes no more can be provided than a box or a basket, but that box or basket should belong to the child and he should come to feel that it is his. Happy the child who can have a playroom of his own. Some of the most satisfactory playrooms have been built in the basements of houses, basements with many windows letting in much sunshine and fresh air, basements that are as dry and as well heated and ventilated as the main part of the house. If this playroom can have an outside entrance that allows the children to come and go without tracking snow or mud into mother's part of the house, then every one will be happier. The fewer the furnishings which can be broken and the greater the opportunity for active play, the more useful the playroom will prove. A cement floor and a drain which permits it to be washed with a hose will simplify things, if small boys are to play there. A playroom with the electric lights protected by wire guards will not be damaged by balls thrown in the air; a playroom with large roomy cupboards will be more satisfactory than one in which all the toys must lie around on the floor or on tables; if a little stage or even just a curtain can be arranged at one end of the room, there will be a chance for many thrilling dramas to be performed; and so on. Most families cannot hope for such a playroom, but they can provide some small room in which the child may play without interruption. Often this will have to be the child's bedroom. Although ideally the bedroom should be reserved just for sleeping, it is nevertheless better to use a bedroom for a playroom, too, than to require the child to play in the adults' living room.

Not only should every child have some small spot in the house which he can call his own, but he should come to feel that certain other things in the house belong to the family as a whole, that they are not "mine" but "ours." If the piano belongs to mother, then, although the child may try not to scratch her property, he will not take the satisfaction in its smooth, shining surface that he will, if he feels that it is partly his. And so about many other things. The child may be taught to be proud of the front lawn and by his own choice to travel on the walk instead of across the grass. He will come to be proud of the chairs that his great grandfather brought from Europe, or of the wall paper that he helped select, if he feels that these things are "ours."

Family Conversations

Obviously the child should share in the pleasures of the family. We have already suggested the joy and the feeling of membership which he gains from playing games with other members of the family. The same sort of fellowship may develop from a group activity which means a great deal to the child but which is often ignored by the adults, the family conversation. Most schools give a great deal of time to teaching children to write compositions, essays, and themes. Such practice may, of course, increase the individual's appreciation of literature, but it has little effect on the later use of writing itself. For most adults, composition is limited to writing letters, and very few of them will fall into the class of essays or themes. On the other hand, all normal adults use spoken language frequently, although it is only recently and only in the most progressive schools that much attention is given to training the child in the use of spoken English. The only satisfactory way to learn to speak well is through example and practice. The child talks as those around him talk. Two sisters spent their early years under quite different conditions. When the older one was learning to talk, she was with her parents almost all the time; when the younger sister was learning to talk, the parents were away from home for nearly a year, and the children were under the care of a Swedish nurse. The effect of the two kinds of examples was seen in the oral language of the children. The older child at the age of three sang, "It isn't going to rain any more," because, as she explained, "I know it says 'It ain't goin' to rain no more'; but that isn't the way to say it." On the other hand, the younger child, at the age of three witnessed something which she thought very funny and commented, "Isn't it a yoke!" Thus, each reflected the speech which she heard daily.

After children go to school, their pronunciation is affected more by that of their playmates than by that of their parents.

The Southern-born woman who rears her children in the Northwest will gasp to hear the rolling *r*'s, the final *g*'s, and all the other twists which sound strange to her, while the children will ridicule her soft drawl. Often these children who hear one accent at home and another at play will acquire both accents but will use the play-speech most of the time. Certain errors can, of course, be stopped. One father, who refused to allow his children to answer, *Ya!*, in the idiom of the neighborhood, taught them to give a clear *Yes,* although they clung to the local usage for other expressions.

In spite of the fact that pronunciation is determined usually by playmates, and is influenced only in part by the example of parents, the parents can exert a great deal of influence upon the children's vocabulary, which like pronunciation, is most easily learned through example and imitation. Talking down to a child, using baby-talk and only very simple words, is an insult to his intelligence and a hindrance to his development. One of the most striking differences between the modern grade school and the grade school of twenty years ago lies in the vocabulary used by the teacher. Children like new and long words. Perhaps they are a bit embarrassed at first to try them out, but it takes only a short time for the sound of such words to become familiar and only a little longer time for the pronunciation of them to become easy. The child who lives in Minneapolis or in Kennebunkport has no more trouble in telling where he lives than the child who lives in New York or in Wells. It is all a matter of familiarity. A Rockefeller child learns to recognize his name just as quickly and to pronounce it almost as early as the Ford child does his name. So any child will learn *soup spoon* just as easily as he will *dreat big 'poon,* and he will be saved from having to learn two names for this utensil. He will learn *beautiful* just as easily as *nice* and probably with less confusion, for he will hear only beautiful things called *beautiful,* whereas he may hear anything under the heavens called *nice.*

English is admittedly a difficult language. We have many words which sound alike but which mean different things according to the context. Who has not had a small child ask, "What does b-o-w spell?" and given the only possible answer: "It depends upon the sentence in which the word is used." In one kindergarten, the teacher was talking recently about the flowers they might raise in the winter and the bulbs they might plant. She had forgotten to bring a crocus bulb as she had planned, but the children seemed to know what she was talking about. When she asked if any of them had bulbs which they could bring to plant in school, several offered to bring some the next day. Then one little girl said in rather a timid voice, "We have an old bulb I could bring but I don't know whether it will grow or not; it won't light any more." The first grade child, who said he had "seed work" (seat work), and the second grade child, who reported that her school started the day with "poems and potations," are in the process of learning new words too. It is only through free conversation in which mistakes are corrected in a kindly way and in which the child is helped and encouraged with the difficult words he undertakes that he can learn a satisfactory oral language. And the most simple and natural way to learn correct usage and to acquire a workable vocabulary is through informal conversations at home. Meal-time can be both a happy time and a time for trying out growing powers of language, if the conversation is conducted as a family affair. The meal that is eaten in glum silence is not digested as well as the meal eaten during happy chat. With a family of ordinary size gathered about a fairly small table, it is obvious that one person cannot be heard unless the others are silent. Thus the child learns naturally to wait until another has finished talking before he begins to speak. With a little guidance from the adults, the opinions and experiences of each member can be given in turn, and the youngest can have a chance to speak as well as the oldest. In some families the different members save interesting bits of news to relate at the family table. Certain of these items will be more interesting to some persons at the table than to others, but all can acquire the habit of listening politely, and all will learn that many things which do not seem interesting at the beginning are intensely interesting to those who know more about them. If guests are frequent, the children will gradually learn two important things: first, that the polite thing to do is to let the conversation run on matters of interest to the guests, and second, that they must speak briefly and only when they have something to add to the general talk. As the children grow older, their interests will diverge more and more. In many families the mother learns a football vocabulary and goes to football games for the sake of being able to talk intelligently with her growing son about his one absorbing interest. One of the wisest fathers I ever knew subscribed to a moving-picture magazine and read it from cover to cover so that he would be able to enter into the interests of his growing daughter and gradually lead her to more worth-while enthusiasms.

Through informal conversation with the family, then, the child learns to pronounce words, to understand words, to express himself with reasonable clearness; at the same time he learns one of the fine points of conversation—to listen when other people are speaking. He is also doing something else which may prove to be of great value to him. He is gathering information of many kinds. All children are interested in tales of what their parents used to do as children, provided these tales do not set the parents up as perfect examples and great contrasts to the present generation. Through such tales, children learn what life a generation ago was like. To be sure, they often fail to realize that the incidents related were not everyday occurrences but events of banner days, and so they come to overestimate the good times which the parents had; but, on the other hand, they get an atmosphere and an understanding of past years which very few books can give. If grandma enters into the conversation, they will hear of a childhood which knew no electric lights, no telephones, no automobiles, no airplanes, perhaps no railroad, and they may come to realize that the children of those days were happy and busy, often very busy, with no longings for inventions of which they had never heard.

From the adults' discussion of current events, the children acquire facts, points of view, and ideals which will oftentimes color much of their later thinking. The child of the doctor hears more or less of illnesses and epidemics; the child of the lawyer of trials and evidence; the child of the teacher hears of lectures and classes, of studying and learning; the child of the laboring man of bosses and time-clocks and, perhaps, of strikes. From these different children we may hear, "They ought to be quarantined," or, "We're laid off." The children's play and their interest in reading or studying will be affected by the conversation which they hear at home. Lucky is the child who has the opportunity to be present when foreign visitors are being entertained. The mere fact that the child has met a person who lives in France makes France a living country, instead of just a squarish blue blotch on the map. If you have heard a traveler tell of riding in a rickety Ford across a desert with an Arabian driver who understood no English; if you have heard the wife of a Yankee sea-captain tell of her embarrassment at forgetting to take off her apron when they "spoke" a passing clipper; if you have heard a person tell of two days spent in an open life-boat after a steamer had been torpedoed in the war; or if you have heard an Arctic explorer describe a Thanksgiving pie in which vaseline took the place of shortening, then you have learned things almost at first-hand, you have lived through the experiences with the teller, and if you are a child, you have "dreamed dreams and seen visions" which may result in broader interests and greater understanding.

Family Gardens

Besides family games and family conversations, there are
other group pleasures in which the child may well have his
share. Many families have gardens. Whether the garden produces flowers or vegetables, the child will be only too glad to
help daddy plant and water and weed it. The child may really
be a help, too. He can be taught, by the time he is five or six
years old, to recognize certain weeds, and he can do a good
deal of work in pulling these out of the garden. There is no
age limit to pleasure in sprinkling the garden, whether it be
with a watering can or with a hose. With a little direction,
many children will be happy to take over this part of tending
the garden. Usually a little corner can be set aside as the
child's own. Here, perhaps, he can raise the family carrots or
lettuce, and there will be no other part of the garden which
is watched as tenderly. Even if the child does no actual work
in the garden, he may come to enjoy certain bits of it. One
mother brought home three hollyhock roots one day, one for
each of her own children. She consulted with the children as
to the best part of the garden for the plants, allowing them
to pick out the exact spot in which each root should be planted.
All summer long, small visitors were taken down the garden
walk, but they were warned particularly not to step into any
of the flower beds. They were told, "This is John's hollyhock, and this is Katherine's, and this is mine. I come to see
mine every day."

Children who live on farms may do much to help with the
family tasks but their parts should be selected most carefully
so that they suffer none of the bad effects of hard work. The
White House Conference reports [2] that many a farmer "is
accustomed to hard work and fails to appreciate the strain it
involves for young children or the danger of over-fatigue at
the adolescent period." They find that:

[2] *Child Labor* (The Century Co., New York, 1932), p. 213.

"Children are working wherever crops are raised, and they help in every kind of farm job. They carry in the wood, feed the chickens, gather the eggs, hay and bed the horses, fodder the cattle, milk the cows, and slop the pigs. They drive the team to the plow, the harrow, rake, binder and mower. They hoe and weed the garden, potatoes, corn and other crops. They pitch hay, shock, haul and thresh wheat, oats, and rye, shuck the corn, and engage in many other tasks. Children do chores all the year round but work on the garden and crops usually is confined to spring, summer and early fall."

In so far as such work does not overtax the child, and leaves plenty of time during the day for free play, it is desirable. Children who grow up with some particular chore for which they are responsible feel themselves an integral part of the family, and even when they dislike the actual work, they may get a compensatory satisfaction in the feeling that their work is important for the welfare of the family as a whole. Once in a while we find a child who is so impressed with the value of her labor that she explains why she cannot go away for a visit by saying, "There will be no one to wash the dishes," or "Who would feed the canary?"

Family Pets

The family may not have a farm or a garden, but it may have an animal pet of some sort. The child who lives on the farm knows each animal; he learns the personal characteristics and peculiarities of each horse and each cow, perhaps even of each hen and each duck. The city child has no such opportunity. He may be able to see strange animals at the park or in the zoo, but seldom can they become real individuals to him. Sometimes the city child can have a dog, one of the best companions and friends he could possibly find, and the owner of such a pet learns to be kind to him and to other animals. Although a young child should not be required to assume full responsibility for an animal's food, he can be encouraged to share in seeing that his dog has proper meals at regular times. All children enjoy animal stories, and all children enjoy live animals which are not too rough or poorly trained. If it is impossible to keep a dog, perhaps the family can own a cat. Perhaps the yard can be fixed so as to provide for a rabbit hutch or a chicken run. If a child plays outdoors less than seems advisable, an outdoor pet may entice him into the fresh air and sunshine. Then there are indoor pets which are still easier to care for and for which any home can make room. Several kinds of birds are available as cage pets: canaries, love-birds, and sometimes that childhood favorite, the parrot. Then there are the water animals: goldfish, guppies, turtles, and snails, all easy to care for and a source of constant interest to the small child (and adult as well). At first, these may seem to serve merely as a bit of bright color to the room or as something for the child to look at, but the father who was left with the pets on his hands when the family went away for a month and who tried to teach the goldfish to come for food when he rapped on the bowl and who filled the bathtub for the sake of giving the turtles a good swim, will find many other adults who highly approve of his conduct.

The care of pets has the further advantage of giving the child an understanding of animal life. (For a discussion of sex education see Anderson's *Happy Childhood,* Chapter XIV.) The White House Conference suggests that:

"The care of pets is an important aid in universalizing and normalizing the child's knowledge of reproduction. It utilizes his spontaneous interest in living things and makes impressively realistic the significance of mating, pregnancy, the care of the pregnant mother, birth, mother love, parental care, dependence of offspring, family life and its relationships. Usually a child who has had responsibility, under adult guidance and interpretation, for the feeding, care, and home making of a pair of bunny mates through the periods of mating and of breeding and rearing of a litter of baby bunnies, is better equipped to understand his own family drama and to adjust himself in it and in his general environment."—*Social Hygiene in Schools* (The Century Co., New York, 1932), p. 18.

Courtesy of the Minneapolis *Star*
and George E. Luxton

Courtesy of the Minneapolis *Star*
and George E. Luxton

Pets of All Kinds

The Work of the Home

It is not only in the chores of the farm and in the care of pets that the child may be given responsibility; he may assume a share in much of the work and responsibility in the home. Children are usually keenly interested in such tasks. The first plays of the child are, as we have seen, imitations of the activities of the mother. Every family knows where the children will be found when the paper-hanger is redecorating a room, when the storm windows are being put on, when a new chimney is being built, when a Thanksgiving dinner is being cooked, when the guest room is being prepared for company, even when the weekly laundry is being hung out. The children are on hand for anything which is the least bit new or for anything at which some adult is busy. If mother goes upstairs to make beds, she often has an observant group of spectators; when daddy carves a chicken, the children watch him so carefully that the anatomy of the fowl becomes an open book to them.

Now this work of the home, which is naturally interesting to a child, will be still more interesting, if he has some part in it. The child takes greater pleasure in the smooth preciseness with which mother tucks in the under sheet and in the ease with which daddy sharpens the carving knife, if he has had a little practice in doing those things himself. And many times there are opportunities for the child to be a real help to the group. On days when the attic or basement is cleaned, small hands and feet can be very useful with a little adult guidance. When the children's playroom is to be cleaned it is quite necessary, as a matter of fact, to have the children present and helping. If mother separates the things to be saved from those to be thrown away, the results are apt to include tragic misunderstandings as to the value of some cracked doll or crumpled bit of paper. Then, too, if the toys are being looked over before Christmas to find what ones shall be passed on to less fortunate children, the mother may learn a great deal from the discussion as to which are best-loved and why. She may also be able to encourage the children to give away certain things which mean but little to them when compared with what they might mean to some child who has no toys at all.

Often special occasions arise when the assistance of the children may relieve the mother of considerable work. If there are to be guests for dinner, the younger children can help set the table, and the older ones can prepare some part of the meal. Long before a child knows the glory of serving an entire meal which she (or he!) has cooked, she can help in the preparation of a salad or a dessert, can serve as watchman of the dishes cooking on the stove, can open cans, or at least act as errand girl. Sunday night supper is probably the simplest meal of the week for the child to serve, and its preparation will be gladly relinquished by a tired mother. An opportunity to make place-cards for the guests, to greet them at the door and help with the removal of their wraps, or at least to direct them to the appointed room, perhaps an opportunity to prepare a short program for the entertainment of a group of doting relatives will provide both social training and enjoyment for the child. When guests are present, the child may be expected to take an interest in the general conversation. He can listen attentively to the remarks of the guests, answer questions promptly and clearly, and, when appropriate, can contribute his own questions or brief remarks.

When the home is to be redecorated, there is a fine opportunity to teach the children both financial and artistic values. The children's opinions should carry some weight in selecting rugs and wall-papers, especially for their own rooms. Only through actual experience will they learn relative costs, durability, suitability, and so on. If the child selects something which is far beyond the family purse, he has an opportunity to learn from the mother's remarks something he has not realized before. If he selects something which will fade or which will wear out quickly or which will clash with other colors in the room, he may learn that too from his mother's comments. Sometimes the child will learn only through trying something out for himself. Sometimes, it does not really matter which thing is chosen. One six-year-old child had a small play-room, perhaps six by twelve feet, and when this room was to be redecorated, she selected a landscape paper with a rather large design! The mother tried to influence her to select a plainer paper but small daughter insisted that what she really wanted was the paper with the river and the boat. The mother said that after all she herself was in the playroom but little and, if the child wanted the paper so much, she could have it. After the paper was on the walls, the mother remarked, "Really, it doesn't look nearly as bad as I thought it would." So, in selecting the children's clothes, a minor point such as pleats just like big sister's, or knickers just like those of the big boy next door, will often make all the difference between a perfectly satisfactory outfit and one that is not just right.

The committee of the White House Conference which was interested in the home and the child made many suggestions as to the part which children may take in the running of the home. They suggested that one of the first things which can be done

". . . in allowing a child to take part in the selection of the household furnishings is to permit him to 'listen in' on the discussion which precedes the purchase of a piece of furniture or a musical instrument of interest to all the members of the family. The next is to allow him to go shopping with his parents when some piece of furniture or equipment is to be bought for his own use. When a new chair is to be selected for his bedroom, he may go along to the shop to sit in one after another to determine which is suitable for him in size and shape. As his mother decides on one of the several chairs considered, she will explain the reasons for her choice—the chair is not only comfortable for him, but it is also good in design, strong in construction, and suitable in price.

"Through such experiments a child learns what is good and what is bad. He acquires standards. Through such experiences personality develops. He gains self-confidence and power. Even when his choice is poor, it is an opportunity to learn better standards and to profit by his mistakes.

"This privilege of taking part in the choice of personal and family belongings has the advantage also of creating in the child a sense of personal as well as of family pride in ownership, and eventually teaching him that his personality can be expressed through things. . . .

"There is a give and take and an opportunity to develop social traits where a family considers coöperatively the furnishing and equipping of the home. Sometimes in considering and meeting the needs and desires of each member of the family, one individual has to give up his own choice for the best interests of the group or of another person in it. This has a real value in developing in even the youngest members a fine spirit of family consciousness, coöperation, and unselfishness. This is true, not only of the selection of furnishings, but also true of their arrangement and use."—*The Home and the Child* (The Century Co., New York, 1932), p. 40 ff.

Whenever there is any big family project on foot in which all members can take part, everybody is happy. One family bought a small and inconvenient cabin on the shore of a lake and moved in for the summer. And what a summer they had! Father was there for a week at the beginning and then back again for a month later on. Mother and two sons and two daughters were there for the entire season. The family cut down trees, cleared up underbrush, made steps down to the lake shore, made a small but serviceable garden, and, in the month when father was there, actually built a porch and an extra room on the cabin. There was plenty of opportunity in between times for play and swimming. It was interesting to hear that, the following year, the fifteen-year-old son didn't want to go back to the lake unless something needed to be done. He said, "I'm afraid we've done everything there that is fun to do, and we'll be bored to death this year."

For most families there is little chance for any big constructive project like the new camp, but there are many little tasks about the house which children can do and can come to regard as part of their responsibility toward the home. Some writers have claimed that children should not be expected to do any task about the house which is not clearly *educative* in value. They apparently mean that a task which is teaching control of muscles may be required of a child, but not one that is a monotonous repetition of what he already has learned how to do perfectly. Thus, I suppose, a child who can wash dishes perfectly is to be promoted to some other job and a younger child or mother is to be given the dish-washing. In such an interpretation of *educative* it seems to me that those writers err, for what do we have to learn more clearly than that there are many things which need to be done and to be done well, but which are in no way interesting after they have become routine? It is not fair to the child to keep him at the factory-type of job hour after hour, but ten or twenty minutes' worth of monotonous, routine help in the house, may make a great deal of difference to mother, and may give the child quite a different notion of housework and the work of the world in general. If he sees that nobody especially wants to do that particular thing, but that it must be done and done well; that if he does it, every one will be more comfortable; he will learn to do dreary and even tiresome work with dispatch, and he will learn that he can wash dishes (or whatever the work is) and do a good job at it, while thinking of something very pleasant. On the other hand, if he thinks all the while of how much he dislikes the job, the probability is not only that will he do a poorer piece of work and perhaps break some of the dishes in his disgust, but that he will also take longer at it than if he goes to work in a happy frame of mind.

Modern "Chores"

In the days when most children lived on farms (see Anderson's *Happy Childhood,* Chapter IX), they came to take "chores" as a regular part of the day, of the same order as getting up and getting washed and dressed. All of the family were working at the same time and it was to be naturally expected that the children should help. In these days, when so many children are living in cities and in small apartments at that, there are no chores. The father who, as a boy, brought in the wood, pumped the water, and drove the cow to pasture, is hard put to it when he hunts for a household job which he can assign to his son. The heat is now regulated by the janitor; the water comes from a faucet; the milk is delivered at the door in bottles. The mother who as a girl, built the kitchen fire, "did" the dishes, and dusted, is in like difficulty for the kitchen stove is often heated by electricity, the dishes may be washed by electricity, and the vacuum cleaner does not raise so much dust as the old broom. But there are a few tasks which, in most families, can be assigned to the children with benefit to them and to the rest of the household as well. There is, in the first place, the task of washing and dressing himself. The child can learn to do these things when he is still quite small, if he is given a little help in the way of buttoning, hooking, and tying shoe laces and if his clothing is planned for his convenience. He can also learn to wash his face and hands and can frequently take complete charge of his own bath by the time he is five or six years old. These may not seem like household tasks, but if the child does not do them himself, some other member of the family must do them instead. The child of eight or nine can take considerable care of his own room. He can make his own bed, barring perhaps the job of putting on fresh sheets. He can clear up his playthings when he is through play.

Of the tasks which are more clearly related to the family as a whole, the young child can wash dishes, especially if he has a helper to wipe them for him. Frequently the happiest arrangement is for the child to wash, while the mother, with her higher degree of skill, arranges the dishes to be washed next, rinses the ones already washed, dries them, and puts them

There Are Many Jobs a Child Can Do

away. With some such arrangement, the child's work really helps the mother and it gives them time to talk about anything which interests them. The child who is hanging around the kitchen while the mother prepares a meal, can set the table for her with very little guidance. Another task which actually improves the child's behavior at meal-time is that of helping clear off the dishes after the first or second course. The small child frequently becomes restless, if he is required to sit quietly through a three- or four-course meal, whereas, if he is asked to help take the dishes off, he is thus given a legitimate excuse for activity. Older children may learn to cook and often enjoy it greatly. A child of eleven or twelve can often get breakfast entirely by himself. While children do not especially enjoy dusting, and in this respect are not unique, it is a job which they can learn to do. They can run the vacuum cleaner. They can shovel snow, and that is fun, of course. There are many other jobs which may be assigned to them. If the child is spending six or seven hours a day in school, his home tasks should take not more than half an hour. Probably it would be better to have them take only fifteen minutes, but those few minutes will be worth while, if the child is allowed to realize that he is actually helping in the running of the household, that he can learn muscular control just as well through washing dishes as through many of his plays.

Educational Value of Work in the Home

The White House Conference suggests [3] that the child "should be allowed every opportunity to help because of the value to his development—sometimes physical, sometimes mental, sometimes social, and sometimes all three. The range of things he can do increases with his years, but to him the value of doing these things is never greater than in very early child-

[3] *The Home and the Child* (The Century Co., New York, 1932), pp. 54 and 81.

hood when he needs to learn motor control and to feel his importance through the help he gives. . . . The degree to which children contribute their service in the home varies with the skill of the parents in directing them, the philosophy regarding the part they should play in the home, their ages, and the hours that they spend in school.''

The same committee reports various studies on what household tasks were most frequently carried on by children. Unfortunately these studies cover only the work of girls in junior and senior high schools. From them it appears that the work of young girls in the home is usually of the type of making their own bed and caring for their own room, setting the table, washing dishes, dusting, waiting on table, caring for their own clothing, darning stockings, shining shoes, and the like. It is admittedly easier for the mother ''with a full schedule of household activities, to do the work herself than to find time to teach her child to assist her; and for this reason the training of children in the performance of household tasks too often is indefinitely postponed. . . . It would seem that in spite of the changes that have taken place in the work of the home in recent years, it still affords opportunity for training the younger members in manipulative skills, in scientific knowledge, and in artistic appreciation and expression, both as a part of the child's general education and as a training for family life.'' [4]

Family Economics

The child may also have some part in the economics (see Anderson's *Happy Childhood,* Chapter XIII) of the family. He may not only learn the use of money through having a regular allowance of his own, but he can ''take part in the family plans for the use of its money.'' [5] The White House Conference says:

[4] *The Home and the Child,* p. 84.
[5] *Ibid.,* p. 97.

"The economic education of the child is his directed experience, at home and school, with the financial and business problems that come naturally into his life so that he may meet such situations successfully as a child and later as an adult. The adult's money activities include earning, spending, saving, investing, borrowing, lending, and giving money; and the child may wisely experience money in every one of these ways while still a child and youth, under parental counseling, and often in joint experiences with his parents. With this as with other home-directed education, 'living with one's children,' giving them opportunity to make their own plans and decisions, to make mistakes where mistakes are not serious, and encouraging them to talk over their problems with their parents, seems the ideal method. . . . The child as a developing personality needs financial freedom with friendly, companionable guidance from elders; this the modern, democratic, mutual-aid family is competent to furnish. The child by his allowance is given opportunity to learn through experience; but an allowance does not work automatically, it requires counseling and guidance. With it available, and with parents interested to keep in personal contact with their child's financial problems, he will, with their coöperation, find his way while yet a child and a youth into experiences of earning, spending, giving, saving, and investing money, that will equip him with the knowledge, skill and attitudes necessary for a wholesome and successful experience as an adult."—*The Home and the Child* (The Century Co., New York, 1932), pp. 31–137.

Summary

Let us then make the child a real member of the family, sharing not only in the home itself, but also to the limit of his understanding and experiences in the play of the family, in the work of the family, and in the finances of the family. Through such coöperation with parents and brothers and sisters the child will gain much pleasure and much training which will make easier many of the adjustments of adult life.

Chapter IX

OCCUPATION FOR THE ILL OR CONVALESCENT CHILD

THE child who is extremely ill should not play and does not want to, but there are many times when a sick child will recover more quickly, if he has something to occupy his mind and to amuse him. (For a discussion of children's illnesses see Stuart's *Healthy Childhood*.) Desirable occupation at such a time is real occupational therapy. Oftentimes it is important that a child remain quietly in bed, well covered and relaxed, but, if the child is very young, it is difficult for the mother to induce him to stay there. Many a child rebels at the notion of staying in bed all day and thrashes about so much and complains so bitterly that the mother is forced to relent and let him get up. A little care and forethought on the part of the mother may make staying in bed at least as interesting as hanging about the house in a half-sick condition. Sometimes the mother keeps a special group of toys which are to be used only when the child is in bed. Sometimes she allows him to spend the day in some bed which is not his own or to wear a special bathrobe or jacket. Any privilege of the sort will add to the interest of staying in bed.

The tendency is usually to err on the side of offering the ill child too many toys at once. He is more easily tired when he is ill, and the mere sight of his bed or the bedside table littered with old toys irritates him. If one toy at a time is provided, he will probably be mildly amused, and it is a state of mild amusement which we wish to maintain. The sick child who is bored is pathetic; the sick child who is overstimulated is a reason for worry. Any ill child should have some periods in the day reserved for complete rest; all but the most seriously ill should have also periods in which they are enjoyably occupied. (See Stuart's *Healthy Childhood*, Chapter X.)

The Child Too Ill to Sit Up

Perhaps the degree of illness which receives least attention from the mothers as far as occupational therapy is concerned is that at which the child cannot sit up and yet is not so exhausted as to be indifferent to his surroundings. He does not want to be required to attend to anything, no matter how interesting it may be, but he wants to have something to which he may attend, if he likes. One child, who was recovering from a very serious illness, could not bear to have an adult sit down and read to her, even a story in which she really was much interested, but if the adult read the same story to another person in the room, then she lay quiet and amused, feeling herself free to ignore the reading at any moment she liked. This response carried over also to conversations. She did not want the nurse to talk to her, but she wanted to hear conversation going on, and when only the nurse was in the room the youthful patient would cry, "Talk, but don't talk to me. Talk to the radiator!" The child just mentioned was fourteen years old, but there seems good reason to suppose that the same situation may hold in the case of many younger children. We know, for example, that the ill child who is comfortable but unable to play is quiet and relaxed all the time the nurse or the mother is moving about the room straightening things up and arranging the room for the day. Such a child is also quiet when the doctor talks with the mother, whether the conversation be about the child himself or about the weather or the political state of the country. The child who is ill in a hospital is usually happier,

if there are one or two other patients in the same room. The
activities of other persons serve to distract the child's attention from his own state of helplessness and are mildly divert-
ing. Sometimes the mother will provide sufficient amusement,
if she sits quietly sewing. The movements of her hands as she
plies the needle and adjusts the cloth provide just enough to
look at. Whereas the movement of the pen, if the mother is
writing a letter, or the turning of pages, if she is reading, is
not usually quite enough to hold the child's attention.

Something to Watch.

It is, of course, impossible for most mothers to be in the
room constantly with a child who is not seriously ill, and it is
not best for the child to have some one there every single
moment of the day. The question then arises: How can the
child be kept contentedly quiet when the mother or nurse is
not in the room? An obvious answer is: Give him something
else to watch.

There are two sorts of animal pets which are very well
suited to the sick-room. A canary will provide movement and
sound, so that the child may watch the bird or may listen
to him with eyes either closed or open. If the singing disturbs
the child, then, of course, the bird should be removed from
the room, but usually the canary's song is enjoyed. If the
bird-cage is placed where the child can see it easily and where
the light is such that the child's eyes will not become strained
or fatigued, then the canary will provide quiet amusement
for many an hour. Goldfish are also well suited to sick-room
use. For some children, the quiet of the fish is more pleasing
than the noise of the bird. The graceful movements, the glint
of light on the scales as the fish swims about, the care with
which it passes through the openings of the castle, the nibbling
of the tiny mouth at the food or weeds, even the placid waving
of the fins as it rests, will provide just the right amount of

amusement for the child who has not the strength for any activity more strenuous than mere looking.

Other objects which are not alive may be provided to give the child something to look at. Many adults remember the careful attention they gave to the patchwork quilt which covered them in their childhood illnesses—not the beautiful quilts done in elaborate designs, but those which were really patchwork, small squares or diamond-shaped pieces of mother's old apron, Sarah's last summer's checkered gingham, John's striped shirt, and some quaint old bits from grandmother's piece bag. The quilts were not furnished with amusement in view, but by the time he was well the child could tell just how many different patterns were used, which ones appeared most often, and many details of the individual bits. Every person knows the attention which the wall-paper receives from invalids. Children do not usually object to the obvious repetitions in the pattern as the "nervous" adult may, but children will be best entertained by paper with details which can be studied day after day. Best of all they like landscape paper, which, unfortunately for the ill child, is seldom found in bedrooms. Draperies may provide something to look at, especially if the child is in a room where the curtains have been selected with his interests in mind. Some of the prints with Mother Goose figures or farmyard scenes provide a huge picture book for the child lying in bed. Sometimes interesting toy figures may be placed within the child's vision. Celluloid animals lined up on the bureau, a doll in a foreign costume, foreign toys carved from wood or made from straw may provide something interesting to look at. Large pictures may be pinned on the draperies or on a screen and changed every day or so. Then there are the glass chimes which can be hung in an open window and which tinkle pleasingly when swung by the wind. The prisms, which, when hung in the sunshine, scatter dots of color all over the room, are full of interest to the child. Later on, when the child is stronger, many hours can be spent happily in turning the prism in the sun and making the dancing spots of light travel up and down the walls and into the far corners of the room.

Flowers and growing plants provide interesting objects for the child to look at. No flowers with a heavy odor should be chosen, for heavy fragrance may become so disagreeable as to counteract all the good done by the appearance of the bloom. Plants are frequently more satisfactory for the sick room, but, if possible, they should be plants which change somewhat from day to day. Seeds which develop quickly may be planted in a shallow dish and the child will be interested in watching their development. Corn, peas, and beans sprout readily and later may be transplanted into a real garden. A carrot may be made into a growing vase to hang in the window by cutting out a little hollow in the wide top and keeping this hollow filled with water. A sweet potato may be persuaded to produce a most delightful vine. Stick toothpicks or long pins part way into the potato about half way up. Rest the pins on the mouth of a water-filled jar so that the root-end of the potato is in the water. If this is set aside in the dark for a few days till the roots get well started, vines will grow from the upper end of the potato very quickly.

Something to Hear.

As the ill child becomes a little stronger, he will be glad to have an adult read to him. The stories which are read at first should be short and very simple, with a meager plot—nothing which can possibly worry or frighten the child. Probably a story which he already knows and loves will be more suitable for the convalescent than a new story. If he does not have to remember new characters or listen too attentively to follow the development of the tale, he will enjoy it more. Just as the adult who is very tired can read with pleasure a story with a very simple plot and a small number of characters (like the average detective story), so the ill child can follow a very simple or familiar story without fatigue, when a newer or more detailed story would confuse and bother him.

Something to Hold.

As he progresses toward convalescence the child will also enjoy holding and handling light toys. Celluloid animals, soft dolls, and the like will be held for hours at a time and furnish considerable entertainment. A doll that cries when she is tipped over, a rubber animal that squeaks when it is pressed, or a clown that flies over a trapese when the standards of the rope are squeezed together, will provide attraction in the way of sound and movement. Playing a toy accordion takes a little more effort, but it is most entertaining to some children. At this stage in his recovery, the child is interested in regaining some power over his environment and is no longer contented with mere looking and listening. Perhaps a light-weight book can be found which has large and interesting pictures. Any home can produce some old picture-postal cards, which are almost perfectly adapted to the use of the child too weak to hold a book. The young invalid who has a thoughtful aunt or grandmother to send a card each day in the mail has something to look forward to until the mail comes, and something to look at and compare with the previous cards for the rest of the day.

The Convalescent

As soon as the child is able to sit up in bed and use his hands easily, even if for only short periods at a time, a host of occupations are at his command. When he first begins to sit up, he needs some sort of a back-rest. If it is inconvenient to obtain one of the good ones now on the market, a simple one may be made from a piece of canvas about half as long as the bed itself. Attach it to the upper half of the mattress under the lower sheet, so that one end of the canvas is securely tucked under the child. The upper corners of it can be fastened to the upper part of the headboard of the bed, and this sloping back-rest will make innumerable pillows unnecessary and yet give the child sufficient support. If no table is available for use in bed, a fairly satisfactory one may be made from an orange crate or apple box by using the end-pieces as legs and cutting away enough from the sides of the box to allow the child to move his feet without upsetting the table. If this improvised table is covered with oilcloth, it will be still more useful.

Cutting and Pasting.

Almost any of the handcraft occupations, suggested in Chapter V, can be provided for the child in bed, if the mother is willing to have a few paper scraps about. If the child has the use of a bed-table, he is most fortunate, but many things can be done even without it. Paper-dolls, which will delight the heart of any girl—and almost any boy—may be purchased from the five-and-ten-cent stores. Cutting out the dolls and their costumes and trying on all the clothes will occupy many hours. Many children will go on from this point to play house with the dolls. Delightful scrap-books of six or eight—or even more—pages can be made from the ordinary wrapping paper to be found in any house. The most convenient scrap-books will be about eight inches square when finished. To make one, cut three or four sheets of brown paper into pieces eight by sixteen inches. They can be smoothed with a hot iron, if wrinkled. Pile these pieces one on top of another and sew with heavy thread and very long stitches down the middle of the sheets to hold them together. Fold the book neatly at the sewing, and the result will be a scrap-book which will make a fine neutral background for any gay pictures the child may have. The advertising sections of any of the magazines designed for the homemaker will supply quantities of pictures. Some of these magazines are too heavy and too awkward for the child to handle himself, but the mother can easily rip out the advertising pages, sometimes without destroying the reading matter, and then give the child simply the loose sheets to look over and to choose for himself. If several scrap-books are available, they may be used as houses for different families of paper-dolls. Wall-paper may be pasted across the upper half of the page to make the wall of a room, leaving the brown paper for the floor. Furniture may be cut from magazines or catalogues and pasted on in appropriate places, and so every pair of pages in the scrap-book may provide one room. With two paper-doll houses thus arranged, the dolls may visit back and forth. A third book may provide for travel: one pair of pages for a trip to the lake, another for a railway journey, another for a shopping trip down town and so on.

Patience for more exact work is required in pasting the books of posters which may sometimes be secured from the five-and-ten-cent stores and always (at a higher price and with better materials) from school-supply houses. Most of the stores handling play materials will have some books of things to cut out and paste together: baskets, houses, or jointed dolls. If several children are sick at once, one of these books will be sufficient to furnish patterns which the mother can transfer to plain colored construction paper. If the article made is to be moved about after it is finished, the paper will have to be mounted on thin pasteboard. The family waste-baskets will usually supply this: cardboard which comes home from the laundry with daddy's shirts, cardboard which comes around things bought at the dry-goods store, and, of course, all sorts of pasteboard boxes. Jointed dolls have the added advantage of being good playthings when the hour for sitting up has passed and the child has to lie down for a time. He will lie quietly, moving the arms and legs and getting the doll into all sorts of odd and interesting postures.

Easy Hand Work.

Another type of material which can be supplied very cheaply and which furnishes easy occupation is found in the sets of gummed paper strips which can be purchased in most stores for play materials. The strips may be very easily fastened into a simple chain, woven into various color combinations, or even made into animals and dolls which are still amusing when mother pins them to the curtain or hangs them from the bedpost.

Crêpe paper has many possibilities because it may be puckered and pulled into all sorts of weird shapes. It may also be used to fashion the clothes for a clothes-pin doll, especially if mother will furnish a few elastic bands to hold the paper clothing in place.

Stencils, coloring books, and crayons are perhaps too commonplace to mention, but there are other things which many mothers may not have tried. An ordinary picture on a card, a large pin and a pillow make an interesting combination. If the child holds the card on the pillow and pricks holes around the outlines of the picture, he will be fascinated to find he can recognize it when he turns the picture side from him and holds it up so the light will shine through the holes. For the child who may be trusted not to swallow them, a paper of safety-pins will furnish all sorts of possible combinations in chains and bunches. Paper clips, also, may be used to make chains, necklaces, and bracelets. If the bedding can be protected with papers, oilcloth, or even an old sheet, plasticene or modeling wax may while away many a weary hour and may even furnish practice for the budding sculptor.

Solitaire.

There are some card games of solitaire which even a seven- or eight-year-old child can play with pleasure. The simplest of them starts with eight cards laid out in two rows of four,

one row below the other. If no two of the cards are of the
same denomination, i. e., if there is no pair of "fours" or
of "Jacks," the cards must be shuffled and dealt again. If
any pair appears in the eight, these two cards are to be
covered with two more cards taken from the deck and placed
right side up. The array is then inspected again, and any
pair which now appears is covered as the first pair was. When
there is no pair to be covered the game is lost and all the cards
are shuffled for a new game. The game is won if all the deck
can be used in covering successive pairs of cards. If the child
is at all irritated by the infrequency of the times when he wins,
the game may be further simplified by having him lay out ten
cards at the beginning instead of eight.

A solitaire which is a bit more complicated is played as
follows. With the deck shuffled and held as for dealing, the
cards are turned over one by one and placed one after another
from left to right. Any card which is of the suit or of the denomination of the preceding card or of the card which is third
from the right-hand end of the row may be placed on top of that
card. Thus, if the first card to be turned over is the "two
of diamonds" and the second is the "King of diamonds," the
King is placed on top of the two. If the third card is another
diamond or another King it is placed on top of the "King of
diamonds"; but if it is, say, the eight of clubs, it is placed
to the right. Then suppose the five of spades is turned, this
is placed to the right of the others. Then another card is
turned. If this is the "King of spades" it may be placed on
top of the five which preceded it because they are both spades,
or it may be placed on top of the King of diamonds because
they are both Kings and the King of diamonds is third from
the right-hand end of the row. This King of spades cannot
be placed on top of the five of spades and then that whole
pile put on top of the King of diamonds. The game is won
if all the cards are finally piled in one pile.

Puzzles and Simple Games.

Simple puzzles—picture, block, or mechanical—will provide good entertainment for many children, but care must be taken not to provide puzzles which are too difficult. The ill child needs to be contentedly busy, not excited, not tense, not under any strain.

Some games can be played by the child alone. He can play tiddly-winks, for example, and either count the number of hops he takes to get all the men into the cup or he can play one color against the other and count the color which gets all its men in first as the winner. Jack-straws can be played either to see how many "turns" the child requires to remove all the pieces, or to see which of two imaginary players wins, the child taking the part of first one player and then the other.

Any of the paper and pencil games which we have discussed in Chapter VII can be played by the child in bed if some other person is free to play too. Another game which furnishes great amusement for children of eight years and older is called "Salvo." [1] In this game each of two players is provided with a sheet marked off in squares, upon which he locates with a pencil his "battle fleet," without telling his opponent where these "ships" are. Each square can be located by means of a letter and a number. One player "shoots," telling the other where his shots are falling. When this first player has fired a "salvo," the opponent reports whether any of his fleet were hit. The opponent then fires a salvo. Each player keeps a record both of his own and his opponent's shots, and the firing continues in rotation until all the ships of one player have been "sunk." One great advantage of this game is that it does not require both players to use the same material or to work at the same board or table. In fact, two children in

1 Copyright, 1931, by the Starex Novelty Company.

separate beds in the same room can play the game without ever coming near each other and without making use of a messenger.

Invention and Imagination

The child who is interested in inventing stories or writing verses may welcome staying in bed as an opportunity for quiet, a chance to write down the stories and rhymes that are running in his head. Even if a child has no aspirations as an author, he may use many hours happily with pencil and paper making lists of various sorts: all the sounds which he can hear, all the objects which are colored blue (or green or purple) which he can see or can remember, all the girls' names or all the boys' names which he can remember, names of animals, and so on. Sometimes the child is amused by keeping a very detailed diary, recording at what exact minute he saw certain people go past his window, just when he took a drink of water, etc. Older children who are not very ill may be given a toy typewriter to use.

The child who likes to pretend, will spend considerable time in day-dreaming (for a discussion of day-dreaming see Anderson's *Happy Childhood,* Chapters IV and X), which is not a bad occupation at all for the child who should lie quietly. He may pretend he is a prince who has to stay in bed because of a ''spell'' of some sort; he may be a warrior who has been wounded in combat, and so on. Sometimes a paper soldier hat, a paper crown, a paper feather head-dress will be sufficient stimulus for this type of play. In one hospital for children, the worker who is responsible for their occupations collects extra buttons and badges from the conventions that meet in her city and distributes them among the children with the result that many imitation Shriners, doctors, and railroad men spend hours talking as they imagine the persons who wore the badges talked.

Summary

The alert mother and the inventive child will devise many other occupations for the sick room. Such occupations will, of course, vary with the interests of the child, the restrictions of the particular illness, and the material which is available. Every household will be able to provide something which can be used for the amusement of the child who is too ill to be out of bed but not ill enough to require absolute rest and quiet. Whatever is provided will be satisfactory, if it does not strain the child's eyes or tire him in any way and if it keeps him contented, for in contented relaxation we find one of the greatest of recuperative agencies.

Chapter X

STORIES AND BOOKS FOR CHILDREN

ONE of the most striking differences between man and the other animals lies in man's ability to benefit from the experience of other individuals. As it has been phrased, "Each generation stands upon the shoulders of the preceding one." In prehistoric times, men handed on their acquired wisdom by word of mouth, and so sons learned many things from their fathers and grandfathers and other adults whom they knew personally. With the development of writing, it has become possible to learn from people who live far away or who have died many years before. Nowadays, the average successful individual probably learns a great deal more from books than he does from oral teaching. If a man has acquired the ability to read understandingly, he has within his reach a vast wealth of information and of pleasure.

Importance of Reading

If we should be asked, then, "Why should a child read or why should he be read to?" we would probably answer that, in the first place, reading is the most important tool which he will ever have for acquiring the information that he needs. As adults we tend to forget how much we ourselves learn through reading or how much of the time many of us spend in reading. A professor in one of our great universities was requested by a new student to outline a course for her which wouldn't use her eyes very much, since they "were too weak to endure much reading." After frantic searching

through the catalogue of courses the teacher announced that it would be better for the young lady to find something else to do for she simply could not go to school without either reading a great deal herself or hiring some one else to read a great deal for her. Although reading is not quite so necessary for the child in the grades, a mere glance at the books on geography, history, and even arithmetic, will convince any person that it is a fundamental skill for the child in the modern school.

Stories, which are practically the only type of reading suitable for the youngest children, may be expected to broaden the child's knowledge of the world, and, as his knowledge broadens, so will his sympathy for and understanding of other people increase. The person who has read stories of all sorts of people will be much better able to comprehend points of view which are different from his own. Stories will also aid in clarifying the ideas which the child has already acquired. Perhaps he has formed a notion of a boat, for instance. His ideas will, in many instances, be inexact, but a story involving boats will correct some of them. A little girl who had been much interested in a kindergarten "boat project," in which the children had drawn boats and built them of blocks, was taken on a small steamer the following summer. As she stepped from the gang plank and looked around the interior, she stopped in amazement and gasped, "I didn't know there were stairs in boats. We didn't put any stairs in our boat in kindergarten." In this instance, it was through actual observation that the child's notions were cleared and enriched, but it might just as well have been through reading a story of a child traveling on a boat and walking up stairs in the course of the trip. A story may also increase the child's fund of information by increasing his vocabulary. Into any ordinary story will enter words which the child has not met before. They will perhaps be explained to him, but

even if they are not, he will gradually come to learn their meaning through finding them in various combinations.

In the second place, books serve as sources not only of much information but of much pleasure as well. In these days of labor-saving and time-saving devices, we are coming to realize the necessity for training the child for the profitable use of leisure time. When he has nothing interesting to do, he may be either unwholesomely bored or actively delinquent. Such undesirable states are seldom found in the individual who has acquired a taste for good reading. In fact, there is probably no other one occupation which so well fills the requirements for leisure-time activity. So we give the child stories—orally in the early years or to read to himself when he is older—in great part because they give him something pleasant and interesting to do.

There is still a third way in which stories offer very definite training for the child and that is in giving practice in imagination. At first the child is unable to imagine anything which is not present to his sight. Later, however, he learns first to revive past experiences in the form of memories and then to combine them in new ways. He may pretend, for example, that a number of people whom he has seen separately are all together with him; or he may pretend that he is riding on the train which he sees passing, but on which he has never been. Gradually as his reading grows more and more mature, he becomes able to imagine himself and other people in all sorts of new combinations and places. It is an absolute impossibility for any one to imagine anything wholly new. All that even the most ingenious of us can do through imagination is to combine in new relationships bits of experience which we have picked up in various places. In such a recombination of experiences lies all invention. Vicarious though it may be, reading multiplies the child's experience.

The White House Conference suggests that:

"As a nation we have failed to realize that it is not enough to teach our children to read. They must also be guided and directed in their reading, encouraged to read for enlightenment, recreation, and pleasure, trained to have permanent habits of reading and given easy access to all kinds of worthwhile reading matter. . . . Teachers, librarians, and specialists in child training and child psychology seek to stimulate reading by making it an integral part of work and play activities. Storytelling, reading clubs . . . the use of posters and pictures, visits to places of interest, the distribution of reading lists and exhibits of books, are all suitable methods for stimulating a desire in children to read. . . . Most normal children will read good books and periodicals if they are easy to obtain. . . . If bookstores and libraries are not near at hand, children and their parents will usually content themselves with the offerings of local newsstands and subscription book agents. The nation-wide popularity of certain books of cheap fiction, particularly of books in series, is not always so indicative of the undeveloped tastes of boys and girls as of the prolonged and successful activity of some publishers and book dealers in making these books easily available. . . . At no time in the history of printing has there been such a wealth of suitable books as are produced constantly to supply book stores, and hence homes and libraries. . . . There are now approximately six thousand public libraries in the United States. . . . Systematic, specialized library service for children began about forty years ago. Today in practically all good public libraries, except the very small ones, it is a distinct unit of work organized to meet the demands of a special group of people who, though limited in experience, are none the less entitled to good reading, authentic sources of information, and dignified aid in using this material. . . . It is this voluntary feature, this sense of being left alone in a pleasant pasture, that accounts for the hold which children's rooms have upon reading children and which attracts the non-reading child. The librarian does, however, stimulate and guide reading by storytelling, by exhibits, by distributing reading lists, by talks to classes in the schools and to individuals at the library and in many other ways. . . . In conclusion the Committee repeats that the problem of promoting good reading among American children is, above everything else, a problem of making good reading matter accessible."—*Children's Reading: A Study of Voluntary Reading of Boys and Girls in the United States* (The Century Co., New York, 1932), p. 4 ff.

The First Stories

If, then, we are to provide the child with literature for
his pleasure, for his information, and for the training of his
imagination, the question which naturally arises is: What
stories should a child be given first? There seems to be no
doubt that the first "stories" should be very simple and
should be originated by the parent or nurse and not read
from a book. In her *Here and Now Story Book*,[1] Lucy Sprague
Mitchell has outlined the early stories in a most interesting
fashion. She calls them "here and now" stories because they
are accounts of what is going on at the present time. The
baby understands only the present and so the mother talks to
him about that. Every mother does this, though few of them
realize that they are beginning the child's education in the
story line. When the baby is getting dressed to go out for a
ride, he will often lie quietly, if mother tells him what she
is doing: "Now mother is putting on David's right sock and
now here comes David's left sock. Here is David's right shoe
and now mother has to tie the bow. She is tying an extra
knot in the strings so that young David cannot pull it out,
etc. etc." This is the simplest form of a story. It tells about
what the child and the mother are doing at the moment. But,
you will object, a five-months-old baby or even a nine-months-
old baby will not know what his mother is talking about. He
is quiet only because his attention is held by the modulations
of her voice. It is quite true that he does not know what a
good deal of the talk is about, but it is also true that only
through such means will he acquire the vocabulary which
he will need for further stories. It will take him an astonish-
ingly short time to learn that the word "sock" comes when
that particular article of clothing is put on.

[1] The books mentioned in this chapter are listed on page 217 ff. The
reader who is interested in a more exhaustive survey of children's literature is referred to *Realms of Gold in Children's Books* by B. E. Mahony
and E. Whitney (Doubleday Doran and Co. Inc., New York, 1929).

The next type of story which the baby should hear is the account of some past experience which he has had, perhaps an account of what he did on the preceding day. "Yesterday David and mother were in the living room and the front door bell rang and Fido barked 'Bow-wow' and when Mother went to the door, who should be there but Aunt Mary? etc. etc." This kind of story obviously is inappropriate until the baby is able to remember something of his past experiences. Along with this type or following soon after it, may come the story which forecasts the immediate future: "After David's hat and coat are on, he will go out in the automobile for a ride and the car will say 'Honk, honk,' etc. etc."

The selection of this type of story as the introduction of the child to the realm of literature is well justified by what we know of the psychology of a baby's learning. We know that he learns his words through the frequent repetition of the word at the same time that the object named is presented. Thus *cap*, spoken every time that the baby's cap is put on, will soon result in the child's associating the sound with the article and will mean that that word has been added to his vocabulary. We know, moreover, that if any person is to learn anything new, he must begin with what is already familiar to him. A mountain may be explained much more easily to a person who already knows a hill; a tiger is more intelligible if the child has seen a cat or at least some four-footed animal. Thus it is practically impossible for the average person to understand what blindness is like, for he is apt to assume that it is like what he experiences when he is in the dark. He forgets that he is actually seeing the dark, whereas the blind person does not see anything. But ask this average man what he sees behind his head, and he will answer that he sees nothing; it is not black, it is merely nothing. Through realizing what "nothing" looks like, he will come to some conception of blindness.

Mother Goose.

Along with these early simple *Here and Now* stories the beginnings of poetry should be offered, and, of the various poems for children, nothing is so satisfying, so appealing to the baby, as the old, old *Mother Goose* rhymes. The White House Conference has shown [2] that up to the age of seven years *Mother Goose* is almost without a serious rival as the favorite story of young children. The fact that *Mother Goose* is particularly popular with children of the lower socio-economic groups probably means merely that these children are less likely to hear other verses and stories than are the children of the more fortunate classes.

Over and over we find adults asking, "What is the sense in *Mother Goose?*" or "Why do children love *Mother Goose* so much?" The answer seems to be that although there is no sense, or very little sense, in *Mother Goose*, this does not disturb the child in the least. What he loves is the swinging rhyme and the jingle. What little sense or story appears in the rhymes is almost always action—"Jack and Jill went up the hill," or "The mouse ran up the clock," or "Little Miss Muffet sat on a tuffet," and so on. Although many of them include children and animals as actors, the content of the verses does little to explain their fascination. Above all else *Mother Goose* is rhythmical. The lines scan perfectly and, when read with strongly marked accents, they have a perfect rhythm of a simple and regular type. Moreover, the ends of the lines rhyme, and the words in the earlier part of the line jingle in a delightful fashion and with considerable alliteration. "Hickory dickery dock" or "Intery mintery cutery corn," are combinations which we never forget. Children delight in odd sound combinations in words and frequently the sound is much more important to them than

[2] *The Young Child in the Home: A Survey of Three Thousand American Families.*

the possible sense. At first children seem to be attracted by the sound alone; later they are highly amused at the making of sounds which seem like words but which really mean nothing. This adds the element of humor to the verses. There is no doubt that even the tiny baby enjoys a clearly accented rhythm. Some persons see in the baby's kicking with alternate feet the beginning of a rhythmic sense, but whether or not we follow them to that point, we all agree that the baby enjoys the rhythmic motion of being rocked or the steady bouncing up and down in his buggy. Now *Mother Goose* makes an excellent accompaniment to rocking, to bouncing, or to almost any other regular motion, and so fits in with the baby's first experience of rhythm. Blank verse which has been written especially for children is highly unsuccessful; they simply don't like it, but nonsense with a definite swing and rhythm—that is a different matter!

The First Books

As the child grows out of babyhood, as he learns to understand simple things which are said to him and to say a few words himself, his stories will gradually develop into a somewhat more complex kind. By the time he is two, he is ready for simple stories with picture accompaniments. The first books which are put into his hands should be made of cloth or of linenette. His motor coördination is still too poor to turn paper pages without tearing them. The pictures in these books should be large, simple in outline, with little detail, and printed in fairly bright colors. Children are most interested in pictures of animals, of other children, and of objects or places with which they are familiar. The lure of the familiar is something which is rather difficult to explain psychologically. Of course we all tend somewhat to return to places and to people we know. In attending a large tea, the average woman will spend the majority of her time in talking to women whom she knows very well, and will give little effort to getting acquainted with others whom she knows less well but might come to like even better. So in the commuters' train we find the same individual occupying the same seat day after day even when it would be easier to try some other position. These returns to the familiar are without doubt partly due to habit. It is easier to keep on doing the thing in the same old way than to try out a new way. They may also be partly due to the memories which the familiar calls up. In glancing through a book of pictures of many different places, the average person will spend almost all his time looking at pictures of places with which he is very familiar. He will inspect other pictures intently only when there is something very striking or unusual about the place or when it is a place of which he has read or heard. So the child returns again and again to the familiar. The picture of a cat is much more interesting than one of a dinosaur; and the picture of a cat resembling the family cat is much more interesting than one with different coloring or marking.

To satisfy this interest in pictures of the familiar, Mary Steichen Martin has published *A First Picture Book* in which the pictures are black and white photographs of objects familiar to any baby. They are beautiful examples of photography and that they are lifelike is shown by the way in which certain babies try to grab the cup and the ball. Very young children seem to like these pictures just as well as colored ones, but among the two-year-olds and the three-year-olds there is one objection to the book. They say, "It isn't a book. There isn't any reading in it." In other words, they object to the lack of printing. It is amusing to note here that even three- or four-year-old children do not object to books in which the text is written in Swedish or German or Russian. Perhaps they would object to Chinese characters, but I doubt it. The printing is something which completes the book, regardless of the child's ability to understand what it says.

The recently published *Peggy and Peter* provides both good pictures and a charmingly simple, jolly text and is a great favorite.

Children seem to have a natural interest in animals as well as in other children. The baby in the baby-buggy will turn to watch a dog and will smile at a passing child when he ignores adults, buildings, and trees. Why this should be we can only guess. Perhaps, since the child and animal move a great deal and since moving things attract the attention, the baby watches other children and animals in part because they move. It may be, too, that the faces of other children are more nearly on the level of the baby's eyes than are the faces of adults, and faces are more interesting than clothes. At any rate we know that animals and children and familiar objects are interesting to the young child not only in actuality but in pictures as well. The content of the stories which the child of two or three enjoys is very simple, usually a mere series of unrelated incidents. In a picture book of farmyard animals, and in the recent *Picture Book of Animals,* a brief remark about each animal, giving the sound it makes or something of the kind, is perfectly satisfactory. There need be no plot nor any connection between the text accompanying one picture and the remarks under the following picture.

Simple Story Books

However, we find that as the child grows older he becomes more interested in books in which one central character passes through a series of experiences. These stories need no plot, no climax, and certainly no development of character; they need only one character (usually a child or some particular animal) to bind together the various simple incidents. As some one has said, this character is like the cord which holds a string of beads together, and the events of the tale are the beads, any one of which may be dropped without hurting the others in any way. A character is thus the integrating force in *A Day with Betty Anne;* a bullet in Peter Newell's *Hole Book.* Sometimes it is a line repeated in a sort of refrain which holds the story together, as in the case of *Johnny Crow's Garden.* Most adults would be just as well pleased with this book, if the clever pictures were accompanied by jingles wholly unrelated to each other, but probably the refrain "In Johnny Crow's Garden" aids in holding the child's interest.

Of the stories with a very, very simple plot, Elsa Beskow's *The Tale of the Wee Little Old Woman* is an excellent example. Here is the entire story:

"There once was a wee little old woman who had a wee little house and a wee little table and a wee little chair and a wee little stool and a wee little milkpail; and a wee little cat that said 'Meow,' and a wee little cow that said 'Moo-o-o.' One day the wee little old woman took her little wee stool and went out to milk her little wee cow. She put the wee bit of milk on the little wee table. Just then the little wee cat came in— First he jumped on the little wee stool, then on the little wee chair and then on the little wee table, and drank up all the milk!— But then the wee little old woman came back— 'Scat, cat!!!' and the cat ran away to the woods and never came back again."

Just seven sentences! Less than one hundred and fifty words and yet from the point of view of a small child, it is a very satisfactory tale. If we analyze the story to discover just wherein the charm lies, we find first that most of the characters are animals. Beside the old woman herself (who is, of course, a perfectly understandable character), we have a cat and a cow. These are two of the most familiar animals, and the other objects coming into the story are also familiar— the house, the table, the chair, the stool—and the less familiar milkpail and woods. Nothing, then, of the material of which the story is made is unfamiliar to the average child. If he does not know a milkpail, he certainly knows a pail, and even if he does not have personal acquaintance with a cow or with woods, a vague idea of either is all he needs to understand the story. The action of the story is also extremely simple. The little woman *had* certain things, she *took* the stool, *went out, milked* the cow, *put* the milk down. Then the cat *jumped* on various pieces of furniture and *drank* up the milk. The woman *came* back and the cat *ran* away. Of all these verbs none is unfamiliar, and most of them are used by the child himself every day. There is no description in the story save for *wee* and *little* which repeated over and over have the effect of a refrain. The material of the story, then, is familiar and the events well within the range of the child's understanding. The story appeals to children through the repeated phrases (not only *wee little,* but the series, *stool, chair, table*), through the use of animals and through the introduction of animal sounds. The gay illustrations which accompany this story are in every way as simple and as pleasing as the words themselves. Combined with the story they make one of the most charming books for the young child's library.

That the material of the story must be familiar to the child is seen very clearly, if you try to tell any story involving a special dialect. Brer Rabbit is a most delightful figure to a Southern child of almost any age, but to the young Northern child he is a complete mystery, so much so that there is no fun in trying to find out what the story is all about. If the reader tries to explain the Southern dialect to a Northern child, he will often evoke the retort, "Well, if that's what it means, why doesn't it say so?"

We find, then, that for these earliest stories, plot is not essential, logic is not essential (there is no logic to *Johnny Crow's Garden* nor to *Little Black Sambo*) and complete comprehension is not essential. In fact, if the child understands *Little Black Sambo* too well, he begins to ask, "Why didn't they do this or that?" and the story is spoiled. There are, however, certain characteristics of the story which are essential to its success with young children. The topic or the material must be interesting to the child, usually animals or other children. The story must contain action of a simple sort that a child understands, like running and jumping and crying. The various animal sounds always arouse interest. The cat in the *Wee Little Old Woman* is the more interesting because it says "meow." An adult would assume this vocal activity on the part of any cat and think it silly or insulting to his intelligence to include that detail in the description of the animal, but the child loves to hear it over and over. Moreover, the story must be short to be effective. The child's interest is a very temporary affair and he may be tired out by too long a story. Last but by no means least, the story should be accompanied by pictures which have comparatively little detail, but which have good outlines, pleasing colors, and details which do not contradict the story. To older children and adults, an inaccurate illustration is far worse than no illustration at all. We do not know at what age the child begins to be critical of the pictures, but we do know that a faulty drawing may actually provide faulty information and make it harder for the child to learn the correct points afterward.

The White House Conference reports [3] that for ages one, two, and three the favorite stories are either verses (almost invariably *Mother Goose*) or stories of animals, among which *The Three Bears* is without a serious rival. At the age of four most girls begin to lose their interest in *Mother Goose* and to show interest in fanciful tales of the talking animal or fairy type. They become much pleased with stories of other children by age nine, while books of facts and stories of heroes hold the boys' attention from about the age of seven or eight on up to age twelve. Stories of animals are popular at all ages with both boys and girls, although the type of story

[3] *The Young Child in the Home: A Survey of Three Thousand American Families.*

shifts with the increasing age of the child from that of talking beasts to true stories of real animals.

Verses

The verses which the older child likes are somewhat more complex than *Mother Goose*. He still loves jingles, but he prefers verses which make some sense instead of pure nonsense. Probably the Milne poems are the greatest favorites with the child of preschool age. The jingling "Christopher Robin goes hoppity, hoppity, hoppity, hoppity, hop," is a favorite as are the animal verses, "Once upon a time there were three little foxes" and "Ernest was an elephant, a great big fellow." *The King's Breakfast* has some of the characteristics of the cumulative tale; has the fascination of kings and queens, almost the equivalents of fairies; has a real swing and the familiar delightful suggestions of bread and butter and marmalade. Many of Robert Louis Stevenson's verses, also, deal with topics which are of interest to children. "The birdie with a yellow bill," "In winter I get up at night," "The rain is raining all around," "We built a ship upon the stairs," and so on are interesting because of subject matter and pleasing because of rhythm and rhyme. Almost any acceptable rhyme that tells a story fascinates children of this age. An old favorite is Moore's poem beginning, " 'Twas the night before Christmas." In this we can pick out dozens of words which the average child will fail to understand— *sugar-plums, sash* (of the window), *lustre, miniature, coursers, obstacle, tarnished, pedler, pack, thistle,* etc.—but they are words which aid the rhythm and ignorance as to their meanings in no way injures the main thread of the story.

Simple Plots

By the time the child is four or five years old, he is ready for a story with a more definite plot than the tales which have held his interest so far. *Snipp, Snapp, Snurr and the Red Shoes* and Alice Dalgliesh's *Blue Teapot* illustrate the simple form of plot where the movement of the story is impeded by one incident, happily cleared up in the course of a few pages. In the former, three children want to please their mother by giving her a pair of red shoes for which she has expressed a desire. They lack the money for buying the shoes, but each child (with remarkable ease) locates a job and earns his share of the cost. The shoes are purchased and the presentation made amid great rejoicing. The emotions which the book portrays are typical of any young child—love for the mother, desire to give her something, interest in occupations and in color, and pleasure at being praised by the mother. In Miss Dalgliesh's story, Miss Letty, living alone with her cat, does not realize that she is lonely until she buys a charming blue teapot, cream pitcher, and sugar bowl, with four cups and saucers to match. (Every child will understand the desire for a party large enough to use every dish.) Miss Letty adopts two little girls and they are all very happy until they run short of money. As in the other tale, the children find ways to earn money and the story ends happily. Here the emotions are ones which the child has no difficulty in understanding—the affection for the cat, the delight in the blue dishes, the desire to have children come to live at the house, the fun of buying things, the interest in earning money, and the satisfaction in pleasing and helping the person who makes their home for them.

And so we might go on with illustrations of more and more complex stories, until we reach those where the action is nearly as complex as in a story planned for adults and where there is even some character development. But before we go on to stories for the older child, let us review the natural interests of the child of kindergarten age, the child of four, or five, or even six. From that review we may be able to predict whether or not any given new story will prove to be a popular or well-liked book for young children or not.

Children's Interests

Rhythm and repetition in speech or in singing is a characteristic of many of the most popular games of this period and it seems not unlikely that rhythm and repetition in a story may add definitely to its charms, as for example, "hundreds of cats, thousands of cats, millions and billions and trillions of cats."

A striking characteristic of children's play is constant activity, and, even at a very early age, the child will notice moving things. The younger the child the greater, roughly, is the proportion of action words which he uses in conversation. Children of two use about twice as many such words as the average adult. When children make up stories of their own, the characters are doing something all the time, perhaps in response to the restlessness or need for action which child psychologists list among the native motives of the child.

Another characteristic interest of all children is in sound. The tiny baby will notice a sound before he will notice a sight. All children, of course, babble and make a varied assortment of experimental noises, many of them apparently just for the joy of the noise. When they are old enough to listen to stories, they are fascinated by sound combinations, from the early *Mother Goose* to the soul-satisfying "man of infinite-resource-and-sagacity," "Bi-Colored-Python-Rock-Snake" and "great grey-green, greasy Limpopo River" of the *Just-So Stories*. Perhaps it is this interest in sound and joy in its production which gives children their great interest in animal sounds. There is good psychology back of letting a child call a dog a *bow wow*. It is the sound and not the appearance of the dog which he likes most, and the term *bow wow* sounds more like the animal than the term *dog*. So with his earliest pictures the child likes to be told that the dog says *bow wow* and the cow says *moo*. Many a mother has been embarrassed by having an interested child ask, "What does the elephant say?" and

"What does the crocodile say?" Any sound will satisfy them and one mother was thunderstruck to find that her son took one of her answers perfectly seriously and that he was informing his playmates that the elephant said, "Please give me a peanut." Not only are animal sounds of interest, but sounds of machinery are also fascinating. In *Jingleman Jack,* now unfortunately out of print, the child is held enthralled with "Clickety-clack, clickety-clack, the weaver's loom goes forward and back." In all stories of trains the *toot toot* adds vividness; in stories of hunting, *bang, bang,* adds realism; in stories of domestic life, cooking which says, *bubble, bubble* or *sizzle, sizzle,* is much more satisfactory from the point of view of the child.

Perhaps the natural interest in movement and the natural interest in sounds combine to make the great interest which young children show in transportation. This interest in trains and boats and cars and wagons comes long before the average child has had the joy of traveling and visiting strange places, so the charm cannot lie in the fact that the vehicle is capable of carrying him to foreign places. Certainly transportation is interesting throughout life, but apart from the features which interest the adult, the child delights in the movement and in the sound. A trip in a car or train or airplane would lose all interest for him, if there were no feeling of movement either in the vehicle itself or in the landscape, for most small children have little or no interest in the places they pass by. Without motion all that would be left would be the pleasure at reaching the goal. As it is, the majority of people, both children and grown-ups, enjoy traveling unless they are forced to spend so many days on train or boat or car that they come to ignore the view and the motion. Be that as it may, the young child enjoys stories about all sorts of transportation, just as he enjoys playing train with a toy train or with a series of chairs. The child who lives near a river, lake, or ocean will naturally be most interested in boats; the child who lives near

an airport will be most interested in planes; and the child
who lives near a railroad track, most interested in trains; but
they will all be interested to some degree in all kinds of
transportation. Of course, it happens not infrequently that a
small child will be severely frightened by a loud bark from a
dog, but if the animal makes sounds not too sudden or too
violent or too close, then the sound adds to the child's pleasure.
Probably small animals are more interesting than large ones;
they are not frightening, and they are on the child's level. A
dog may not be as interesting to an adult as an elephant, but
he is much more pleasing to a young child. Perhaps that is
because the larger animal is somewhat overpowering, whereas
the smaller one can be taken in at a glance. Whatever the
preference, the fact remains that all young children are interested in animals and in stories of animals. There seems to
be no doubt that they think of the animals as individuals more
or less like themselves and at first are content with stories in
which the characters are animals who behave just as children
would behave and who have experiences similar to those which
children have. Although, later on, the interest will be in true
stories of animals in their native habitat, for a considerable
number of years, the children will prefer to have the animal
humanized, at least in ideas and emotions, if not in actual
speech.

The child's thinking and imagination are at first limited, as
we have already said, to his own experiences. Gradually he
becomes able to imagine himself in other situations. When he
reaches this stage, he is interested in stories of other children.
The child reads himself into everything which goes on, for he
cannot understand anything except as that thing is related to
himself, and a simple story of a child in circumstances and
surroundings not unlike his own gives him his first experience
in imagining himself in another environment. It is probably
largely for this reason that he is interested in stories of children.

We have already suggested that children are interested in action and things which move. They are also interested in hearing of what animals or trains or whatever *do*. They are beginning to be interested in the activities of adults, and so we find interest at this age in the *Social Science Readers*, the accounts of the activities of the fireman and the policeman and the motorman. Some of the interests which appear in the child's play, in his conversation, and in his reports of what he has seen include the following: play, fighting, imitation, eating, making sounds, touching and handling things, being with other persons, helping mother about the house, playing with pet animals, going on picnics, having new clothes, pleasing other people, doing as other people do, deciding what to do themselves, being with other people, and so on. Some of the emotional experiences which they understand are: sympathy; affection for members of the family and friends; gregariousness; suspense and danger, if it is evident that the outcome will be satisfactory; hunger; recognition; and security. And so we find among the favorite stories of young children, tales of houses made of candy, of animals making noises, of hungry children being fed, of ragged children being adorned in beautiful new clothes, of children playing with others, of children helping their mother, of children receiving praise for their efforts.

Books for the Child of Six to Nine Years

By the time the child is six or seven years old, he has usually begun to read for himself, although children vary greatly in the age at which they begin to enjoy so doing. Some people have felt that the child who is accustomed to hearing books read aloud may object to the slower and more laborious process of reading to himself. Experience shows, however, that, if a child is very fond of stories and hears them read aloud only at set times of the day, just before bedtime, for example, he shows no objections to reading to himself at other times. Most children learn to read at an age when they need considerable outdoor activity. The fact that the child is spending regular hours in a school-room means that in his free hours he needs outdoor play in the sunshine much more than he needs the mental stimulation of books, so that, although he should be supplied with the books which he craves, he should not be encouraged to spend too much time in reading.

The type of book which the child of this age enjoys is somewhat different from the type which the preschool child liked best. *Mother Goose* has lost some of its charm, though it is still popular with some children at the age of six and even seven. Stories of animals are still among the best liked, but the animals are expected to do more complicated things than those of the picture books. The child is now old enough to enjoy a fanciful element, such as the thought of Peregrin traveling around on a goldfish, and to be attracted by the notion of elves and trolls and fairies.

The plot of the story must now be more complex. The child of the early grades frequently feels a lack in the simple recounting of a sequence of unrelated events. He likes a definite plot, working toward a climax and ending in a satisfactory conclusion. He likes a story which is longer than the ones he formerly enjoyed, and he prefers a book with a number of chapters in which the same group of characters pass through a series of events to some desired goal. He likes to select certain chapters to read over and over, and he is much better satisfied when each chapter has a happy ending. For some children *Pinnocchio* is disturbing because, at the end of many chapters, the marionette is left in some precarious position with the outcome in suspense and we hear "Oh, Mother, read just enough farther so that he is all right again." On the other hand *Hittie,* though in general more suited to an older group of children, is very well arranged into chapters, each of which comes to its own climax and happy ending while, at the same time, it foreshadows interesting events to be told in the following chapter.

The material for stories for the child in the early grades is still largely made up of animals. The animals are a bit more lifelike and there is less and less attempt to make them think and act like human beings. The child has now left *The Three Bears* and *The Three Pigs* and *Billy Goats Gruff* largely behind him, and he is ready for *Wag and Puff, The Twins and Tabiffa, The Runaway Sardine, Tigers 'n Things, Karoo the Kangaroo, Little Black Sambo,* and *Peter Rabbit,* if these are not already favorites, and for Thornton Burgess's animal stories. The last are very well known among children, probably in part because they appear in many evening papers.

Other children enter into many of the animal stories, for almost any story is more interesting to boys and girls at this age, if other children figure in the plot. Some children seem to throw themselves into the character of the child in the story and rejoice or suffer with him. Frequently the story is interrupted with, ''Don't you hope he gets it?'' or, ''Oh boy! I wish it was me!'' Sometimes the stories for this age are concerned wholly with children—at first with children in the same general circumstances as the child who is to hear the story and later with accounts of children in other countries.

Still another type of content which is most interesting to the children is that of the order of the *Social Science Readers,* stories of the fireman, the policeman, the farmer, and so on. The children are now interested to some extent in the occupations of the adults whom they see. If the child has visited a fire-station or a farm, then the story of the fireman and the farmer will be much more interesting, will call up memories, and will actually clarify the experience which the child has had. He can review his experience in the book, or he can discover the differences between the two.

Mechanical things are yearly becoming more interesting, especially to the boys. Trains and derricks and steam-shovels will hold many an adult entranced at their behavior, and there is hardly a small boy who has not wanted at some time to run a steam-shovel when he "grows up." This interest in mechanical things is reflected in the type of stories which are best liked. Sometimes the story is one of a humanized machine, as in the ever-popular *Engine That Could;* more often the machine comes in as part of the story, and a human hero pulls levers, pushes brakes, and whirls wheels to the accompaniment of shining eyes and tense muscles in the listener.

Fairies and trolls and giants offer many thrills. Most of the children of this age recognize perfectly clearly that they will never meet such beings in life, but this does not make the characters a whit less fascinating. Few people outgrow the fun of pretending to believe in Santa Claus. Often such pretense is kept up more on account of the adult's feelings than on account of the child's. It is a case of grandpa having to take his grandchildren to the circus even after they are perfectly capable of going alone. Perhaps, if the child believes too firmly in the existence of fairies or of Santa Claus, he will be too much upset when he has to give up all hope of meeting them, but most children get just as much fun out of pretending that there are fairies as they do out of actually believing in their existence. The small child, of course, is much happier believing that ogres and giants are imaginary, than that they are real. The fairies that are best loved are those which help human beings, often secretly and certainly unostentatiously. The bad giants or the bad trolls must receive their due punishment, and no sympathy is wasted on them. So to be perfectly satisfactory, the hero of a fairy tale must be perfect and must be rewarded amply; the villain must be wholly bad and must receive a very severe punishment. If the punishment results in the reform of the villain, all very well; if he simply disappears from the story, no tears are shed.

Another interest which continues strong throughout the early school years is the interest in food. Part of the pleasure in *Poppy Seed Cakes* lies in the recurrent mention of food—the poppy seed cakes themselves, the green tops of vegetables for the goat, and the picnic basket with its enumerated edibles, —these are things which every child can appreciate. Ameliar Anne's umbrella full of scones and buns, the Millions of Cats drinking the pond dry and eating every blade of grass on the hill, Peter Rabbit enjoying Mr. Macgregor's carrots, the Little Red Hen eating her own cakes, the Three Little Kittens anxious for their pie, and Alice responding immediately to labels of "Eat Me" and "Drink Me," all strike a responsive chord in the child.

The treatment of the material in the stories for the child of this age may, of course, be more mature than it was for the child of five or less. The story may, for example, stress various emotional experiences which up to this time have been beyond his comprehension. He is beginning to be patriotic and to see that the land of a person's birth or of his ancestry will mean more to him than other lands. He becomes interested in children of other countries and to some extent in the countries themselves. Milne's books have made England into "the country where Christopher Robin is," just as Elsa Beskow's books have made Sweden seem like a home of real people to the child, and just as the Alps are "where Heidi lives." The child is also forming a fairly clear notion of bravery and courage, and he understands and sympathizes with the other child who is brave in the face of difficulties and dangers. He takes joy in owning things himself, and he rejoices with the story-child who receives presents or who succeeds in making a collection of butterflies or stamps. At this age the child is also more or less belligerent, and he revels in the story of a fight, provided that his hero wins. The fight must be fair because the primary child is quick to sense injustice and "I don't think it was fair for his mother to do that" will ruin a story. Most children of this age can assimilate fairly large doses of excitement, and the hero of the tale can have adventures that thrill the young child, however unreal they may seem to the adult. The child of the early grades has come to understand something also of death, and, if a death is necessary to the development of the story, there is no need to make a mystery of the event. The child will take it as a matter of course, accept the death as a fact, and pass on to the rest of the story.

Other features which are desirable in stories for children from the age of six on are the giving of temporal or causal relationships, answering the child's "Why?" before he utters it, and introducing bits of humor of a simple sort, amusing word sounds, laughable situations, and so on.

Books for the Child of Nine to Twelve

Along about the age of nine, we find an ever-increasing difference between the interests of boys and of girls. The boys show a growing concern with books of facts, and we find parents reporting that their son is interested in any book about airplanes, trains, animals, and so on. These are the years when the children's encyclopedias are most cherished.

The White House Conference reports that:

"There are about forty subscription sets [of books] designed for children, of which five or six are really excellent. One, a collection of general literature, has been sold to the number of 240,181 in the ten years of its existence. Of another, a work of geographical and historical information, 78,000 sets have been sold. An encyclopedia for children, now in a new revised edition, has gone through three printings of 25,000 each in its first year. Some of the encyclopedias (and) . . . a few of the general collections of literature are valuable . . . but the subscription set has been one of the means whereby well intentioned but uncritical parents and teachers have wasted thousands of dollars. Many of the sets are thrown together without careful selection, and with slight regard for facts; and though cheaply compiled and cheaply printed, are often overpriced. Due credit should be given for the few well edited sets, published and sold in good faith."
—*Children's Reading: A Study of Voluntary Reading of Boys and Girls in the United States* (The Century Co., New York, 1932), p. 16.

One recently published article [4] suggests as desirable collections of informational material for children such sets as: *The Book of Knowledge, Compton's Pictured Encyclopedia, World Book Encyclopedia,* and *Pictured Knowledge.* Each of these sets has certain advantages over the others and the parent who is considering the purchase of one might do well to investigate the others at the same time.

Boys at this age want information about things which they see and about real people. The simpler lives of Washington and of Lincoln and the old familiar Bible stories are read and re-read. P. T. Barnum's accounts of wild animals, Byrd's story of his flight to the pole, Lindbergh's *We,* and the story of Daniel Boone are all favorites with the small boy.

The story of the boyhood experiences of great men; the tales of the adventures of other real boys, like *David Goes Voyaging;* and the Boy Scout books are much more satisfying to the boy than any amount of fanciful stories. Both boys and girls eagerly absorb Hillyer's *Child's Geography of the World* and *Child's History of the World.* The animal stories which are most in demand at this age concern real animals of the type made popular by Ernest Thompson Seton. If the boy does not read of real heroes, he likes imaginary ones who have adventures which might be real. These he can find in *Robinson Crusoe, Treasure Island,* and Hawthorne's *Wonder Book.* This is the age for legends and for fables. The child may enjoy the mere story of the fables, whether or not he is able to understand the "moral" or to apply it to his own conduct. The heroes of the old legends are moved by fairly simple motives which are intelligible to the pre-adolescent.

This is also the age of the books in series. Just what the fascination of a series is, it is hard to say, but the boy who reads and likes one of the Henty or the Alger books and the girl who likes one of the "Elsie Dinsmores" or the "Dotty

[4] M. D. Lynch, "When Children Ask How and Why," *The Parents' Magazine,* VI (December, 1931), 28.

Dimples," or preferably the "Margarets" or the "Katy Dids" or the "Twins" is more apt than not to run through the entire list by the same author.

Girls from nine to twelve years of age are chiefly interested in stories of other children and in fairy tales. The stories of other children may be those of home and family life, the *Little Women* sort and the kind which Laura E. Richards has written. They may also be stories of other lands. Lucy F. Perkins's *Pioneer Twins, Dutch Twins,* and all the other twins are very popular although no one of these seems to stand out in the way that *Heidi* does. *Hittie,* the story of a doll, is largely concerned with the travels and experiences of her young mistresses and shows plainly the differences between successive generations of children in this country. As for fairy tales, we find that anything is enjoyed as long as there is a fairy or some sort of magic in it. If the child has opportunity for considerable experience, she will probably rank Hans Christian Andersen first, Lang second, and Grimm third; but the avid fairy-story reader will read anything and may live in a world of princesses, fairy godmothers, and enchantment. It seems possible that the coincidence of a sudden increase in interest in fairy tales and the period of quickened growth known as the "pre-adolescent spurt" may have a causal relationship. May it not be that the feelings of fatigue which so often accompany accelerated growth may make the magic assistance of fairies particularly enticing?

Girls as well as boys enjoy tales of animals and they, unlike boys, are ready to read stories about children of the opposite sex. Although we get marked sex differences in their favorite books, we find a goodly number of girls enjoying boys' books just as heartily as do their brothers. The opposite rarely occurs, however, and, if an occasional boy does enjoy a typical girls' book, he usually gloats over it in some secret retreat rather than suffer the tortures of teasing.

With both boys and girls, books with a strong patriotic tang are popular. The national heroes and their struggles are interesting to both. Moreover, children of this age understand not only the cruder forms of courage and heroism but also altruism, devotion, and sacrifice. It will not be long before they will thrill over Dickens's *Tale of Two Cities,* and they are even now ready for the tales of the devotion of the monks in the Alps. Their animal stories frequently have this sort of tone as witnessed in *Black Beauty, Bob, Son of Battle, Wild Brother, Dog of Flanders, Lives of the Hunted,* and so on. Another interest which is common at this age is the interest in earning a living, often resulting in a relish for the most impossible tales of the path from the cottage to the mansion. They appreciate the importance of and the satisfaction in leadership and enjoy a tale in which one individual molds the behavior of many others. They have a very strong feeling for justice and are ruthless in its application, much less ready to concede the desirability of offering a second chance to a malefactor than an adult would be. They are perhaps becoming more religious and have very high ideals of saintliness. Particularly for the girls there seems to be a definite period when books of the "goody-goody" type satisfy a need. Children of this age often enjoy beauty and appreciate beautiful poetry or the description of scenes of beauty. They are also critical of the illustrations and object violently to pictures which contradict the text.

These young people want the development of the story to be logical and to seem possible, at least to their limited experience. They are becoming alert to inaccuracies and will give a book up in disgust if "there is no sense to it," which usually means that they cannot follow it from one point to another. They understand and value resourcefulness, and they admire the hero who knows just what to do upon all occasions. One of the old favorites, *Swiss Family Robinson,* seems to many adults an unutterable bore with its pedantic exposition of useful information, its preaching, and in the way in which each mistake made by Jack or Ernest teaches the other characters a lesson which they never forget. No member of this unusual family is real; we cannot believe in the perfect forethought with which Mrs. Robinson filled her remarkable bag, nor in the encyclopedic information and spotless character of Mr. Robinson; Fritz is surely too good to be true, Ernest too scholarly, and Francis too consistently charming; only Jack produces a bit of mischief at times which classifies him with the humans. But to the average child these difficulties are not apparent. A child can believe that his mother might foresee every possible contingency; that his father might have read every useful book and have remembered all the details; that his older brothers might be practically perfect, each in his own line; and the baby without sin. Every child admires forethought and information and resourcefulness; he would like to believe that if he were left on a desert island he, too, might be a most successful colonist whether in a tub-boat, a tree-house, or a rock-cliff dwelling. We must not, therefore, judge the logic of a child's book from the point of view of the informed adult.

Poetry

The poetry which the child enjoys after he leaves the years of *Mother Goose* and the jingles falls into various classes. Somewhat allied to the alliterative words of the early jingles are the nonsense poems which the older child appreciates. "Twas brillig and the slithy toves" rolls off his tongue as do many others written by Carroll. He enjoys Carroll's fashion of fitting new words to old verses and he tries fitting new words to old rhythms himself. This is the age when "My country 'tis of thee, I come from Germany, of thee I sing, I love thy sourkraut, etc." is terrifically funny.

In the second place, they like poetry which tells a story. They enjoy parts of "Hiawatha" and the ballads of wars and blood and thunder. "Paul Revere's Ride," "Barbara

Frietchie,'' ''Horatius at the Bridge,'' and many others, carry a thrill of courage and patriotism which breaks out in spontaneous declamations by the early adolescent.

Humorous Books

No account of children's books would be at all complete without special reference to humorous books. Good humor (see Anderson's *Happy Childhood*, Chapter X) for children is rare, probably for the reason that adults and children laugh at different sorts of things. Anything subtle is outside the range of the child's understanding. Clever dialogue, hidden implications and insinuations, situations in which the humor lies in a comprehension of standards and attitudes of foreign peoples, are simply not at all funny to the child. On the other hand, jibberish; repetitions of phrases with slight, if any, modifications in sound; accidents; deliberate embarrassment of others, seem to the adult crude and too senseless for consideration. One mother sat in an adjoining room watching three children between seven and ten as they played. Their ''play'' consisted of making up faces, twisting their bodies into unusual attitudes and making up ''words'' which meant nothing but ''sounded funny.'' This play had gone on for nearly half an hour when the mother called out, ''Why don't you children find something interesting to do instead of just acting silly?'' A thoughtful-minded nine-year-old came to the door and remarked, ''Do you know —what grown-ups think is silly, children think is funny.'' It is an unusual grown-up who can write and draw things which children consider really funny.

Of the things which children laugh at, one of the most common is the so-called ''slapstick,'' the kind of thing we used to see in moving pictures when Charlie Chaplin was hurling custard pies. Slapstick is somehow funny when it happens to other people. The person who falls down on the ice and drops

all his parcels is screamingly funny to children and to some
adults, but he is far from funny to himself. So, too, the person who by chance is dressed in an incongruous manner—the
grand lady who arrives at a dinner party in evening dress and
a pair of bedroom slippers, the man who absent-mindedly
sports large black vest buttons in the front of his dress-shirt,
the person on the street-car whose broken garter allows his
stocking to drop about his ankles—all provide much amusement. This type of humor includes the practical joke. When
it is at its best in children's books, it is, of course, incidental.
Not even the most giggly of children could laugh at a whole
book of slapstick. Some of the comic strips in the funny
papers, the old Katzenjammer series for example, are con-
vulsing to most children. *A Book of Cheerful Cats* presents
humor of this same general type in a bit more refined form.
In most of the best children's books, touches of this humor
come in. In *Aunt Green, Aunt Brown and Aunt Lavender* the
sentence, "Mr. Blue dropped both his cane and his hat and
sat down on his hat" seldom fails to bring forth a snicker,
partly for the illustration in the book but mostly for the mental picture which the words call up. Hugh Lofting is an artist
at producing this sort of humor for children. Parts of his
Dr. Dolittle books show a keen understanding of the child's
humor. One of the funniest (to the child) is in *Doctor
Dolittle's Circus* when the animals are rehearsing for a play
they are to give.

"For a club he used a cucumber—until he broke it in half over
Pantaloon [Gub-Gub], whom he was supposed to chase all around
the wagon for stealing the string of sausages. Then the prisoner took
the policeman's club away from him and ate it. . . . Gub-Gub [the
pig], in his part of the comic Pantaloon, had a hard time. He had to
make many entrances and many exits—bounding in and out with the
red-hot poker or the string of sausages. And in spite of the Doctor's
warning him repeatedly to go out carefully, he always forgot that the
wagon was moving, and, making his flying exit, he almost invariably
fell out of the wagon, upside down, into the road. Then the rehearsal

would have to be stopped while Mr. Pantaloon picked himself up and ran after his moving theatre to get on the stage again."

On the subject of clothes, this part is especially fruitful of laughs:

"Fitting suits to animals is not easy. Gub-Gub gave the most trouble. At the first dress rehearsal he came on with his suit upside down, and his wig back to front. He had his hind legs through the sleeves of the coat, wearing them as pants. . . . But Pantaloon's greatest trial was his trousers. When at last they did make him understand how his suit was to be worn, he at first fastened his trousers to a belt. But his stomach was so round and smooth his belt would keep slipping off it. And at the first few dress rehearsals whenever he ran on the stage (always chased by the policeman of course), as often as not he would lose his pants on the way and arrive on the stage wearing only a coat and a wig."

Then we have the type of humorous situation in which the amusement lies in the incongruousness and ridiculousness of the situation, the type of thing which some adults find so very funny in *Pickwick Papers*. The child's book which is the best example of this type of humor is Lear's *Nonsense Book*.

"There was an Old man with a beard,
Who said, 'It is just as I feared,
Two Owls and a Hen, four Larks and a Wren,
Have all built their nests in my beard.'"

*   *   *

"There was an Old Person whose habits
Induced him to feed upon Rabbits;
When he'd eaten eighteen, he turned perfectly green,
Upon which he relinquished those habits."

Practically all of these limericks are about old people; a few mention "young person" "young lady" or "young man," but none mention children. Does this daring to ridicule the elders perhaps make the limerick seem funnier to the children themselves? "The Owl and the Pussy Cat" and "Mr. and Mrs. Spikky Sparrow" are probably the best known of Lear's longer verses. "Calico Pie" has been reprinted in a charming little booklet. Part of Lear's charm lies without doubt in his drawings and many a child pores over the *Nonsense Botany* and snickers at the *Manypeeplia Upsidownia* and the *Piggiwiggia Pyramidalis.*

A picture book which is somewhat like *A Book of Cheerful Cats* and somewhat like the *Nonsense Book* is Benjamin Rabier's *Scènes Comiques dans la Forêt.* A lack of understanding of the French text will interfere with the comprehension of some of the pictures, but many of the situations are so clear that no explanation is necessary.

Along with the incongruous and the ridiculous come the things which are out of proportion. Many of Lear's jingles are about persons with very long noses, and the illustrations show noses so beyond the range of possibility that not even a tiny child could miss the intention. Then there is the element of surprise which often comes into humorous rhymes of this type. The story leads the reader to believe that something very important is going to happen and then suddenly stops with a "So he very soon went back to Dover."

A third type of humor which appeals to the child is that which gives him a feeling of superiority. This type is also very common among adults who laugh at things which make them feel wiser and more able than their fellows. There are few books which are composed entirely of this type of humor. One of the best is Lucretia Hale's *Peterkin Papers* in which the Lady from Philadelphia is the heroine, but in which children are made to feel somehow that her solutions were exactly the ones they would have given themselves, if their opinions had been asked. Much of the content of the *Peterkin Papers* is now definitely "out-of-date," and the average child fails to understand by himself the difficulties which arise, for example, when the horse is tied to the hitching post, but all can get the full fun out of the cup of coffee into which Mrs. Peterkin put salt instead of sugar. Then, too, if the necessary explanations are made, the modern child may feel superior to the characters in the *Peterkin Papers* because he realizes that people can meet such situations now by telephoning, by going in an automobile, and so on. This not only increases his understanding of the environment of children forty years ago, but adds to his own feeling of competence and so to the fun of the tale.

In other books the humor lies partly in the child's foreseeing the climax which is approaching, in his knowing what is going to happen to the persons in the story, even when these characters do not realize it themselves. "The White Goat" in *Poppy Seed Cakes,* where the children understand that the goat will come down off the roof in the end, is an example of this. The children feel the approach of the climax and listen for it with giggles and self-satisfied grins. This joy is all the greater, if they have heard the story before, just as riddles are more interesting to the child who knows the answer than to those who do not. In other stories the fun is supplied by the odd-sounding words or names. The stories of Andrewshek and his Auntie Katushka lose half their fun when a shy story-teller avoids the pronunciation by substituting "John and his Aunt Laura." Much of *Winnie-the-Pooh* will bring forth chuckles from the child of eight or nine, particularly the stories in which Pooh goes through experiences like those which they have known themselves. Some of the verses of *Funday* give humorous comments on everyday occurrences which strike a responsive note in the child.

Books Chosen by Children

The White House Conference suggests that certain factors other than subject-matter influence the child's choice of a book:

"Within certain age limits, children's reading preferences are often reflections of esthetic interest; when they say they dislike a book they often mean that they dislike the format and the type in which the book has been presented to them. . . . Children's own selections are influenced by the make-up of the book, by the illustrations, by the subject matter, by passing interest in the subject of the book, by its relation to a hobby, and by other things as well."—*Children's Reading: A Study of Voluntary Reading of Boys and Girls in the United States* (The Century Co., New York, 1932), p. 9 ff. and p. 49.

A child's choice of books will without doubt be influenced by his mental development, by his previous experience, and by the stories which are read and discussed by the older members of the family. There seems to be some tendency for the children in bookless homes to have a school reading-book or some adult book as their favorite, probably because they have no other books at hand. We know little at present about the influence of race upon the popularity of various books, though some librarians have reported that Negro children tend to select a somewhat different type of books from those chosen by the white children of the same neighborhood. Thus we note in the book on children's reading referred to above:

"Qualities of imagination cause Negro children to take an interest in imaginative literature long after most white children of the same age have turned to books of an informational character. To books on Africa they turn with tremendous interest."

It may be also that the child's state of health may influence the kind of reading which he enjoys at any particular time. Some of the library workers in hospitals have made some advance in working out lists of books which are desirable for different physical conditions: books for the very weak patient, books for the patient who is apt to be depressed, books for the patient who must not become too excited, and so on. Much more could be done in this line. We know far too little about the effect of different sorts of reading. It may be that the young girl, who amused her friends by selecting a book of arctic exploration as reading-matter for a long train trip in the hottest part of the summer, had some notion of the effect which reading had upon her. There is a whole field of research work waiting to be done in solving the problems of the effect which reading has upon the individual.

Summary

Whatever the type of book which the child selects or which is given to him to read, we may be sure that an interest in reading will in the end prove beneficial. We may gradually lead the child to more worth-while books and, if we expose him to a large number of them, he will come in time to recognize the ones which interest him most and which tell him most of what he needs to know at any given time. More and more the libraries are understanding the needs of the child and giving understanding attention to the problems of children's reading, but as the White House Conference Committee on children's reading puts it, "Public, school, and institutional libraries cannot completely cover the child's reading needs. Books that are personally owned have a deep influence, since they are read and re-read and lent by the child to his friends." The few (or happily, the many) books which a child owns himself need, of course, to be carefully selected, for they become old friends to whom the child may turn at intervals for years.

Selected List of Books for Children

Alice's Adventures in Wonderland by Lewis Carroll (Appleton, Macmillan)

Ameliar Anne and the Green Umbrella by Constance Heward (Macrae Smith)

Aunt Green, Aunt Brown, and Aunt Lavender by Elsa Beskow (Harper)

"Barbara Frietchie" in the *Poems of John G. Whittier* (Houghton Mifflin)

Blue Teapot, The, by Alice Dalgliesh (Macmillan)

Bob, Son of Battle by Alfred Ollivant (Nelson Doubleday)

Book of Cheerful Cats and Other Animated Animals, A, by
  J. G. Francis (Century)
Billy Goats Gruff (published separately by Macmillan and in many
  collections)
Child's Geography of the World by V. M. Hillyer (Century)
Child's History of the World by V. M. Hillyer (Century)
David Goes Voyaging by David B. Putnam (Putnam)
Day with Betty Anne, A, by Dorothy Baruch (Harper)
Dog of Flanders by Louise de la Ramee (Macmillan, Lippincott)
Dr. Doolittle's Circus by Hugh Lofting (Stokes)
Dutch Twins, The, by Lucy F. Perkins (Houghton Mifflin)
Engine That Could, The (in many collections such as *My Book-*
  house)
Fairy Tales by Hans Christian Andersen (Nelson, Dutton, Lip-
  pincott)
——————— by Grimm (Scribner, Macmillan)
——————— by Andrew Lang (Longmans Green)
First Picture Book, A, by Mary S. Martin (Harcourt Brace)
Funday by Ilo Orleans (Martin)
Heidi by Johanna Spyri (McKay, Ginn)
Here and Now Story Book by Lucy Sprague Mitchell (Dutton)
"Hiawatha" in the *Poems of Henry W. Longfellow* (Houghton
  Mifflin)
Hittie by Rachel Field (Macmillan)
Hole Book, The, by Peter Newell (Harper)
"Horatius at the Bridge" in *The Lays of Ancient Rome* by Thomas
  B. Macaulay (Dutton)
Jingleman Jack by J. O'Dea (Saalfield)
Johnny Crow's Garden by L. Leslie Brooke (Warne)
Just-So Stories, The, by Rudyard Kipling (Doubleday)
Karoo the Kangaroo by Kurt Wiese (Coward McCann)
Little Black Sambo by Helen Bannerman (Stokes)
Little Women by Louisa M. Alcott (Little Brown)
Lives of the Hunted by Ernest Thompson Seton (Scribner)
Mother Goose. Three of the best editions are: *Mother Goose* illus-
  trated by Blanche Fisher Wright (Rand McNally); Mother
  Goose in Silhouettes (Houghton Mifflin); and *Nursery Rhyme*
  Book collected by Andrew Lang (Warne)
Nonsense Books by Edward Lear (Little Brown)
"Paul Revere's Ride" in the *Poems of Henry W. Longfellow* (Hough-
  ton Mifflin)
Peggy and Peter by Lena Towsley (Farrar and Rinehart)

Peterkin Papers, The, by Lucretia Hale (Houghton Mifflin)

Peter Rabbit by Beatrix Potter (Warne)

Picture Book of Animals, A, by Isabel E. Lord (Macmillan)

Pioneer Twins, The, by Lucy F. Perkins (Houghton Mifflin)

Poppy Seed Cakes, The, by Margery Clark (Doubleday)

Queen Hildegarde by Laura E. Richards (L. C. Page & Co.)

Robinson Crusoe by Daniel Defoe (Houghton, Doubleday, Cosmopolitan)

Runaway Sardine, The, by E. Brock (Knopf)

Scènes Comiques dans la Forêt by B. Rabier (Librairie Garnier Freres, Paris)

Snipp, Snapp, Snurr and the Red Shoes by Maj Lindman (Whitman)

Social Science Readers by H. S. Read and E. Lee (Scribner)

Swiss Family Robinson by Johann D. Wyss (Harper, Dutton, Rand McNally)

Tale of the Wee Little Old Woman by Elsa Beskow (Harper)

Three Bears, The, illustrated by L. L. Brooke (Warne)

Three Pigs, The, illustrated by L. L. Brooke (Warne). This story and the preceding one appear in many collections such as *Chimney Corner Stories* by V. Hutchinson (Minton) and *Best Stories to Tell to Children* by Sara Cone Bryant (Houghton)

Tigers and Things by A. Kaufman (Macmillan)

Treasure Island by Robert Louis Stevenson (Scribner, Harper)

'Twas the Night before Christmas by Moore (Gabriel) and in many collections

Twins and Tabiffa, The, by Constance Heward (Macrae Smith)

Uncle Remus by Joel Chandler Harris (Houghton)

Wag and Puff by Marjorie Hardy (Wheeler)

When We Were Very Young by A. A. Milne (Dutton)

Wild Brother by William L. Underwood (Little)

Winnie-the-Pooh by A. A. Milne (Dutton)

Wonder Book, The, by Nathaniel Hawthorne (Houghton Mifflin. Also Doubleday)

Children's Encyclopedias

    Book of Knowledge, The (Grolier Society)

    Compton's Pictured Encyclopedia (Compton)

    Pictured Knowledge (Marshall Hughes)

    World Book Encyclopedia (Quarrie)

Chapter XI

MUSIC FOR CHILDREN

PROBABLY no person interested in the education and training of young children would disagree with the statement that all children should have the opportunity to become well acquainted with good literature. Nearly as many persons would agree that all young children should have a chance to hear good music, but there might be considerable vagueness in the replies, if the latter group were asked why music should be provided for children.

Importance of Music for the Child

The reasons usually given for offering music to children stress the fact that music provides a variety of opportunities for interpretation and creation (sometimes grouped as "self-expression"), emotional response, and intellectual response. Interpretation of music almost always takes the form of rhythmic movement. Rhythmic responses appear, as we have already said, very early in the life of the child. The baby waves his arms in fairly well-defined rhythms, not in isolated movements which are never repeated or which are made now very quickly and now very slowly. Later he kicks his feet alternately, and later still, walks, runs, skips, and gallops in various degrees of complexity of rhythm. Spaeth [1] has said that most of us listen to music with our feet. If a band is playing, all the pedestrians on a street will march to its time; when the orchestra plays in the concert hall, most of the

[1] S. Spaeth, *The Common Sense of Music* (Boni & Liveright, New York, 1924), p. 49.

audience will keep time with a foot, or a hand, or with movements of the head or throat. These are unplanned and often
unnoticed rhythmic responses to music.

The White House Conference has shown [2] that approximately half of the homes studied owned radios, and about 40
per cent owned phonographs or pianos. While these percentages are rather small when compared with the 70 per cent
which have automobiles, yet they indicate that most children
have access to some form of music. As might be expected the
higher socio-economic groups are more likely to have musical
instruments than are the less fortunate classes. The differences
are least marked in the ownership of phonographs, but they
come to more than four times as many pianos in the higher economic groups as in the lower.

Self-Expression in Music

When the opportunity is given for planned rhythmic responses, young children will respond with joy. The four- or
five-year-old will clap his hands enthusiastically in time to
music played in a clear simple rhythm, or he will show still
greater interest if given two blocks to clap together. Rhythm
sticks may tap the time on the floor, a block, or table, or they
may be struck together. And nothing is provocative of much
more hilarity than a march which may be stamped loudly as
a procession winds down a street or around a room.

Creation in the field of music most often takes the form of
singing. Improvisation of melodies in developed form requires,
of course, a special technique, but the improvisation of brief
series of tones is one of the natural types of response in children. Harriet M. Johnson [3] has reported a large number of
remarks which children in her nursery school have sung of

[2] *The Young Child in the Home: A Survey of Three Thousand American Families.*
[3] H. M. Johnson, *Children in the Nursery School* (The John Day
Co., New York, 1928), p. 107 ff.

their own accord without instruction or example. Almost any group of small children will develop short sing-songs which are repeated endlessly with great evidence of satisfaction. At one time the children in the nursery school at the University of Minnesota, coming in the bus in the morning, acquired the habit of reporting what they could see from the bus windows after this fashion:

These notes were sung with the words "I see a statue," "I see a street-car," "I see a ma-an" and so on. A few years later this song was partially revived in:

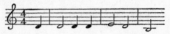

with the words "I see a funny ma-an." One brother and sister in the group varied the song in the summer vacation when driving about the city to:

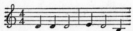

"Now I know my way home." It is interesting to note that these sing-songs vary only in rhythm and not at all in the succession of tones used. Another pair of children developed a rhythm which was spoken in a loud monotone. They were visiting in a small town which boasted of an old-style covered bridge as one of the two means of crossing the river. The children were fascinated with the bridge and every day when returning from a ride would chant together, *"Un*-cle *John* will *you* go *through* the *cov*-ered *bridge* when *you* go *home,* PLEASE!"

There is still another form of self-expression through music and that is in the expression of the emotions through music. For most children, this means merely singing when they are happy, being quiet or moaning when they are unhappy. For the true artist, in command of the necessary technique, expres-

sion of emotions through music may result in something of
beauty which will live for years, but such an expression is not,
of course, for the ordinary mortal.

Enjoyment of Music

Aside from providing opportunities for self-expression,
music may give the individual much happiness and a great intellectual interest. In all modern education, teachers try to
provide desirable forms of amusement and enjoyment for the
children. It is distinctly worth while to give a child an ample
acquaintance with music, if it means that, as an adult, he will
be able to enjoy concerts or enjoy making music for himself.
In this sense a musical education is a training for the profitable use of leisure time. If the individual enjoys listening to
music, there are many avenues open to him. Even if he lives
far away from a musical center with its symphony concerts,
its recitals, and its choruses, he may still have music from a
phonograph, from a mechanical piano, and from a radio. The
person who enjoys making his own music can whistle and sing
at will and can spend many happy hours with his piano, his
violin, or his flute.

Music may be listened to solely for the sake of the emotional enjoyment of the harmony, but it may, instead or at the
same time, be for the sake of the intellectual appreciation of
it. A fairly large number of persons probably get more intellectual than emotional enjoyment from music. This group is
composed of those who understand the technique of musical
composition and performance. They range from the individual
who ignores the sound of the music in his wonder at the speed
and accuracy with which the pianist can move his fingers over
the keyboard up to the individual who has a clear understanding of the music itself and of the performer's interpretation
as well. Such listeners get their enjoyment at least in part
from the understanding of technicalities which are beyond

the imagination of the ordinary audience, just as the expert
painter studies a painting from the point of view of technique,
while the average observer judges wholly from general im-
pression and the type of emotional response which the picture
calls up.

Opportunity for All

In view of the fact that music has so much to offer in the
way of self-expression and enjoyment, it is obvious that all
children should have contact with it and that all of them
should be at least exposed to musical training. The child who
seems to be non-musical really needs this training more than
the musical one, for the musical child will enjoy music with
or without training, while the child whose gifts are less evident may still learn to enjoy it under the proper tutelage. It
has been said that every child who possesses normal hearing
and a normal speaking voice can be taught to sing. Probably
the most important thing in the training of the un-musical
child is not to let him come to believe that he is not musical.
If he is made to feel that he has no ability in music, he will
lose all incentive and will fail to make the progress which
he could make, if he realized that his musical development depends only in part upon his inherited abilities.

The child who is really musical can often be detected at a
fairly early age. He will show a correct sense of rhythm and
an appreciation of pitch and melody. He will often pick up
any sort of a musical instrument and play familiar tunes
"by ear." He will learn songs very quickly from hearing
others sing them, and in many other ways he will display his
interest and ability. If a child is really musical and wants to
learn to play some instrument well, however, he will need not
only his native musical ability but good muscular control over
his fingers and a great deal of persistence, and he must be
willing to work hard. Many a possible musician is lost because
he is unwilling to spend the necessary hours in practising.

Singing

Although there are many forms which the child's musical training may take, every child should be encouraged to sing. Children learn singing through imitation, and the baby who has a singing mother is fortunate indeed. It does not take many months before the baby tries to sing with or in answer to the mother's songs. The songs which the two-year-old can manage are very simple, but they are true songs. They must be short for the child's attention soon wanders; they must appeal to his interest; and they must be pitched within the range of the small child's voice. One of the most popular songs among the youngest nursery school children is, ''The cow says 'Moo, there's milk for you,' '' where the air uses but two notes "G C' C' C', G C' C' C'" and where there is no complexity of rhythm. Many of the easy songs for young children are based on the tonic chord, C-E-G-C'. The child learns to sing accurately, just as he learns to pronounce words accurately, through trying over and over, through being corrected occasionally, and through listening to good examples. Teaching the child to sing music from the printed notes is, of course, a more difficult process than encouraging him to sing by imitation, and it is one that most parents do not feel qualified to undertake, but many of the modern schools are including this as part of their regular program.

One of the questions which one committee of the White House Conference asked parents was whether or not their child was learning to sing songs. The results show [4] that some children of even less than two years of age are learning songs and that more than a third of the two-year-olds, more than half the three-year-olds and nearly three quarters of the five-year-olds are learning to sing. In this type of learning we find little difference between the various socio-economic groups,

[4] *The Young Child in the Home: A Survey of Three Thousand American families.*

with a little more than half of the three highest groups and a little less than half of the four lowest groups represented.

Dancing

Another form of musical expression which develops early is dancing, of which one of the simplest forms is simple running to a musical accompaniment. If the pianist is alert and adapts her time to the movements of the trotting feet, the children will gradually get the feeling of the rhythm of the music. Although we have already suggested that children early show rhythmic movements of the body and that all young children love to march, marching is a bit more difficult. It is more satisfying, if it is accompanied by music, especially by music which has a clearly marked rhythm. Soldiers march better, if the band plays; sailors pull better on the ropes, if they sing a chantey; many a carpenter swings his hammer in time to his own whistling; and hikers often find that they walk up a long hill more easily, if they sing a marching song as they go. In fact, all effort is easier and less tiring when done rhythmically and the march rhythm is the simplest of all rhythms.

Unstudied rhythmic response to other types of music is just as natural for children as marching. If the two-year-old is offered a chance to "dance," while the piano is played, he will ordinarily produce a sort of jig with arms and feet in lively motion. The older child who is "turned loose" in a rolling meadow on a sunny day will spread her arms and dance through the grass, perhaps humming or singing, perhaps pretending she is a bird or a buttercup, perhaps just reveling in the sunshine and freedom of movement. Often when bands and orchestras give outdoor concerts, children will be seen dancing just beyond the group of adult listeners. Graceful movements, representing a butterfly, or a wave, or a threatening storm, are but little removed in the child's mind from crawling around on the floor and barking like a dog. They are all forms of expression through movement, and, if the child is encouraged at a fairly young age to interpret music through movement, he will do it as naturally and with as little self-consciousness as he plays bears and tigers.

Not only is this sort of dancing an outlet for self-expression, but it gives definite training in relaxation, for the natural dancing movements cannot be carried out with tense muscles. Satis Coleman suggests "the dead game" as a means of teaching relaxation. In this game relaxation is taught by requiring the children at a given signal to drop down, absolutely relaxed, as if they had been shot. Mrs. Coleman uses the word *dead* deliberately and finds no unpleasant reaction to the word on the part of the children.

"It is the 'grown-up' who is afraid of the word, but to children it appeals to the dramatic instinct as few words do. If I should ask Johnny to relax, he would probably see no use in it, and I would have a big undertaking in attempting to teach him how to relax; but if he is a bear walking on all fours through the forest or doing a wonderful bear dance, and a hunter appears and shoots him, he is instantly a dead bear, and more relaxed than anyone could teach him to be. I have also tried sleeping games, but the response is not so quick nor so effectual. Sleep is too common an experience with children to have the same effect. It is not dramatic enough. A little 'dead music'—very soft, quieting strains—will help to keep the children absolutely lifeless as long as seems best for them. Later the dramatic preparation may be omitted; and the moment I see signs of fatigue in a child, all I have to do is to point my finger at him and say, 'Bang!' and he is instantly flat on the floor or on the couch." [5]

Other workers believe that playing "rag doll" accomplishes the same effect. Whatever the method used, surely a child who has learned to relax completely upon occasion will be less likely to succumb to serious fatigue than will be the child who has not learned this valuable art.

Folk-dancing is often introduced into the physical activities of young children and should hold an important place there.

[5] Satis N. Coleman, *Creative Music for Children* (G. P. Putnam's Sons, New York, 1922).

Many of the folk-dances are simple forms of a pleasing rhythm, performed in a group as a sort of game. The interest in these dances is, of course, increased, if the children see pictures of people entering into the dance in native costume. Although it is not practicable always to supply the children with the costumes, surely we may tell them something of the people who originated the dance. All of this broadens the child's interest in other countries and increases his understanding of other peoples. The chief fascination of folk-dances, however, seems to lie in the feeling of unity which they give; all the group are doing the same thing and each individual is an integral part of the whole.

Most persons would agree that every child living in a community where most of the people like to go to dances should learn social dancing. The age at which different children are taught social dancing is extremely varied. The White House Conference has found [6] that, as we would expect, more girls take dancing lessons than do boys. While some 15 per cent of girls of ages six and seven take some sort of dancing lessons, this figure drops to 9 per cent for ages ten to twelve; for boys, the corresponding figures are 3 and 6 per cent. Also to be expected is their finding that dancing lessons are almost wholly confined to the three highest socio-economic groups. There can be little doubt that the children from the poorer groups learn to dance from other children instead of in definite classes, and that much of this learning comes at the high school age which is not covered by the White House Conference work.

It is safe to say that the child who has been encouraged to respond naturally to music; who has become fairly well acquainted with various rhythms in music; and who has, perhaps, had lessons in interpretive or natural dancing, will learn social dancing in a very short time.

[6] *The Young Child in the Home: A Survey of Three Thousand American Families.*

Music Lessons

Singing and dancing are forms of musical experience which every normal child will encounter in some form or other. There are other forms of musical training, however, which are offered to only a limited group of children. When we speak of *music lessons* we usually mean lessons in the playing of some instrument, nine times out of ten, the piano. It is unfortunate that the piano has come to be used so much because it is one of the most difficult instruments for the young child to master. The next most common instrument, the violin, is also exceedingly difficult for small children to manipulate. The easiest of all instruments is the drum. Here, of course, there is just one tone which is to be sounded at the appropriate time. The drum gives the simplest combination of tone and rhythm. In the children's bands in the earliest grades, the instruments used are sometimes just drums and bells, each in a single tone. The children learn the appropriate time for the introduction of each of the instruments (drum and bells) and so combine two tones with rhythm.

There are a number of simple percussion instruments in which the child may be given as many or as few notes as he is ready to use. Musical glasses can be made in any home. Some glass has a purer musical note when struck than other glass, but any ordinary drinking glass will give a usable tone. Since the pitch of this tone may be raised by pouring water into the glass, a set of three or four glasses may be tuned to desired tones and will then furnish a "keyboard" on which the child can play any melody which uses those particular notes. The eraser at the end of a lead-pencil will serve as a satisfactory striker. One advantage of this musical instrument is that it can be constructed by the child. In such construction, the child learns a great deal about the physics of tone to say nothing of the added joy of using something which he has made himself. Sets of bells which are tuned to one key may be obtained and the presence of tones which are not to be used will thus be avoided. Another simple instrument is the marimba or xylophone. Here, as in the case of the glasses and bells, a few notes may be supplied at a time. For the youngest children it is probably better to get a marimba with the four notes *C, E, G,* and *C'* or, if this is impossible, to remove the notes that are not to be used. Given these four notes and plenty of opportunity to experiment, the average child will improvise all sorts of little melodies and will play without effort the songs which he has been taught, provided, of course, that these songs are based on the tonic chord. One of the greatest difficulties with the piano and violin is the presence of a great number of notes and the necessity for selection. When the number is strictly limited, this confusion largely disappears.

The instruments which have been suggested are all percussion instruments, and they require only a moderate degree of muscular control. The playing of stringed instruments, excepting the piano, requires considerable strength in the fingers of the left hand as well as steadiness in the hand which draws the bow or plucks the strings. This means that for children below the age of eleven or twelve there is little chance that the use of a stringed instrument will produce any real music or will be anything more than a plaything. The same age limitations appear in the use of the wind instruments. Younger children can perhaps handle a harmonica or a very simple form of the pipes of Pan, but they have not the muscular control of the lungs or of the lips to make their performance on the ordinary wind-instrument anything more than occupation for an idle hour.

Frequently a child who has to be forced to practise, when he is taking music lessons by himself, will work for hours at a time learning to play an instrument in a school orchestra or band. One reason lies doubtless in the joy of being a contributing member of a group. Just as piano-practice is less drudgery, if you are working on a duet or if mother sits nearby to offer an appreciative word now and then, so it is much more fun to rehearse in a group. The objective is closer at hand. After a few months of work, the orchestra can play together with credit to the whole group, but the recital of a lone person who has been working for the same length of time on a single instrument is often an agony for performer as well as for audience.

If an individual can acquire some degree of skill in playing any one instrument, he will have laid the foundation for a greater understanding of all music as well as for a source of enjoyment to himself. In learning music it is not a case of a "little knowledge being a dangerous thing," but rather a case of the more we know of the various arts the better. Just as understanding one foreign language broadens our cultural horizon, so does the playing of some one musical instrument deepen our appreciation of others.

As in the case of dancing, we find[7] that girls are given music lessons more often than boys. A good many children (15 per cent of the girls and 8 per cent of the boys) have begun their musical training by the time they are six or seven years old. By the time they are from ten to twelve years old, we find 26 per cent of the boys and 42 per cent of the girls taking music lessons. Music lessons are not so strictly limited to the higher economic groups as are dancing lessons, for although we find 40 per cent or more of the first and second socioeconomic groups being given these lessons, the percentage does not fall below seventeen until we reach the two very lowest groups.

A generation ago the child who was given piano lessons received much training in scales and exercises planned to develop finger control and technique. This sometimes led to considerable dexterity in execution and perhaps to an ability to read music at sight. Usually such musical education, if it can

[7] *Ibid.*

be so called, stopped at that point. It left the pupil with no realization that there were any laws of musical composition or that there was any sense to music other than a more or less pleasing series of tones when the teacher and the more able pupils performed and an agonizing acrobatic struggle, accompanied by intermittent nerve-wracking discords, when the playing was undertaken by the less gifted pupils. The modern music lesson, on the other hand, recognizes the importance of teaching the child theory as well as technique. Some teachers of music believe that musical theory can be taught best through the actual construction of various instruments, the work of tuning them to the desired key, and the composition of melodies to be played upon the instruments after they are made. As in the case of almost all forms of knowledge and especially of all the arts, the more we know about the subject, the more we understand and appreciate the work of others.

Appreciation of Music

Closely connected with the teaching of the theory of music is the appreciation of music. More and more we are coming to realize that this depends, at least in part, upon our understanding of the language of music, of the ways in which musical tones are combined, and of the laws of form and structure of music. Children are taught, for example, to recognize the theme or melody, to know when it reappears and what the changes are which have been made in it, and to understand why the melody isn't simply repeated over and over, and so on. They learn the meaning of some of the most common musical terms, so that they can better understand any discussion of music which is not strictly technical.

But musical appreciation does not depend wholly on the intellectual comprehension of what the composer is trying to do. It depends to an even greater extent on familiarity with good

music. Just as the classics of literature and the masterpieces of painting are well worth a second, a third, and even a tenth and eleventh study, so the masterpieces of music are worth hearing many, many times. As in the case of literature, each time that we renew our acquaintance with a masterpiece we see beauties which we have passed over before, and we experience the pleasure of renewal of old friendships, a relief like that of abandoning strenuous work to sink into the familiar comfort of a favorite arm-chair. Children may learn to enjoy the melodies of great musical compositions long before they can appreciate the masterpiece in its entirety. Other simple melodies—folk-tunes and the great hymns—are well within the comprehension of the child.

It is no longer necessary to seek the city, if we desire to hear the best in music. The reproducing piano brings to any home the most famous of piano selections, played with a technique and an interpretation which is seldom found at the concerts given in a small town. The phonograph brings us the best-loved songs in history, sung by the best of singers, some of them no longer living. Perhaps we miss the glory of exaltation which our grandmothers felt when they heard Patti sing, because for them that singing stood out from a mass of inferior singing, whereas the irreverent great-grandchild may retort, "Sure, I put on Caruso every night"; but there can be no indecision in choosing between one superior evening of song and many such evenings. The phonograph brings us also the music of many instruments, and the child may learn not only to distinguish between the different ones but also to listen critically to the same composition played by various artists on different instruments and in different keys. Of the radio and what it has done to bring music to isolated sections of the country, it is impossible to say too much. We may complain about much of the music which comes from the radio, and yet there is seldom a time when we cannot find some sending station which is broadcasting really good music. It is amazing to

find the number of people who have been, until recently, almost isolated from musical centers but who now recognize not only the voices of the announcers but also those of the soloists. They have learned a great deal about the best music and have found great pleasure in that which they are now able to hear. Nor can too much be said in praise of the contribution which Damrosch has made to the musical education of the country.

Summary

In summary we may say that every child should be given the opportunity for acquaintance with music. The child may dance, or sing, play an instrument, or merely listen to others. His type of response is of far less importance than his need for opportunity to enter into one of most accessible fields of culture and enjoyment.

Chapter XII

VACATIONS AND SPECIAL DAYS

THERE is an old saying that "All work and no play makes Jack a dull boy." This saying is true but no truer than that "All play and no work makes Jack a dull boy." Psychologists have shown experimentally that we do not accomplish as much or work as easily when we keep at any occupation without rest. Certain factories have shown that more work is done in a shorter total time when the laborer has brief rest periods at fairly frequent intervals. Teachers recognize the fact that the children do better work and are more contented, if their occupations are varied and if action and rest alternate. Not only is it tiring to be steadily active for a long period, but it is also tiring to sit still for a long time. Even the most enthusiastic church-goer is glad to stand to sing a hymn at the end of an hour-long sermon. Industry has found that one day or one day and a half off in seven or the reported Russian plan of one day off in five will bring about better results than work every day. Certainly many people would prefer to work six hours a day for seven days rather than seven hours a day for six days.

The Value of Variation in the Child's Schedule

The reasons cited above for periodic interruptions of school work or any other type of occupation have been those concerned largely with efficiency and the feelings of fatigue. But there are other reasons for occasional breaks in routine. From the point of view of physical health, every one profits from an occasional rest. Frequently a beginning cold can be

checked by a day in bed, if there is an available day to spend there. In schools for young children or in any grouping of young children, the two-day week-end frequently serves to stop the spread of a contagious disease. For example, a child may be feeling not quite his usual self on Friday. The mother thinks, "Oh, well, it won't hurt him to miss one day of school," and she keeps him home that day. If some contagious disease develops before Monday, the other children have not been exposed.

Still another advantage of a break in the usual routine comes in the form of a social advantage. All of us are fonder of each other and get along together more happily, if we are not constantly together. Whether we glibly repeat, "Absence makes the heart grow fonder," or talk in the more erudite terms of Virginia Woolfe's "Room of One's Own," we come to the same conclusion. The mother who spends twenty-four hours a day, seven days a week, with her children does not enjoy them nearly as much as the mother who has an hour or two "off" each day and a half-day off a week. A little precious absence removes the need for the remark that the children "get on her nerves." So with the children themselves. The constant society of other children or of the same group of children means scraps, fights, bickerings, exhibitions of selfishness, and so on. Nursery schools have found that the one seldom-failing cure for emotional difficulties is the separation of the children concerned. A fierce enemy rarely seems so horrible the next day. One tends to forget the unpleasant when it is not forced upon him and this fortunate forgetting means that, although a child could not bear a certain playmate in June, he may find him friendly and interesting in September. They have both grown up in the meantime and are no longer suffering under the disadvantage of fatigue.

And so we find that occasional breaks in schedule, whether they be at the week-end or for a longer vacation, serve to heighten efficiency, to increase resistance to disease, to lessen

the probability of exposure, and to smooth out minor social maladjustments.

In order to accomplish these ends, the break in the schedule, or let us say, the vacation must provide a real change of occupation. The child who is required to spend Saturday and Sunday making up school work which has been missed or in which he has failed, the mother who leaves her convenient city kitchen to slave for still more ravenous appetites in a crowded camp lean-to over an unpredictable stove, the father who leaves his office only to sit on a hotel porch talking his same old business problems with half a dozen other men whose recreational possibilities are likewise limited—none of these is having a real vacation. There is in each case a change of scene, but the occupation remains practically the same.

A change of occupation in itself provides some small amount of rest and relaxation, but in order to derive the greatest benefit from such a change, the vacation occupation should be interesting as well as different. We have all heard people say that they were so bored on their vacation that they enjoyed getting "back in the harness again." Sometimes it may be worth while to be uncomfortable on a vacation just to learn what pleasure we do get out of our work, and those of us who have held positions in which we literally did not have enough to do to keep us busy realize that there are worse states than that of feeling that we have too much to do. Yet neither of these states is the ideal one for a real vacation in which our forces—physical, mental, and emotional—are to be recuperated.

All that is true of adults is still more true of children. Children fatigue more quickly than adults, and they also recover more quickly. Some years ago the writer saw a five-year-old child who had been on a rather tiring shopping-trip with her mother. The child seemed to be enjoying her experience greatly until they started to take the street-car home. Then she almost collapsed on the street, and it was only under urging and continued encouragement that she walked the necessary three blocks to the street-car. The car which they boarded was fortunately almost empty, and the little girl stretched herself out, completely relaxed, on one of the long seats. A few blocks were traversed in silence, and then the child jumped up, alert and fresh as a daisy, saying, "I wish I could jump rope right now on the car." In the space of some fifteen minutes, fatigue had come and passed. This rapid fatiguing and rapid recovery on the part of the child mean, in the first place, that no child should be expected to stick to a job as long as an adult could. It means that school periods and school days for young children should be short. It is perfectly possible that, if we were logical, we might say that it means, too, that the vacation periods should be short also. Maybe children would be happier and would learn more easily, if their nine months of schooling were distributed evenly throughout the year. Suppose, for example, that their school vacations were the entire months of July, November, and March, or even that they had two weeks vacation in each of the months July, September, November, January, March, and May.

We have come to take for granted the three periods of public schools with short vacations at Christmas and Easter and a long vacation in the summer, but, if we hunt back in the history of the elementary schools, we find that the length of the school year once varied with the finances of the town concerned. Brookline, Massachusetts, for example, had twelve months of school in 1727, ten months in 1730, and only four months in 1732. The length of the school week also varied. Between 1800 and 1830 school kept every day of the week except Sunday and did not have even Christmas or New Year's as holidays. Between 1830 and 1860, some schools did not keep on Saturday afternoon, so that the teacher would have a time for "doing her washing." Other schools in this period allowed "the customary Wednesday and Saturday afternoons" without specifying the reason, while one of a little earlier period allowed the teacher "two days in every quarter of the year to visit his friends if he sees cause to take up with it." Between 1860 and 1900, Saturday became a full holiday and has remained so ever since. This seems to be the result of a custom which was arranged to meet the convenience of one particular section and has settled into a confirmed habit without consideration of its present value.

The Summer Vacation

Whatever may be, theoretically, the best distribution of schooldays and vacation, as things are now, parents and children are faced with the problem of what to do in the long summer holiday. We have already suggested that this occupation should be different from the school routine and that it should be interesting. It should also be worth while, not mere futile amusement for week after week but something constructive that will teach the child more than he has known of nature, of animal life, of machinery, or of anything in which he is interested. In the choice of worth-while occupations for the vacation we need not be sugar-coating a pill of information for the child, but we can give him something which he really enjoys. The average child has a consuming curiosity about everything he sees. It is absolutely impossible to satisfy this curiosity in every respect in school, so why cannot the vacation help?

There is probably no play or recreation which can compete in health-building possibilities with the play which the child gets at the seashore or at a lake. In sand and water and mud the child finds almost perfect play materials; and in the sunshine, fresh air, freedom of movement, absence of strain, and relief from the dangers of the city street, he finds the best agencies for rebuilding the bodily vigor and nervous control which shut-in winter life may have weakened. The farm offers endless delight with its friendly animals; its contact with men doing things which are interesting to children and which leave plenty of time for the workers to answer questions and to carry on all sorts of fascinating discussions; with its space to roam; its fields to explore; perhaps its brook to wade; its bountiful meals; and, perhaps most delightful to the child, the need for wearing old clothes, and the expectation that every one will get dirty before the day is over.

For the child who has neither a home near a lake nor relatives on a farm, and for every child once in a while, the modern summer camp is a joy. Sometimes we find children who have started their yearly sojourn at camps at so young an age that the novelty has worn off before they are old enough to get the greatest joy from the camp activities. Most children, however, who spend from two weeks to two months in a well-run camp, revel in the sports, in the rough life, and even thrill over making their own beds and obeying camp rules in a way that produces a never-ending wonder in their parents. It is largely a case of every one doing the same thing. An early bedtime is a pleasurable thing in a camp where every one else has it too, whereas it seems a disgrace and a punishment in a neighborhood where others are allowed to stay up later. The ''lights-out'' bell of the boarding-school or the call to early prayers in the convent school do not seem harsh, unnecessary intrusions on personal rights when every one else is obeying them at the same time.

The White House Conference says:

"We are interested that each one of all the children of all the people may have during vacation time . . . that life which shall mean most to him. . . . The well run camp is one of the most educative of available institutions. But not all children can go to camp. . . . One fact stands out clearly from the survey of vacation activities of the school child. There is grave need for thought, planning and provision for these periods in the child's development. The vacation time is an empty one for the majority of children in this country. The reports show that of 32,000,000 children, 4,000,000 urban and at the utmost 1,000,000 rural children have advantages of playgrounds; about 100,000 are in camps for a period as long as two weeks. A few

All Children Revel in Lake and Ocean

attend vacation schools, and a comparatively small number—about 3,000—are given all-day care in summer play schools. Of the remaining 27,000,000 a few travel or find constructive home life on vacation tours, or in the country, in the mountains or at the seashore with their parents. The vast majority are without facilities for enriching experience."—*The School Health Program* (The Century Co., New York, 1931), p. 266 ff.

Summer in the City

For the family who has to stay in the big city during the summer, there are many possibilities. That is the time to make full use of the public library and of the art museum and of the parks. That is the time to visit the factories and industries which are typical of the city. That is the time to enter into the games which are conducted in the public playgrounds, to take swimming lessons at the Y.M.C.A. or the Y.W.C.A. Perhaps that is the time to take those music lessons or those dancing lessons which could not be crowded into the busy winter time. Perhaps that is the long-awaited opportunity to have mother teach the children to cook, or to have daddy teach them to use tools. Summer offers a good opportunity to give children more responsibility than they have had before. The younger children may be made responsible for washing the breakfast dishes, or for making their own beds and keeping their own belongings in order; older brothers and sisters may take charge of the yard, seeing that it is mowed, raked, and watered sufficiently; or they may be responsible for preparing one of the meals, preferably breakfast for that is the simplest and does not interfere with the day's play. Many homes can find special tasks which can be handed over to some child: the sweeping of the porch every morning; the picking of certain flowers, like pansies, which need daily attention; the feeding of pet animals, and so on. Such duties may be too much for the child during the school year, but they will provide excellent experience during vacations when other routine tasks are at a minimum. If a child is to spend the summer at home, plan ahead to let him do some big thing which he has been wanting to do for a long time, like starting some big construction or learning to play some game of skill. Any good-sized town or small city will provide tennis courts and golf links; almost any back yard will make a good croquet ground.

Most families can arrange a number of trips and picnics through the summer. If these include camping out or staying at a cottage over a night or two, they are all the more profitable and enjoyable; but if they last merely for one day, they still have much to offer. They should be planned so that the place is interesting. We cannot take a group of children to a vacant lot, in which there is nothing to do but roll in the grass or attempt to climb an unclimbable tree, and expect them to be happy for an entire day, but we can turn them loose in a wooded dell with a brook, or on a sandy lake shore, especially if we have been foresighted enough to bring balls or a game of quoits or something of the kind to fall back upon when other plays pall.

If, however, there is no wholly desirable place like a camp or a cottage or a farm for the child and if the child must adapt his vacation to the vacation needs or desires of the adults, then there may be trouble. The ordinary summer hotel with its fastidiously kept golf course and its row of gossiping bridge players is no fit place for a lively child. Some of the more alert summer hotels are equipping playgrounds and are actually engaging playground instructors and swimming teachers for the children. Such a hotel is obviously a better place for the children, for they will be under fairly reliable supervision while the parents engage in their own amusements. At least one of the women's colleges offers every summer courses which provide information and intellectual stimulation for the mother and at the same time offers nursery-school training for any preschool children she may wish to bring to school with her. Such a scheme provides a high type of vacation for a mother who has become rusty in her college work or who wants to learn more of the development and training of young children. It solves her problem of how to have her child cared for while she returns to school, to say nothing of the great benefits which the child may be expected to derive from six weeks' training at a good nursery school.

Long Trips

Long automobile trips are not the joy to most children that they are to the average adult. Children of seven or eight or less do not enjoy sight-seeing; they cannot get from watching the unfolding landscape the rest and relaxation which comes to the tired grown-up, although an occasional child can be found who thoroughly enjoys long hours of riding. Usually these are children who have, for most of their lives, been accustomed to longer or shorter trips or they are the children who are naturally placid and prefer sedentary occupations. The typical small child, however, is a bundle of energy which demands and should, whenever possible, be provided with greater opportunity for lively play than is possible in an automobile. Generally speaking, a vacation which involves taking children of the preschool age on long trips is in reality a vacation for neither mother or child and is followed by a distressing period of a week or two of getting rested from the strain of the journey. When, however, it becomes necessary to take the child on a long automobile, train, or boat trip, there are certain things which the parent may do which will make the trip much happier for every one concerned.

Boat trips are ordinarily monotonous for the small child. Children are bored with sitting on deck after the first half hour or so; they are frequently an annoyance to the other passengers in the saloon and a source of anxiety to the parents, if they roam the decks. One two-year-old child nearly exhausted her parents on a four-hour boat trip on Long Island

Sound. She did not want to sit still and play with her doll; there was too much breeze to play with bits of paper; she had no kite or other wind plaything; her mother objected to her climbing around the seat which ran along the railing. She was fairly contented only when she walked round and round, so the parents took turns walking with her and at last she found just the plaything she wanted—a fire-bucket half full of water! Then a sailor came up to say that even that was forbidden! Her nap was some hour or so overdue, and her mother succeeded in getting her to sleep on a fairly comfortable bench only to have the boat blow off steam. The child awoke screaming and was fretful for the rest of the trip. Needless to say, such journeys should be avoided! For longer boat trips, where the family has a state-room, the problem is much less acute. In fact, there is little problem at all. The state-room gives ample room for fairly active play; the boat is steady enough, except in very rough weather, to allow the use of pencils, crayons, and scissors; and the surroundings, the berths, the passing steamers, the waves, and so on, provide added local color to the play.

If one is taking a long train trip with children, there are certain essentials to be met in selecting the play materials. Obviously they should be light in weight, if they are to be carried from one train to another; and they should be fairly small, if they are to be packed and repacked. Obviously, also, if the family is traveling in an ordinary sleeping-car, the toys must be small enough to be used adequately in a sleeping-car section; if the family is provided with a drawing-room on the train, then, of course, the child has somewhat greater play space. The limitations of space and the rights of the other passengers on the train require that nothing like balls or horns or mouth-organs be taken. The material must also be fairly easy to clean up. Paper scraps can be swept up by the porter with little difficulty, but clay or plasticene imposes unnecessary work on the person who cleans up. If possible, the

toys should have a variety of uses so that they may be used one hour for one thing and another for another, and they should be something which the child can use without assistance—unless, of course, some adult happens to want to spend the day playing with the child. Usually old toys are not as desirable for trips as are new ones or those which are variations of some loved toy. Often a new doll or a new outfit of clothes for an old doll will give much more pleasure on a journey than something the child has been playing with for months at home. The material must also be something the child can do something with.

For children of nine or ten or less a mother who has for many years taken an annual train trip lasting several days suggests the following: crayons and books to color; scissors and pictures to cut out; pads of paper in assorted colors; a note-book and pencil (which can be used by an older child to keep a record in words and pictures); a magic drawing-book in which the pictures are produced by rubbing a pencil over an apparently blank page; a note-book with a carbon paper such as is used in stores for making sales-slips; paper-dolls with clothes to cut out; gummed picture puzzles, with small parts to cut out and stick on the appropriate place in an out-line picture; small nests of boxes and small sets of blocks for very young children; miniature sets of doll furniture and tiny paper-dolls; a celluloid doll some three or four inches tall; scraps of cloth, scissors, and rubber bands to make "dresses" for the doll (the rubber bands hold the cloth in place and take the place of pins or sewing); a magnet and set of things to be lifted with it; puzzles which do not have to be held steadily (the motion of train makes certain ones too difficult, but puzzles where the trick is to take things apart in a certain way are often amusing); trick boxes where a hidden spring produces remarkable results. If there are two or more children traveling together, then, of course, there will be opportunity to play Old Maid, or similar card games. This same mother sug-

gests that the adult, planning for a long trip for children, see to it that the children be kept in ignorance of what play material has been provided and that one bit of play material be produced at a time, with no suggestion that there is more to follow. When the child tires of one material, it can be put away and something new produced. It is a good idea to have some five or six things along on any trip, although the child must not come to feel that he will be given something new every ten or fifteen minutes. If he gets this notion, he will fail to settle down to play with any one thing. If the trip is to be a long one, the foresighted parent will save something particularly interesting for the last stretch. For such a trip, the big five-and-ten-cent stores are a mine of possible material. Keeping in mind the tastes and interests of the particular child one is planning for, one can walk slowly up and down the aisles of such a store looking at each section, whether it be postal-cards, pencils, safety-pins, or hardware, asking oneself all the time, ''What could the child do on the train with those things?'' By giving just as much, if not more, attention to the counters of household supplies and favors as to the ordinary toy counters, one can leave the store loaded with fascinating material and with one's purse still unstrained and ready for tips and taxi-fares.

For automobile trips, many of the same rules apply that hold for train trips. There are certain exceptions, however. In an auto, if the immediate family can stand it, the child can have noise-makers, such as horns, whistles, or toy accordions. It may be possible to take along the family dog, and the child will usually spend much time playing with him. There are, of course, limitations to the car. It is much more difficult to draw or color or cut accurately in an automobile than on a train, and probably this should not be permitted on account of the child's eyes. Dolls, toy trains, sets of toy animals, or tiny trucks and cars can sometimes be used, particularly if it is possible to give the child the back seat to him-

self. Some children will settle themselves on the floor of the car, use the back seat as a sort of table or shelf and play happily by themselves for long stretches of time, relieved by periods of sitting up on the seat to see what is passing by. One advantage of the automobile is that the adults are not ordinarily trying to amuse themselves by reading, as they so often do on the train. They are much more in the mood for chatting with the child informally about the things they pass and they are generally more companionable and less easily upset than they are on the train. Another advantage of the trip by car is that it is possible to stop occasionally during the day and, of course, every evening so the child can have some really active play. For these periods of the day it is desirable to have some toys which encourage vigorous activity such as balls and jumping ropes, although often just a chance to run and caper is sufficient.

Games for the Car

Children frequently become restless on a long automobile ride, but they need not, if some one in the group will remember one of the dozens of delightful games which may be played from a car. One of the oldest of these used to be called ''Traveler's Whist.'' According to the rules of the game, the occupants of the car (once, of course, it was the carriage) are divided into two teams, according to whether they sit on the left-hand or the right-hand side, and each side tries to count the people and animals that are passed on their side. Sometimes the rules give one credit for each animal or human being. Sometimes there are more detailed rules, one set allowing ''25 for each cat, 50 for a cat in a window, and 500 for a school-teacher.'' Since the team on the left-hand side of the car has more chance to pass other people in cars, sometimes the teams exchange sides at some predetermined time, and sometimes, neither side is allowed to count persons in other cars.

Then there are the games which can be played with the

signs which are seen from the two sides of the car. Sometimes the rule is that the first sign you can count must have an "A" in it, the second a "B" and so on and the side that first finds the entire alphabet in signs wins. In this game street signs, store signs, bill boards, all count.

There are also many games which may be developed out of the license tags of passing cars. Sometimes a family divides into two teams and records every different State license which they see. This game need not, of course, be played on the road, and it may last over several days or even weeks. Another game which uses license tags is to see who can first get a whole set of numbers, i. e., first a tag with a "1" in it, then a tag with "2," and so on up into the hundreds, if it is desired to set the limit there. The goal of still another game is to see how many license tags contain three of the same number. Thus, the requirement might be "numbers containing three 2's." In this case 122-342, 212-324, and so on, would count a point each, but 252-333 would not.

The Week-End

We have been discussing the longer holidays which come only once a year. But every week we have a shorter holiday in the week-end, Saturday and Sunday. To provide the utmost of rest, the week-end, like the longer vacation, should provide a real change from the schooldays. Some way or other, these days should be different from the rest of the week. If the child has to be hurried every school morning to get through his dressing and his breakfast, it is a good plan to give him more time on Saturday and Sunday; let him lie abed, if he wants to; let him dawdle with his dressing; let him stop to philosophize while his cereal cools in its dish; let him for a while forget the clock. Many children, of course, don't consider it a privilege to lie in bed late. In fact, all too often, they dread Sunday because they must keep still and let the grown-ups sleep late. Such children obviously should not be forced to stay in bed. Let them get up provided they can do it quietly, and what child will not creep about and tiptoe downstairs to avoid an hour of boredom in bed?

Often the mere fact that they do not have to go to school makes Saturday an interesting day for the children, but, if it is merely a day of tiring shopping-trips, of trips to the dentist, of music lessons and practising, most of its joy is gone. Part of every Saturday, the child should be left to his own devices, allowed to choose his own occupation, his own companions, and to feel that for the time being he is a free agent. Saturday should be a happy day, a restful day, and an interesting day.

Sunday

Sunday also should be a happy day, a restful day, and an interesting day, and it should, moreover, be a family day. For most families Sunday is outstanding because it is the day that daddy is at home. It is often different because the schedule for meals is not the same as that for other days. Many people carry happy memories of foraging in the ice-box for impromptu Sunday night suppers, for weird collections of food which would be scorned by any self-respecting cook and utterly prohibited by mother at any other meal in the week. Why mothers should consider that what you eat Sunday night won't hurt you, when they are most careful about other meals, I do not know, but I have not heard of stomachaches being more common Sunday night than they are on any other night. Perhaps the delightful informality of standing round the kitchen, lunching on odd left-overs, or sitting by the open fire, eating all sorts of toasted creations, serves as a counteracting digestive force.

The time-honored way for the children to spend part of Sunday morning is in attending Sunday School. One committee of the White House Conference asked families whether or not the children had ever attended Sunday School. They found [1] that attendance increased steadily from about 15 per cent of children between the ages of one and two to 78 per cent before the age of nine. This does not mean that 78 per cent of all the eight-year-old children are now attending Sunday School, but that that per cent have at some time attended Sunday School. "It is clear . . . that as children grow older attendance at Sunday School becomes much more regular. Only thirty-six percent of the one-year-old children attended Sunday School four times within the month previous to the interview, as contrasted with some seventy percent for the ages eight to ten and sixty-six percent for the ten to thirteen year-olds. Furthermore, children of the upper socioeconomic groups attend Sunday School more frequently than do those of the lower groups.

Sunday School may perform a double function in the life of the child. In some homes, the day seems a long drag of quietness and repression of activity, in which case Sunday School provides a happy break. As most modern Sunday Schools are conducted, they offer a pleasant place to learn Bible stories, to hear moral tales of all sorts, and to join in singing the hymns which should be a part of every child's experience.

The second function which Sunday School may perform is that of introducing the child to religious education. The question of how much creed, what notions of immortality, of divine intervention in human affairs, and so on, should be taught to a young child will have to be answered by each individual family. Childhood is certainly not the time to introduce Biblical criticism or conflicting notions. The young child is sometimes much upset by not being able to believe whole-heartedly in supernatural forces. Much that happens in the world around him seems to him supernatural, and he easily adopts the faith of his teachers. If the adults do not

[1] *The Young Child in the Home: A Survey of Three Thousand American Families.*

insist upon crystallizing his ideas into too firm a shape at this time, he should have no more difficulty in adjusting his notions and beliefs to his maturer wisdom than he does in changing his ideas of the process of the evaporation of water when he comes to study chemical changes.

Of the relationship between the child and the church, the White House Conference says:

"Among the child's security needs is the satisfaction in an ever widening field of a craving for affection and understanding that comes from beyond the widest of human relationships. . . . Furthermore, in the growth needs of the child lies basically the need of accepting himself as being in harmonious relation with an ordered universe and with an ultimate destiny. While these needs undoubtedly are answered for many children through the apparent security of those adults who immediately surround them, yet it has been the church which has through the ages ministered to these cravings. Through the assurance of a Supreme Power, in one manner or another, the security cravings of individuals have been satisfied. . . . The child can be educated to those sacrifices that are inevitable in meeting the duties and responsibilities of living with others only when he has in some way accepted himself as being in harmonious relation to all that is about him."

And again:

"For one who sincerely accepts religion, of whatever creed or denomination, even when it departs from generally accepted formal doctrine, a scale of ultimate values is established which permeates and gives direction to the whole life of the individual. Religion is involved in a sense of beauty, of worth, of ideals, of belonging to or being in relation to something transcending one's immediate life. Throughout human history these concepts have been stated in words of deep significance. The statements have varied throughout the ages but perpetually some attempt is made to meet this need for ultimate values. Some religious awareness is there to be cherished and cultivated. . . . In so far as they [home, church and school] accomplish their purpose, they give the child, from his earliest days, a sense of stability and security, a feeling of personal dignity that comes from a knowledge of his infinite worth, a responsibility for directing his life in harmony with highest ideals."—*The Delinquent Child* (The Century Co., New York, 1932), p. 41 ff. and p. 138.

Most persons working with children, particularly with adolescents, will agree that there are many individuals who feel the need of the church and that these persons will feel free to turn to it, if they have had sufficient acquaintance with it to make it easy and natural to throw themselves into church work. The simplest way to give the child this feeling of familiarity with the church is through encouraging him to attend Sunday School.

Sunday afternoon is sometimes a series of irritations, of querulous demands for ''something to do,'' or of idle teasing of other children. Sunday afternoon may, on the other hand, be the most delightful time of the entire week, and whether it is or not depends almost entirely on the attitude of the parents. If mother and daddy will devote a couple of hours wholeheartedly to some family enterprise, they will find that before many weeks are passed, they will be looking forward to Sunday afternoon as eagerly as the children themselves. It is the ideal time for family expeditions—on foot, in the auto, or even the street-car—for tramping, or for picnics; or it might be the time for repairing broken toys which have been saved up for masculine skill during the week. It might be the time also for group games such as have been suggested in an earlier chapter; for family choruses or orchestras; for pasting snapshots in the family album; for making plans of all sorts —for a new house, a new garden, a new trip. This is the time also for family calls on friends living outside the immediate neighborhood, especially friends who also have children. If the family is at all musical, Sunday afternoon may give an opportunity for attending the concerts which the symphony orchestras of many cities give and which are well within the enjoyment of fairly young children; if the children get too tired when they stay for the entire concert, they may enjoy at least a part of it. Then, too, there may be family trips to museums and zoos, where each member will find something of interest and where the children's pleasure and interest will be doubled by the fact that the whole family is there together. For winter week-ends or holidays, when outdoor play is impossible for any length of time, older children may well plan out some fairly elaborate program to be staged (after practice and rehearsal) before friends and the adults of the family. In one family, fortunate enough to possess a reflectoscope which throws pictures on the wall or a screen, the children frequently work up lectures on various subjects, selecting the pictures to be shown from their own magazines and books, arranging the material logically, and presenting it in an interesting manner. Other families may contrive plays, either original or memorized from a book of plays, constructing their own scenery and costumes, and so on. Such plays require the coöperation of a number of children, but a puppet show may be put on by a child alone. Such a show may demand many days spent in happy work making the puppets, learning how to manipulate the strings, and how to alter the voice as each character speaks. No performance, whether of the lecture or the dramatic type, will amount to anything without an audience, and the audience should contain some appreciative and critical adults. If they refuse to attend any play which is not worth while, they can raise the standards of the children's playing; if they understand and praise improvements which one performance displays over the previous showing, they are giving the children a real reward for their efforts; if, however, the adults attend only to ridicule, they will widen the breach which probably already exists between their children and themselves and so lay the foundations of unhappiness and misunderstanding in later years.

Holidays

Not only do the children have long summer vacations and short week-ends, but they have also occasional holidays scattered throughout the year. Christmas and Fourth of July ordinarily fall outside of the regular school time but Labor Day, Washington's Birthday, Good Friday, Memorial Day, and the rest interrupt it.

The manner of celebrating any particular day will, of course, vary with different families, but one fact seems to be fairly evident: If the day is worth remembering with a holiday, the children should be given some opportunity for reminding themselves of the man or the event which the holiday celebrates. We do not want our children to grow up like the little boy who, upon his return from a Lincoln's Birthday party, reported that it was a good party, but Lincoln wasn't there. Many schools pay considerable attention to the various holidays. If the school fails to do this, the family should see that the children understand the significance of each particular day. Many, which are not school holidays, lend themselves to some family notice. Sometimes a mere suggestion of special emphasis, green dishes or favors on St. Patrick's Day, watching for shadows on Candlemas Day, a little discussion of the calendar on the twenty-ninth of February and on the first of January, give the child a living interest in history and tradition. One family makes a ceremony of reading the Declaration of Independence aloud on the Fourth of July. It would, however, take away half of the joy of the holiday, if every family did the same thing. The holiday is a time for cementing family traditions and customs, but it cannot be expected that every family will celebrate every holiday. There must be selection, and so we find some families who make a great day of Thanksgiving and practically ignore New Year's Day, while other families reverse the procedure.

Older children can often be interested in the national holidays of other countries. Mr. Rowe of the Pan-American Union says that in many of the Latin-American countries the public school buildings are named for the other countries of this Western hemisphere, that each school takes particular interest in the country for which it is named and makes some special observance of the holidays of that country. It would seem that there could hardly be a simpler way to interest the younger generation in its neighbors. If we cannot have schools so named, it is still possible to have the family study now one country and now another, or perhaps to have each of the children choose a special country for his own special interest.

The White House Conference suggests that:

"The integrity of the family is maintained partly through traditions—its own successful way of meeting life in the past. Its tendency to preserve traditions, therefore, is its effort at self-preservation. Out of this stable background comes much that has richness and worth for the child. . . . Wise parents will give the children those formulations of tradition which they have found most valuable, teaching the child as he grows older to find their vibrant elements for himself."—*The Delinquent Child* (The Century Co., New York, 1932), p. 87 ff.

Birthdays

Certain days, such as the birthdays of individual members of the family, are necessarily family days. They offer a perfect opportunity for making each child feel important in his turn. It is one day in the year when even the shyest child may feel that he is the center of attention. The giving of presents is of less importance than is the endeavor to make the "birthday child" as happy as possible all day. It is a good thing for the other children to try deliberately to make their brother or sister very happy one day in the year. If they understand that their own turn will be coming in a few months, there will be no cause for envy or jealousy. Even the four-year-old who remarked at his baby sister's birthday party that mother was making him wait until next month for his birthday realized that his turn was coming.

Probably the great event of the birthday is the party. It is good social training for the child to be hostess to a group of small friends and to try to see that every one is having a good time. It is good mental hygiene for the child to be the center of attraction once a year. Some parents object to the custom of having the children who come to the party bring presents and are apt to refer to the present as the "ticket" to the party. The children, however, have no such feeling about presents and they enjoy selecting them and giving them almost as much as they do receiving them. If there is no competition as to value of presents and if there is practically an exchange during the year, there need be no feeling on this point. Many parties are planned so that each guest goes home with a little souvenir which is as important to him as the present which he brought is to the birthday child. One warning might be given and that is: Don't expect young children to understand the theory of prizes. A group of four-year-old children may be quickly reduced to tears, if a competition results in a prize for one and not for others. Failing to comprehend the meaning of competition, they see only that one child has been singled out for a reward. If the adult in charge feels a need for prizes for young children, then let there be a prize for each one, but let the winner of the contest have first choice. Another rule for parties: The food is next in importance to the present. Often, in a group not very well acquainted, conversation and games are stilted and lifeless until after the refreshments have been served; therefore it is sometimes more satisfactory to feed children early in the afternoon and then let them play games afterward. Most parties for very young children should be very short. Two hours is plenty long enough for children of six or seven. For older children the hours may be increased somewhat, but for all youthful parties the rule holds that a short, snappy one is more enjoyable than a long, dragging one.

Summary

In conclusion, we may say that vacations and holidays should be in some way special days, offering occupations which are different from those of other days and which are real opportunities for recreation and recuperation. No general rules can be laid down, for vacations and holidays should be pre-eminently family days. Unless the observance in some way marks a family as "queer" in the neighborhood, the more individual the observance of special days, the closer will the child feel to his family group.

Chapter XIII

EDUCATION AT HOME AND AT SCHOOL

ONLY a comparatively short time ago the term *education in the home* would have covered all education, for the only teaching was that done by parents and by private tutors. Gradually, with the introduction of schools, the notion spread that children were to be educated outside the home, though at first children were admitted to schools only after they had learned to read at home. With such developments as the incorporation of the primary school in the public school system, the compulsory education laws, the introduction of the kindergarten, of vocational schools, of "play schools," "nursery schools," and summer camps, the child's education has been taken over more and more by agencies outside the family itself.

Division of Responsibility

As the schools have thus assumed more and more responsibility toward the child, it has been only natural for many families to drop their own feeling of responsibility at approximately the same rate. We find mothers who no longer take their children for regular medical or dental examinations on the assumption that "they get those examinations in school." Some parents likewise no longer feel any need for planning recreation for their children. It is, "Oh, I can't take you to the Art Institute. I guess the school will take you sometime," or "Can't you be quiet? Go down to the playground, if you want to make a noise," or "No, my children can't skate. The city doesn't have any rink they can walk to." If the school or the city provides educational or recreational facilities, the child is free to enjoy them; if not, he must do without them and without help from his family.

There are, on the other hand, many intelligent parents who are only too anxious to coöperate with the schools and who realize that the child can attain his highest and most desirable development only when home and school each does its share. Occasionally we come across a mother who is so much interested in the school and so concerned over her child's progress that she tries to make herself part of the school situation. The result usually is that the teachers and perhaps the children feel that she is interfering, that she does not belong in the school. To a certain extent it is desirable to have the child feel that at school he is in a different world from the one which he knows at home.

Objectives of the Modern School

We can hardly discuss the relationship between home-education and school-education, unless we remind ourselves of just what the modern school is undertaking. No longer do we call an individual "well educated," if he has merely acquired a great mass of information, for we have come to feel that the ability to use knowledge is more important than the knowledge itself. We realize also that even the most superior person can never learn or remember each individual item which may at some time be of importance to him. Experts in any line are rare enough, and an expert in all lines is simply an impossibility. It is feasible, however, to learn where and how to get any specific bit of information which we need and, to some extent at least, to learn how to think.

The modern school, then, is not concerned chiefly with cramming facts into children; it is endeavoring to train the child so that he may best fit into the civilization in which he finds himself, and even more than that to train him so that he may somehow improve civilization, so that the world may in some way be a better place for his having lived in it. In order to provide the child with this training in citizenship, the schools try, in the first place, to give him the utmost of physical and mental health: to make him strong in body, respecting the laws of hygiene; and strong in mind, free from any of the twists of temperament and kinks of character which sometimes upset an otherwise promising future. The school aims to provide the child with the fundamentals of learning: to teach him to communicate with others and especially to use spoken language well, to teach him about our civilization and the part which various individuals play in the work of that civilization; the school aims to teach the child to read so that he may be able to learn many things by himself, to teach him to use numbers efficiently; and, most important of all, the school endeavors to teach the child to think. The person who can think accurately and to the point and who knows where and how to get various sorts of information is well prepared for whatever may come.

The school also tries to give the child some specific training as a member of a social group. This includes such points as learning to help himself, learning to respect the rights of others, and so on. The school stresses the development of character. The model child in school is no longer the timid pupil who sits perfectly quiet at his desk, but is rather the alert, self-reliant, responsible child, who displays initiative and leadership, who is able to think and to express himself clearly.

Lastly, the modern school offers training for the profitable use of leisure time. All too often leisure time is wasted, even when it is not used to the detriment of the individual himself or of society at large. The modern school is trying to give each child some interest which may provide for many happy and useful hours of leisure. Appreciation of the beautiful— whether in art, music, literature or what not—hobbies, and all types of self-expression may furnish desirable outlets for leisure-time activity. Every person has an urge for self-

expression, a desire to leave his mark in some way, a longing to do some one thing well, whether it be to draw the plans for a palace, to cook a dinner, to drive a nail straight, or simply to make a pleasing personal appearance. In this effort to develop self-expression the schools do not delude themselves into thinking that they are turning out artists; they realize that few of the inhabitants of the earth will ever produce anything of lasting beauty or of permanent interest or edification. They are trying, however, to encourage every child to express himself, because so doing may give definiteness to his thinking or imagination, may broaden his horizon, or may help him to understand some other individual.

The Methods of the Modern School

When we ask just how the modern school is endeavoring to give a child this ideal training for citizenship in the world, we find that there are two main methods. In the first place, there is the stress on work with actual materials, learning by doing. To many a grandmother, a modern schoolroom is a place wholly without discipline, a place in which to play; to the person who understands the aims of the school, the room is a living laboratory, a place where children try things out for themselves and learn from actual experience. The motto of many a present-day school might well be, "You can tell by trying." We are often called upon to admire some "self-made" man—a stable, rugged, persevering individual who has graduated from the "school of hard knocks"—and to some extent we have modeled the modern school after his school. We do not, to be sure, arrange a Spartan program of deliberate "hard knocks," but we allow the child to learn that water expands upon freezing, not from reading about it but by trying it out; to learn that two and two make four, not from a table but from working with bits of actual materials; to learn what behavior is acceptable to a group, not from a book of

etiquette or a series of proverbs but from watching and discussing the attitude of an actual group when some member infringes upon the rights of another; to learn the duties of various officers in a government, not by memorizing an uninteresting list of duties and privileges but from actually taking the parts of these officers in a small group of children. Much that looks to an outsider like mere play in the schoolroom is part of a carefully thought-out program planned to give the children an understanding of some situation or to give them practice in the use of language, numbers or cooperation with their peers.

The second method which the modern school uses is that of giving the child opportunity, time, and incentives for thinking. In our modern world where we dash madly from one thing to another, where every hour of the day is scheduled for routine or socially ordained and sometimes rather senseless activities, perhaps there is no one thing which any of us needs so much as the opportunity to think things out for ourselves. In school such a need is at least partially met by the so-called "project method," in which the child is given or is encouraged to find a problem which needs to be solved and is then helped to work out a solution for himself. He is taught to think ahead and foresee difficulties and complications, to weigh the comparative values of methods by which the situation may be met, and then to try out the method which seems best. When the chosen method has been carried out, the child is helped to criticize his own performance, to see wherein his planning was correct, and where he erred. Perhaps in the end he will throw the whole thing aside only to start fresh from the clearer viewpoint which he has gained through his own experience. The problems on which the child works are not the unreal hen and a half who by some mysterious process was successful in laying an egg and a half in a day and a half or the eagle who flew three miles an hour inside a train which was moving in the opposite direction at some stated speed, for nobody with

the possible exception of the teacher cares a bit how far the eagle flew or how many fractional eggs were laid by the fractional hen. The modern problems are, rather, problems of real life, with real significance for the child: the construction of a delivery truck for the first-grade grocery store, making change at the third-grade's lemonade sale, or the representation of what was learned on a trip to the post office.

Preparing the Child for School

With some notion, then, of what the school is trying to do for the child, we may ask how the home can work with the school. Obviously the education of the child before he goes to school falls upon the shoulders of the family. If the child happens to attend a nursery school, there are still the first two years when the family's influence is without a rival, and even the nursery school does not pretend or desire to act as a substitute for the home. For the great majority of children who do not attend any school before they are five years old, there is much which the home can do in the early years to make the child's adjustment to school more simple. In the words of the White House Conference:

"Child health and welfare efforts sponsored by the state and fostered in the schools will continue to come to naught if parents are to be left untrained, to fail in their share of the business of education." —*Home and School Coöperation* (The Century Co., New York, 1932), p. 6.

"There is a growing realization by parents and school administrators of the necessity for having children enter school in the best physical condition. The Summer Round-Up of the National Congress of Parents and Teachers is a country-wide movement. . . . The parent teacher associations coöperate with the local school authorities in providing a health examination during the spring term for children who expect to enter the kindergarten or the first grade in the fall. Follow-up work is carried on during the summer months."—*The School Health Program* (The Century Co., New York, 1932), p. 131.

Another volume of this series discusses the ways in which the child can be put into the best possible physical condition. (See Stuart's *Healthy Childhood*.) Of course, no child who is suffering from bad eyesight, from aching teeth, or from chronic fatigue can be at his best at school. The White House Conference suggests two specific points to which the home should attend before the child enters school: one, that during the months preceding school entrance, the parents should endeavor to ''discover health handicaps and correct remedial health defects of preschool children, so that they may commence their school life in a physical condition favorable to making the best of their educational opportunities'';[1] the other, that ''every child should be vaccinated against smallpox and present a certificate to that effect before he is allowed to enter school and should be revaccinated at about the time of entrance into the junior high school.''[2]

After the parents have made sure that the child is in good physical condition, they may turn to the other forms of preparation for school. The child who has learned to be contented in the absence of his mother and who is accustomed to playing happily with other children is ready to join a group of children under the direction of a stranger. We find this type of preparation for school life stressed by a number of the committees working in the White House Conference. The group concerned with home and school coöperation writes:

"Preschool contacts with the school should assure a correlation of the home and the school programs and an adaptation of home life to the new requirements. The child must be gradually taught self-reliance, especially in personal habits such as washing, dressing, and eating. His family relationships should create in him a friendly attitude toward adults, and in contact with other children he should be trained in adjustment to the group. . . . Continuous contact of the

[1] *Home and School Coöperation* (The Century Co., New York, 1932), p. 62.
[2] *The Administration of the School Health Program* (The Century Co., New York, 1932), p. 28.

parent with the school is essential in the preschool years, so that there may be no break, but only development, as the child's horizon widens. The home is the first school, and should be recognized as such, and the parents must be trained, since they are inevitably the first and the only continuous teachers."

In another connection the same committee says:

"During the preschool years, the mother gradually should free the child from herself. The child should be trained to wash, dress, and feed himself. He should have right attitudes toward the adults in his world and a faith in the reasonableness of those upon whom he depends for guidance and companionship. He should have experience with other children so that he is already adjusted to group life before entering school. An attitude should be created toward the school that will make the child eager to enter into this larger life."—*Home and School Coöperation* (The Century Co., New York, 1932), pp. 5 and 39.

The report on the delinquent child [3] suggests that a "hazard of major importance exists in those situations where the child has been so permeated with over-protection and over-solicitousness that the freer competition of the classroom is a source of terror and dismay" to him, and goes on to say that "Common as these situations are in school there still exists a peculiar blindness to the fact that over-solicitousness by parents means lack of richness in their [the parents'] other emotional outlets."

The child who has had some practice at home with scissors and crayons and paste will not be at a loss when these materials appear at school. The child who has had opportunity for response to music enters more quickly and more fully into the kindergarten music hour. The child who has become accustomed to the use of the simpler pieces of gymnasium apparatus —swings, bars, ladders, and the like—is much more able and gets much more fun from the apparatus which he finds in the kindergarten. Training of this kind is offered in the best nursery schools, but it need not be omitted in the home, if the parents are alert to their opportunities.

[3] *The Delinquent Child* (The Century Co., New York, 1932), p. 114.

More important than any of these points, however, is the mental attitude which the child has assumed. The child who comes to school ready to try anything which is offered, confident that he can attain some degree of success in any reasonable undertaking, the child who is friendly, who has learned to take part in a conversation without monopolizing the center of the stage, who has learned to take turns, who relies upon himself, who takes some responsibility for his own toilet needs and for putting on his own wraps, this child is much happier and a much more valuable member of the school community than the overbashful, clinging-vine, spoiled-baby type of child, no matter how appealing the latter may be to the doting mother.

The list of "preparatory courses" given above may seem like a large order, but, if we remember that the young child is learning something all the time and that the parent is able to determine to a large extent whether he shall learn desirable habits and attitudes or whether he will have to un-learn in later years much that he learned at first, then we will realize the importance of getting started right.

Coöperation of Home and School

After the home has coöperated with the school to the extent of preparing the child for school entrance, there comes the question of coöperating with the particular school which the child is attending. We tend to think that the child is at school most of the time, but a little arithmetic will show that less than half of the days of the year are schooldays, and, of these, not more than six hours or some 43 per cent of the waking hours are spent at school. The home, then, remains the influence which is working on the child for the greater part of the time, even when he is of school age. The child's education, therefore, cannot be handed over entirely to the school. One obvious way in which the home can help the school greatly is in the matter of physical health. The school attempts to keep its children in the best possible condition and parents can help by reporting cases of contagious disease and by interviewing the school nurse or the teacher when their own child has been exposed to contagion. They can also help by seeing that small children wear clothing suitable for the weather so that they need not have special permission to remain indoors at recess time.

Some of the kinds of coöperation which the school needs from the home are listed by a committee of the White House Conference as follows:

"Parents should provide for a periodic health examination of children during school years by the family physician, which will result in a continuous health record available to the school, to be associated with other school records of the child's growth and development. . . . [They] should, at least, coöperate in whatever examination or inspection the school offers and be present at the examination, if requested by the school. Children should also have a semiannual dental examination by the family dentist, or coöperate with the school dental service. . . . Parents should be responsible for securing corrections of discovered defects by the family physician or through such coöperative services as the community may offer. . . . The school should ask for and receive appreciation, understanding and coöperation from the home in the school rules and regulations for the control and prevention of contagious diseases among children, and the prevention of attendance of children who are not fit in health to undertake school tasks."—*Home and School Coöperation* (The Century Co., New York, 1932), p. 62 f.

Another committee of the White House Conference lists causes for which children should be excluded from school, as:

". . . nausea, vomiting, chill or convulsions (fits), dizziness, faintness or unusual pallor, eruption of any kind, fever, running nose, red or running eyes, sore or inflamed throat, acutely swollen glands in neck, cough, headache, earache, other observable deviations from his usual condition. . . . Children with the following communicable diseases should not be permitted to remain in school: common cold, grippe, influenza, tonsilitis, whooping cough, chicken pox, diphtheria, measles, mumps, scarlet fever, smallpox, venereal disease, tuberculosis, trachoma, scabies, ringworm on exposed parts of the body, pediculosis, impetigo. . . . Readmission to school after exclusion because of illness, should be upon approval of the school physician or nurse. . . . Every effort should be made to educate the parents so that they can and will make a daily health inspection of their children before sending them to school."—*The Administration of the School Health Program* (The Century Co., New York, 1932), p. 26 f.

Various of the White House Conference committees stress the fact that, even if the school makes the preliminary physical examination, the action upon the physician's recommendations is the responsibility of the family. Thus we find one group reporting:

"The school through its health service should be prepared carefully to check upon the day-to-day health of its children. It should expect that the home will consult the family physician at frequent intervals and coöperate with the school in the maintenance of adequate quarantine. The school should locate existing physical defects. The home should be expected to take care of remediable defects requiring medical or surgical care beyond that which the school can legitimately furnish. The school should be prepared to render immediate first aid for injuries occurring on the playground, but should expect intelligent coöperation from the home in supplying such additional care as the home financially is able to furnish."—*Home and School Coöperation* (The Century Co., New York, 1932), p. 42 f.

Another committee suggests that the:

". . . school health service should do nothing for the child that can be done effectively by the family, unless it is something primarily for the education of the child or his parents. Remedial and curative work should be left to the family. While the promotion of health is one of the cardinal objectives of the school program, no service should be performed in a manner that takes away the fundamental privilege or responsibility of the home."

They claim that:

"If a curative act involves treatment that is closely related to some phase of the regular school program, its inclusion in the school health program may be justified. Corrective gymnastics, for example, may legitimately be conducted by the schools because of its educational nature and because no other agency could so effectively combine its educational and reparative benefits. . . . There are other forms of corrective or preventive measures that should be applied in the schools so that the child's education need not be interrupted. Such measures are the establishment of sight conservation classes, schools for crippled children, classes for the hard-of-hearing, classes for anemic children, speech defect classes, open-air classes, classes or schools for the mentally deficient, and the like. As a rule no child should be segregated in a special class or school unless the educational and other gain to him and to the normal children from whom he is removed is greater than the loss that usually attends segregation.—*Administration of the School Health Program* (The Century Co., New York, 1932), pp. 10, 11 and 25 f.

The home should arrange not only to have the child's general health good when he goes to school, but it should also be responsible for sending the child to school reasonably clean and neat. It is not only an unnecessary burden to the teacher who has to endure dirty children or to attempt to clean them up herself, but it is poor training for the children themselves, both from the point of view of social habits and from that of work habits.

"The schools demand that the child should come clean and tidy to his work. The doctrine of cleaning up after as well as before work is one common to all phases of industry and might well be begun in the schools as a social and civic responsibility resting equally upon both school and home and thereby becoming automatic."—*Home and School Coöperation* (The Century Co., New York, 1932), p. 14.

A group of one hundred superintendents, three hundred high school principals, and three hundred parents were asked: "How can the home coöperate with the school?" Their answers [4] may be briefly summarized as follows:

The home should see that the child has enough sleep, the proper food, the proper clothing; that he has no remedial defect of vision or hearing; that he has proper habits of sleeping,

---

[4] *Home and School Coöperation* (The Century Co., New York, 1932), p. 106.

eating, studying, playing; that he comes to school regularly and punctually; that he is given a time and place at home to study; that he is industrious, reliable, public spirited (generous, obedient, self-controlled, courteous, truthful, honest, considerate); and that he does the right thing for the right's sake instead of for a reward. Although this list makes rather a large order for any family, they are goals toward which the family can work.

The home can provide experiences which will be of great help to the child's understanding of his school work. There are, to be sure, many things which are learned more easily at school for the reason that many other children are doing the same things at the same time. Reading, arithmetic, and history are the type of subjects which usually depend more on the school's instruction than upon the home's, yet the influence of the home is sometimes highly important even here. Who does not know a child whose ability in reading took an enormous leap when he was given some particularly interesting book at home? Or the child to whom mathematics suddenly acquired sense, when he used it to solve some practical problem of his own? Or the child to whom the World War emerged from the realm of fairy stories only after hearing a veteran tell of his experiences at Vimy Ridge or the Marne? The child of ten or eleven may have learned much from the geography book, even though he has not stirred beyond his own city limits; yet the younger child who has never seen a book on geography, but who has traveled across the continent and seen the oceans, the Mississippi River, and the Rockies may have a far truer understanding of the world. And so in any school subject which we may select, we find that the experience in the home— whether it be actual experience, discussion, or supplementary reading—may enrich and clarify the information which was gained at school.

Sometimes parents refuse to allow children to carry to school outside material like cocoons, pictures, special books, costumes, and food for animals, in the belief that the teachers won't want to be bothered with such matters. On the contrary, most teachers will welcome material related to the subjects which are being discussed at the time, and it does not take long for children to learn to distinguish between what is and what is not appropriate for school exhibit at a particular period. Frequently the material from outside is of great interest to the other children and stimulates discussion and activity.

In a school where many trips are made to points of interest, some mothers may offer to drive groups of children in their car whenever the teacher needs transportation facilities. The fortunate teacher who has a group of such mothers to rely on can do much in the way of arranging for outside experiences for the children.

One of the most important ways in which the home can coöperate with the school is through a friendly listening to the child's account of his day at school. The child who is unhappy because he has failed in a test or has received a lower grade than the one he expected can often be brought to see that grades or "marks" are not the most important thing in the world. In fact one of the common causes for difficulties in school is the overemphasis which some parents place upon school grades. The committee on the delinquent child says:

"There are . . . many factors in the family life of the child that condition him unfavorably for his school adjustment. Important among these is the overweening ambition parents often show for the success of their children. The children's grades and marks in school are quite as ready and as concrete measures of family position as period furniture or income. This is particularly true where the parents are attempting to live out in their children's attainment the poverties of their own earlier lives. School dissatisfaction here means a host of problems coming from the child's inability to consummate in school attainment all of those dreams which his parents have constructed about him. . . . Often school dissatisfaction is but the natural reaction of the child to the records of more brilliant or more favored brothers and sisters!"—*The Delinquent Child* (The Century Co., New York, 1932), p. 114 f.

The Child's Progress in School

Parents often make a mistake in urging the school to advance a child to the next grade. If the child attends a school which is conducted by alert and interested educators, his progress may be regulated by the teachers much better than it can be by most parents. Often the child shows a different side of himself at home and the parent fails to realize in which group of children he will fit to his own best advantage. The modern school attempts to provide for the grouping of children "according to their various abilities and with such relation to the curriculum that they can undertake the activities provided with every chance of being successful. . . . If a pupil is placed in a group in which the activities do not sufficiently stimulate him or the tasks are much to difficult for him to master, mental ill health will probably result. Pupils who are thus wrongly grouped soon develop other symptoms of maladjustment which exhibit themselves in introvert activities of daydreaming or sulking, or extrovert activities of boisterousness, defiance, and the like." [5]

If the child is having difficulties in school, the understanding of the home is all the more important. We read:

"The school is justified in looking to the home for coöperation and assistance with children who are maladjusted or who fail in their response to school work. Frequently all that is necessary is sympathetic understanding between the home and the school in order to secure the fullest possible effort upon the part of the child. Where the home is unsympathetic or critical the child's coöperation frequently is difficult to secure." *Home and School Coöperation* (The Century Co., New York, 1932), p. 43.

[5] *Administration of the School Health Program* (The Century Co., New York, 1932), p. 65.

The Attitude of the Family Toward the Teacher

Perhaps it would be as well to strike a note of warning here. We sometimes find families where the parents are greatly concerned at the kind of information which the child is receiving at school. Unfortunately it is impossible to provide teachers for every grade in every school who have as high a degree of education and culture as the most fortunate of parents. Such parents at times find their children learning mispronunciations of words or even entirely wrong statements of facts. What then is to be done? If the parents attempt to correct the child's error, they will often be met with the reply, "You don't know at all. Miss Smith says it's the other way and she knows." Brave is the parent who can let the matter drop at that point and who can believe that the child's attitude toward the teacher and his confidence in her is more important than a wrong date or a mispronunciation.

One of the greatest of our psychologists learned his classical languages so well at Oxford that in his middle life one of his amusements was composing free verse in Latin. When his daughter began to study Latin in high school, she had as a teacher a young woman who had recently graduated from the university with a rather mediocre scholastic record. The psychologist was naturally keenly interested in his daughter's progress in Latin. One night she brought him the "prose" which she had translated into Latin and the father's comment was, "Technically what you have written is correct, but it is not good Latin," and he showed her how one of the great Latin authors would have written that sentence. The next day daughter returned from school and exulted over her father saying, "You may be a good psychologist, Dad, but you don't know Latin. That sentence was right the way I wrote it first." And father, being a practical as well as a theoretical psychologist, said resignedly, "Very well. Do your Latin as your

teacher says. Perhaps if you ever do any graduate work in Latin, we can get together on it again!''

Sometimes with older and superior children, it is possible to explain that there are two points of view and that the teacher has presented but one. It is even possible sometimes to tell the child that the teacher may not know all that is to be known in some line, but don't make him feel that he is between two fires, that he has to remember to say that Washington was greater than Lincoln at school and the other way around at home. Don't give him a feeling of uncertainty, of questioning the accuracy of the teacher at every point. Most of the details of his information he will forget later on anyway. What adult can name the counties of New York State or the kings of England, and who wants to do it even if he can? As a matter of fact we are apt to regret certain phrases which were learned too well, if, for example, we can never think of any Frenchman as other than a ''gay person, fond of dancing and light wines.'' It is not the details that are important; it is the general attitude toward education and toward life.

The Home and the School System

While it is doubtless wiser for the parents to refrain from criticisms of the schools in the hearing of their children, this does not mean that we should assume that the schools are perfect or that there is nothing that we can do to improve them. The real educators and teachers themselves would be the first to agree that there are many changes which should be made in the present system, many ways in which development should be encouraged and that such changes and developments can come about only through the concerted action of teachers, administrators, and parents. The White House Conference suggests that:

"It rests with the general public, including parents, to assure: increased salary schedules providing for adequate pay for service per-

formed; recognition of the importance of good teaching for the lower grades and adequate financial compensation for high ability at this stage; public demand for better trained teachers, thus decreasing the flooding of the market with unqualified young people; adequate equipment of schools, for instruction and recreation; consolidation of rural schools; improvement of living conditions for teachers, especially in rural districts; regular school attendance; continuation of secondary education to completion."—*Home and School Coöperation* (The Century Co., New York, 1932), p. 15.

Fields Which the School Enters Little

There are many things which the child learns at home which he cannot learn at school. Loyalty to the family is one of the most elemental and one of the strongest loyalties. The school can never teach him the family standards, the traditions, the customs which weld the family into a unit, and to a great degree determine fundamental ideals and attitudes. Almost every family develops definite rites toward Christmas and birthdays. We have only to listen to a group of children comparing notes on what different families do on Christmas to realize how deep are the impressions made by family customs and how the child glories in being conservative, in carrying out each Christmas in exactly the method used on previous celebrations. Family pride in the grandfather who was a judge or the uncle who was a policeman or the ancestor who came over in the Mayflower may inspire the child to live up to their glory.

Then there are things which children can, if necessary, learn at school but only through discussion with no opportunity for practice. Such learning as habit training in sleeping and eating can receive only a slight impetus from the teacher. She may paint all the horrid details of the condition of the stomach of the drunkard, the lungs of the cigarette smoker, or the nervous system of the coffee-drinking child, but such preachments have little effect, if they are met with counteracting experiences at home. To be sure, teaching a child how to behave himself as a worthy member of the family group may be advanced by what the teacher says or by reading stories which stress a happy family working together for the good of the group. The teacher may suggest that the girls can help by washing dishes and the boys by shoveling snow; but, if mother employs a maid who dislikes children and if the janitor objects to small boys with shovels, the school teaching amounts to little more than a charming fairy tale.

Summary

And so we come to the conclusion that from whatever angle we view the child's development and education, we find that the highest point is reached only when those two great agencies, the home and the school, work together for the good of the child. In the earliest years, the immediate family is all-important. Gradually the school comes to contribute its share, always supplementing but never supplanting the home. There is much that the home can learn from the school and much that the school can learn from the home, many ways in which each may help the other.

Both home and school give the child much valuable information and many essential skills and techniques, but in no way do they contribute more to the child's happiness and future development than in the cultivation of desirable habits and attitudes, ways of meeting situations and of facing whatever may come. There is no way of acquiring such habits and attitudes save through practising them over and over, and there is no medium for that practice which can be compared with play. Play is the child's own life. As he learns through play to control his own body; to master the material objects about him; to use his wits in the accomplishment of his own ends and for the fun of the mental activity; to enter into social play, following always the rules of the games and giving con-

sideration to the rights of others; as he learns to enter whole-
heartedly into all sorts of desirable activities and to gain
from them satisfaction and joy, so we may expect him to enter
enthusiastically into the civilization in which he finds himself
and to help carry it onward in its course of progress and
development.

SELECTED BIBLIOGRAPHY

Abbot, A., and Trabue, M. R., "A Measure of Ability to Judge Poetry," Series X and Y, *Teachers College Bulletin* (Teachers College, Columbia University, New York City), Vol. XXII, No. 2.

Arlitt, A. H., *The Child from One to Twelve* (McGraw-Hill Book Co., New York, 1931).

Barnes, W., *The Children's Poets* (World Book Co., New York, 1925).

Berle, A. A., *Teaching in the Home* (Moffatt, Yard & Company, New York, 1915).

Berne, E. V. C., *An Investigation of the Wants of Seven Children,* University of Iowa Studies in Child Welfare, Vol. 4, No. 2 (University of Iowa, Iowa City, 1930).

Blatz, W. E., and Bott, H., *The Management of Young Children* (William Morrow and Co., New York, 1930).

Brewer, J. M., "Guidance for Home Membership," *Journal of the National Education Association,* XVIII (1929), 245.

Brugoon, J., "The Sick Child at Home," *Hygeia,* VIII (1930), 713.

Burnham, W. H., *The Normal Mind* (D. Appleton and Company, New York, 1925).

Cameron, H. C., *The Nervous Child* (Oxford University Press, London, 1925).

Canfield, D., *What Shall We Do Now?* (Frederick A. Stokes Company, New York, 1922).

Cobb, S., *The New Leaven* (The John Day Company, New York, 1928).

Coleman, S. N., *Creative Music for Children* (G. P. Putnam's Sons, New York, 1922).

Cook, H. C., *The Play Way* (Frederick A. Stokes Company, New York, 1919).

Creative Expression Through Art (Progressive Education Association, Washington, D. C., 1926).

Creative Expression Through Music (Progressive Education Association, Washington, D. C., 1927).

Curti, M. W., *Child Psychology* (Longmans, Green & Co., New York, 1930).

de Rusette, L. E., *Children's Percussion Bands* (E. P. Dutton and Company, New York, 1930).

Eng, H., *The Psychology of Children's Drawings* (Harcourt, Brace and Company, New York, 1931).

Farwell, L., "Reactions of Kindergarten, First- and Second-Grade Children to Constructive Play Materials," *Genetic Psychology Monographs,* VIII (1930), 431.

Forbush, W. B., *The Home-Education of Children* (Funk & Wagnalls Company, New York, 1919).

Foster, J. C., and Mattson, M. L., *Nursery School Procedure* (D. Appleton and Company, New York, 1929).

Freeman, F. N., *How Children Learn* (Houghton Mifflin Company, Boston, 1917).

Gardner, E. E., and Ramsey, E., *A Handbook of Children's Literature* (Scott, Foresman and Co., Chicago, 1927).

Garrison, C. G., *Permanent Play Materials for Young Children* (Charles Scribner's Sons, New York, 1926).

Gesell, A., *Infancy and Human Growth* (The Macmillan Company, New York, 1928).

Gilbreth, L. M., *Living with our Children* (W. W. Norton and Company, New York, 1926).

Hall, G. S., *Aspects of Child Life and Education* (Ginn and Company, Boston, 1907).

Hart, J. H., *A Social Interpretation of Education* (Henry Holt and Company, New York, 1929).

Hunt, J. L., *A Catalogue of Play Equipment* (Bureau of Educational Experiments, New York, 1924).

Johnson, C., *The Country School* (Thomas Y. Crowell Company, New York, 1907).

Johnson, G. E., *Education by Plays and Games* (Ginn and Company, Boston, 1907).

Johnson, H. M., *Children in the Nursery School* (The John Day Company, New York, 1928).

Justin, F., "A Genetic Study of Laughter-Provoking Stimuli," *Child Development,* III (1932), 114.

Kaufmann, H. L., "Should Your Child Study Music?" *Parents Magazine,* V (1930), 16.

Kilpatrick, W. H., "The New Point of View in Education," *Journal of the National Education Association,* XX (1931), 133.

——————, "The Place of Creating in the Educative Process," *Childhood Education,* VII (1930), 115.

Kirkpatrick, E. A., *Fundamentals of Child Study* (The Macmillan Company, New York, 1911).

——————, *The Individual in the Making,* (Houghton Mifflin Company, Boston 1911).

Lee, J., *Play in Education* (The Macmillan Company, New York, 1926).

Lehman, H. C., and Witty, P. A., *The Psychology of Play Activities* (A. S. Barnes & Company, New York, 1927).

Leonard, M. S., *Best Toys for Children and their Selection* (Wisconsin Kindergarten Association, 1925).

Mason, M. E., "Amusing the Sick Child at Home," *Child Welfare,* XXVI (1932), 335.

Mitchell, H., *Play and Play Materials for the Preschool Child* (Canadian Council on Child Welfare, Ottawa).

Mitchell, L. S., *Here and Now Story Book* (E. P. Dutton and Company, New York, 1921).

Norsworthy, N., and Whitley, M. T., *The Psychology of Childhood* (The Macmillan Company, New York, 1921).

O'Shea, M. V., edit., *The Child: His Nature and His Needs* (The Children's Foundation, 1924).

Palmer, L., *Play Life in the First Eight Years* (Ginn and Company, Boston, 1916).

Parker, H., McConathy, O., Birge, E. B., and Messner, W. O., *The Progressive Music Series, Teacher's Manual,* Vol. 1 (Silver, Burdett and Company, New York, 1919).

Playthings, Bureau of Educational Experiments, New York, 1923.

Rasmussen, V., *Child Psychology* (Alfred A. Knopf, New York, 1923).

Read, M. L., *The Mothercraft Manual* (Little, Brown and Company, Boston, 1928).

Rugg, H., and Shumaker, A., *The Child-Centered School* (World Book Company, New York, 1928).

Sargent, W., *Fine and Industrial Arts in Elementary Schools* (Ginn and Company, Boston, 1912).

Shedlock, M. L., *The Art of the Story-Teller* (D. Appleton and Company, New York, 1924).

Shirley, M. M., *The First Two Years* (University of Minnesota Press, Minneapolis, 1931).

Sies, A. C., *Spontaneous and Supervised Play in Childhood* (The Macmillan Company, New York, 1924).

Small, W. H., *Early New England Schools* (Ginn and Company, Boston, 1914).

Smith, E. R., *Education Moves Ahead* (Little, Brown and Company, Boston, 1926).

Spaeth, S., *The Common Sense of Music* (Boni & Liveright, New York, 1924).

Stearns, A. E., et al., *Education of the Modern Boy* (Houghton Mifflin Company, Boston, 1928).

Strang, R., *An Introduction to Child Study* (The Macmillan Company, New York, 1930).

Strickland, R. G., "The Contribution of the Kindergarten," *Journal of the National Education Association,* XX (1931), 77.

Sutton, W. S., *Problems in Modern Education* (Sherman, French and Co., Boston, 1913).

Tanner, A. E., *The Child* (Rand, McNally and Company, New York, 1915).

Terman, L. M., and Lima, M., *Children's Reading* (D. Appleton and Company, New York, 1926).

Thomas, L. C., *Body Mechanics and Health* (Houghton Mifflin Company, Boston, 1929).

Thomson, G. H., *A Modern Philosophy of Education* (Longmans, Green & Co., New York, 1929).

Troxell, E., *Language and Literature in the Kindergarten and Primary Grades* (Charles Scribner's Sons, New York, 1927).

Waddle, C. W., *Introduction to Child Psychology* (Houghton Mifflin Company, Boston, 1918).

Whitehead, A. N., *The Aims of Education and Other Essays,* (The Macmillan Company, New York, 1929).

Wiecking, A. M., *Education Through Manual Activities,* (Ginn and Company, Boston, 1928).

Wilson-Dorrett, O. B., *Language of Music* (World Book Co., New York, 1921).

PUBLICATIONS OF THE WHITE HOUSE CONFERENCE ON CHILD HEALTH AND PROTECTION:

Administration of the School Health Program (The Century Co., New York, 1932).

Body Mechanics: Education and Practice (The Century Co., New York, 1932).

Child Labor (The Century Co., New York, 1932).

SELECTED BIBLIOGRAPHY 283

Children's Reading, A Study of Voluntary Reading of Boys and Girls in the United States (The Century Co., New York, 1932).

Delinquent Child, The (The Century Co., New York, 1932).

Home and School Coöperation (The Century Co., New York, 1932).

Home and the Child, The (The Century Co., New York, 1931).

Nursery Education (The Century Co., New York, 1931).

Safety Education in Schools (The Century Co., New York, 1932).

Social Hygiene in Schools (The Century Co., New York, 1932).

Summer Vacation Activities of the School Child (The Century Co., New York, 1933).

Vocational Guidance (The Century Co., New York, 1932).

Young Child in the Home, The: A Survey of Three Thousand American Families. This report has not yet appeared in book form (1933).

INDEX

COMBINED INDEX

TO

Healthy Childhood, *Happy Childhood*, and *Busy Childhood*

(*Note:* This index lists only the main topics of the three volumes. A detailed index is found at the close of each.)

Conversation, family: *Busy Childhood*, 153

Convulsions: *Healthy Childhood*, 279

Corporal punishment: *Happy Childhood*, 107

Creative imagination: *Happy Childhood*, 148

Crippled child: *Happy Childhood*, 253

D

Dancing: *Busy Childhood*, 226

Daydreaming: *Busy Childhood*, 181; *Happy Childhood*, 43, 132

Deafness and hearing deficiency: *Happy Childhood*, 104

Death-rates, children: *Healthy Childhood*, 8

Development, Characteristics of: *Healthy Childhood*, 51

Diet: *Healthy Childhood*, 155, 173

Difficulties, methods of meeting: *Happy Childhood*, 45

Digestive Disorders: *Healthy Childhood*, 205

Digestive System: *Healthy Childhood*, 87

Dinner table: *Busy Childhood*, 156; *Happy Childhood*, 161

Diphtheria toxin-anti-toxin: *Healthy Childhood*, 267

Discipline: *Happy Childhood*, 96

Diseases, Childhood: *Healthy Childhood*, 345

Diseases, Infectious: *Healthy Childhood*, 247, 257

Dolls: *Busy Childhood*, 82, 87

Dramatic play: *Busy Childhood*, 123, 253; *Happy Childhood*, 132

Dressing habits: *Happy Childhood*, 64

Drowning: *Healthy Childhood*, 304

E

Eating habits: *Happy Childhood*, 49; *Healthy Childhood*, 196

Education at home and school: *Busy Childhood*, 258

Educational value of work in the home: *Busy Childhood*, 167

Elimination, control of: *Happy Childhood* 59; *Healthy Childhood*, 90

Emotion, development of: *Happy Childhood*, 38; of fear, *Happy Childhood*, 70; of love, *Happy Childhood*, 84; of jealousy, *Happy Childhood*, 93; of anger, *Happy Childhood*, 97

Emotional independence: *Happy Childhood*, 178

Endocrine System: *Healthy Childhood*, 104

Environment: *Busy Childhood*, 4; *Happy Childhood*, 7, 225; *Healthy Childhood*, 74, 281

Equipment for living, child's: *Happy Childhood*, 13

Exercises for baby: *Busy Childhood*, 29

Exposure to Disease: *Healthy Childhood*, 257

F

Falsehood, truth and: *Happy Childhood*, 127

Family activities, participation in: *Busy Childhood*, 149

Family as a school of behavior: *Happy Childhood*, 283

Family conversations: *Busy Childhood*, 153

Family life and security: *Happy Childhood*, 78

Family Management: *Happy Childhood*, 269

Father: *Happy Childhood*, 281

Reproductive System: *Healthy Childhood*, 110
Resistance to Infection: *Healthy Childhood*, 263
Respiratory System: *Healthy Childhood*, 83
Rest: *Healthy Childhood*, 216
Retarded children: *Happy Childhood*, 261
Reward and punishment: *Happy Childhood*, 30, 106
Riddles: *Busy Childhood*, 146
Running games: *Busy Childhood*, 60

S

Safety: *Busy Childhood*, 7; *Happy Childhood*, 66; *Healthy Childhood*, 297
Sand play: *Busy Childhood*, 97
Schedules, Feeding: *Healthy Childhood*, 173
School Age Child, Care of: *Healthy Childhood*, 335
School and health: *Healthy Childhood*, 291
School and home: *Busy Childhood*, 258
Security: *Happy Childhood*, 69
Self-control and discipline: *Happy Childhood*, 96
Self-expression: *Busy Childhood*, 96, 221
Self-reliance: *Happy Childhood*, 170
Sense Organs: *Healthy Childhood*, 99
Serums: *Healthy Childhood*, 271
Sex differences: *Happy Childhood*, 227
Sex education: *Happy Childhood*, 187
Shoes, Selection of: *Healthy Childhood*, 133

Singing: *Busy Childhood*, 225
Skeletal System: *Healthy Childhood*, 116
Sleep: *Happy Childhood*, 61; *Healthy Childhood*, 217
Social and dramatic play: *Busy Childhood*, 115
Social esteem, the quest for: *Happy Childhood*, 153
Social games: *Busy Childhood*, 124
Spanking: *Happy Childhood*, 107
Special days, vacations and: *Busy Childhood*, 235
Special features of care at different ages: *Healthy Childhood*, 317
Speech defects: *Happy Childhood*, 258
Standards for posture: *Healthy Childhood*, 136
Stories for children: *Busy Childhood*, 183
Stress and adjustment: *Happy Childhood*, 37
Stuttering: *Happy Childhood*, 118, 258
Suffocation: *Healthy Childhood*, 301
Summer vacation: *Busy Childhood*, 239
Sunday: *Busy Childhood*, 249
Sunday School: *Busy Childhood*, 249
Swimming: *Busy Childhood*, 45

T

Teacher, family attitude toward: *Busy Childhood*, 273
Teeth, Care of: *Healthy Childhood*, 121
Temper tantrums: *Happy Childhood*, 97
Tests, intelligence: *Happy Childhood*, 140

(1)